THE
PANIC
YEARS

THE
PANIC
YEARS

DATES, DOUBTS,
AND THE MOTHER OF
ALL DECISIONS

NELL FRIZZELL

FLATIRON
BOOKS
NEW YORK

www.flatironbooks.com

The Library of Congress Cataloging-in-Publication Data is available upon request.

ISBN 978-1-250-26812-9 (hardcover)
ISBN 978-1-250-26813-6 (ebook)

Our books may be purchased in bulk for promotional, educational, or business use. Please contact your local bookseller or the Macmillan Corporate and Premium Sales Department at 1-800-221-7945, extension 5442, or by email at MacmillanSpecialMarkets@macmillan.com.

Originally published in Great Britain in February 2021 by Bantam Press, an imprint of Penguin Random House UK

First Flatiron Books Edition: 2021

10 9 8 7 6 5 4 3 2 1

To Liz, the mother who made me.
And to Nick, who made me a mother.

CONTENTS

INTRODUCTION

I woke up on the morning of my twenty-eighth birthday alone, in a single bed, in my mother's spare room and remembered that my boyfriend of six years was no longer my boyfriend. As I lay there, pinned to the bed by the weight of my own heart, I realized that for the first time in a long time, I was alone: unfamiliar, unsure, and untethered.

The morning of my thirtieth birthday, I woke up in bed with my best friend. She was five months pregnant, had a mortgage, and was engaged. I was single, childless, and soon to be laid off. Looking across at her, the bright December sunshine screaming through the window like a fire alarm, it felt like I was standing on a station platform, watching my friend pull out of view.

The morning of my thirty-third birthday, I woke up in bed beside a man I love, with a two-week-old baby breathing so gently beside me that, for the 578th time in his life, I had to reach out a hand and touch his face to check that he was alive. My stomach was wet mud. My eyes were lychees of restless weeping. I hadn't slept for more than three straight hours since the last few weeks of my pregnancy, I was wearing a sanitary pad the size of a blow-up mattress, and I smelled like fermenting milk. As a pinkish dawn kissed the treetops along the River Lea, I dressed in an XL gray men's tracksuit and my boyfriend's socks, slipped out of my baking one-bedroom flat, crossed the footbridge into Walthamstow Marshes, faced the sun, and howled.

In less time than it took my sister to pass her driving test, I had undergone a fundamental life change. I threw away the security of a relationship, confronted the finite nature of my fertility, acted at times with careless depravity, and took on, eventually, an entirely new identity. These changes resulted in me having a baby, but whether it's ending a long-term relationship, moving to a new country, changing your career, getting married, or having a breakdown, huge things tend to happen to us during this nameless period around our late twenties, thirties, and often into our forties, and many of them are irreversible. Becoming a parent is the only decision that comes with a biological deadline, the only one that cannot be reversed: it is therefore the one decision that throws all others into such sharp focus. You can get a new job, move to a new house, make new friends, find new partners, but once you're a parent, you're a parent for life.

And yet this period has no name. Unlike childhood, adolescence, menopause, or the midlife crisis, we have no common term for the tumult of time, hormones, social pressure, and maternal hunger that smacks into many women like a train at the end of their twenties and early thirties. There is no medical term, no compound German word, nothing in Latin, Arabic, or French. Astrology may refer to the seven-year cycles of the Saturn return, but this nebulous phrase speaks little of the grit and girth, the blood and weeping, the travel and transformation that I have witnessed, both in myself and the people around me. While in the midst of it, you feel as though you are twisting through a web of impossible decisions—about work, money, love, location, career, contraception, and commitment—each one pulling like a thread on all the others, impossible to untangle or move through without unraveling the whole thing. In hindsight, many, if not all, of those decisions were rendered so intense by the pulsing, beating, inescapable knowledge that your fertility is finite, that you are running out of eggs, and that one day your body will no longer give you the option to have children.

These years are compelled by the eternal question: Should I have a baby, and if so, when, how, why, and with whom? That question then creeps into every area of your life. It is the *rat-a-tat* of the tracks beneath your feet. The bassline to everything. Whether you want to be a parent or not, as a person in your late twenties and thirties, perhaps even into your forties, the slow march of unfertilized opportunity brings an urgency to your life that no other period can quite match. You have to decide what you want, now, before your body takes the choice away from you.

That there are several words for adolescence in every major European language and not a single one for this second transformative time in a woman's life speaks of two things: that language often lets us down, and that we have never really taken this period seriously. Too often, our journey out of youth, through fertility, and into a new emotional maturity is dismissed as broodiness, anxiety, or "merely" the ticking of the biological clock. In fact, it is a complex focal point of every pressure, contradiction, and fear faced by Western women today, from fertility and finance to love, work, and self-worth.

When I lost my relationship, my home, and my direction at twenty-eight, nobody told me that this was the start of something. Nobody had a shorthand to explain that out of so much loss would come an entirely new identity, that most of the people around me were also in flux, whether they were in relationships or not. We were all wrestling with the same questions, and many of us were also feeling hamstrung by the pressure to make big decisions: in terms of parenthood, an irrevocable decision. As I stood before the great rolling departure board of my future, I had no idea that I was doing so shoulder-to-shoulder with millions of other women on their own journey through the same maternal quandary.

It is because we haven't identified this period with a name that we're not prepared properly for it when it comes, and we haven't developed the tools to navigate it. This is a problem if women are then made to feel that everything that happens during this time is somehow only our responsibility, ours to confront, carry, and resolve, alone. By adjusting women's bodies with contraception and allowing men to live as eternal teenagers—uncertain jobs, short-term flings, adolescent hobbies—we have placed the burden of whether to try for a baby almost entirely at women's feet. We shield men from the reality of fertility, family, and female desire, because we have been conditioned to consider them uninteresting or unattractive. Throughout my twenties and into my thirties, I tried desperately to appear casual and carefree, believing that any hint at my true, complicated desires—in my case, for love, commitment, independence, a successful career, and ultimately a baby too—would render me single forever. I silenced myself, because I thought it made me more attractive. I tucked my weaknesses, my wants, and my womb out of sight.

I spoke to my friends, of course, but not always with total honesty, which meant that they, also, didn't truly open up to me. By putting on a brave face and acting as if we were in control, we all somehow missed the fact that we were on the same train. Without the common shorthand of language and labels to communicate our experience, we became fragmented, uncertain, anxious, and embarrassed. Well, no more. I am here to crack my neck, unhook my bra, and give this thing a name.

I've come up with plenty of suggestions along the way, formal and informal. Firstly, the jokes: fecund choice, egg roulette, whore crux, ova panic. There are the rural possibilities: winnowing, as in the sorting of grain; lacuna, a gap or space in bone; Rubicon, a river that appears impossible to cross; the dimmet, that magical time between daylight and twilight. There are the Latin ideas: *reortempus*, the time of decision; *procogravidum*, to be heavy with doubt, *quasitinciens*, to be pregnant with questions. Then there are the Germanic options: *Schwangerfast*, to be almost pregnant; *Wechselperiode*, the changing period; *Trockenlege*, to adapt and dry out. All apt, all better than nothing, but none bringing to mind the choking, creeping, bewildering nature of the beast. In the end, like the classification of some newly recognized flower or virulent weed, I'm calling it the Flux: a physical and emotional transformation found growing in the soil of the Panic Years. In the landscape, "flux" means the flowing of water; in our bodies it is the discharge of blood; in physics, the state of constant change. The Flux is the gap between adolescence and midlife, during which women lose that constructed artifice of control over their lives, confront their fertility, and build themselves new identities. The Flux is a specific process, provoked by biology, society, and politics, that drives so many of us through the Panic Years like, well, women possessed.

This is an anatomy of my own Panic Years. It is not a guide to finding the right man, getting your ideal job, learning to love yourself, how to get pregnant, or the best way to raise a child. It is about what happens when you're heading toward the grown-up cutlery and matching sheets of adult life, and wondering if you should have a baby, if you only want one because you were brought up to want one, or if you'd even be able to have one if you tried. It is about trying to establish a career before you disappear into maternity leave; it is about wanting stability while your friendship group splinters into the parents and the not-parents; it's about not just looking for a boyfriend or girlfriend, but a potential parent for your theoretical child; it is about fertility, gender inequality, and social stigma. It is about why you find yourself doing the Panicked Math that if you meet someone, and you date for a year, and if it takes two years to get pregnant, but if you were to aim for this job, and if your period started at thirteen, and your mom's eggs ran out at forty . . . until suddenly you're not doing math anymore but asking something bald and blank and unending: Who am I and what do I want from life?

It is about a second adolescence, not of new bleeding and breasts, but of self-awareness, maturity, and seriousness. So, in order to make the broader point that this period deserves recognition, I am making the personal point of relaying mine, as it happened and is still happening. I am describing how I went from a single, commitment-phobic flatmate to full-blown, flat-booted mother, via heartbreak, push-ups, the smell of boot polish, a trip to a nunnery, summer in Berlin, pregnancy, labor, one very unfortunate bus window, and much, much more. I will explain how the Flux affected my friendships, my relationship, my environment, my mind, my work, my very ability to move my body. For the first time, I am giving the Flux a name and walking through it, step by step.

In my case, the Panic Years began at a house party visiting my friends in Liverpool, wearing a silver dress, standing in the disintegrating kitchen of a dead landlady whose lodger had put her ashes in a corner cupboard and thrown rugs over the rotten floorboards. My period was a month overdue and I was waking at four thirty most mornings with my mouth full of fear and sickness. I'd left my boyfriend behind to come and visit my friends. As I looked around that green kitchen I was gripped with a thought that had been quietly lying under everything for weeks: I might be pregnant. I didn't want to be pregnant. Not like this, not now. I didn't want to be trapped that way. I knew it then with a clarity that frightened me. My body was telling me, before my mind had even realized, that I was unhappy. My womb had let off an emergency flare and, duly, I watched it burn. A month later, I was single, not actually pregnant after all, sitting in a greasy spoon in Walthamstow and marking my twenty-eighth birthday, alone, over a cup of instant coffee.

Without the anchor of a partner, I spun into a world of work, parties, sweat, deadlines, running, travel, and cigarettes. Without the counterweight of love, and with the explosive ambition of a young journalist, I discovered that I could say yes to anything, everything. In fact, the more I said yes, the less I had to think. For a whole year my one professional rule was to say yes to absolutely every commission that came my way. I also went camping, had sex with men who couldn't love me and whom I couldn't love, pitched articles to newspapers I'd looked up to all my life, swam on windy beaches, wrote my heart out, asked myself if I really wanted a baby after all, cried for days before my period, made clothes, went on the radio, cut my hair, and listened to my records.

One morning, in the speckled gray of early consciousness, I woke up with the tang of something familiar in my mouth, like the snatches of a song you used to sing at school. In my own bedroom, under my own pictures, under my own bedding smelling of my own washing powder, I was finally recalling who I was.

Which is all very well, but by this point I was thirty, and my female friends, who until that moment had been eating toast and drinking tea with me, ripping through their heartstrings and laughing in the face of time, suddenly grabbed their bags and were off: boyfriends, houses, engagement rings, weddings, pregnancies, babies. The race was on—against time, against our bodies, against the half-life of sperm and, inevitably, against one another. I knew, because I'd been there when it had happened, that my mother got menopause early—at forty—and so I had probably inherited less time than my peers; I was facing a shorter deadline. As a result, my Panic Years were particularly intense, my sprint for security more acute, my need to get my shit together relatively extreme. And yet somehow, I hadn't heard the announcement, hadn't even bought my ticket. The people I loved most were slipping away from me, while I was left behind, staggering in their wake.

Less than two years later, I was in love. This man, with his shoulders like scaffolding and a chin like a peat shovel, arrived into my life unexpected, unpredicted, and unannounced. Just like that, I had boarded the train. I didn't know the destination, but I knew I was going somewhere. And yet, what I'd imagined to be the solution to my disquiet turned out to just be the doorway to more questions. Big questions. For any woman entering a new relationship during the Panic Years, the future is pockmarked by the sort of existential decisions that can bring you to your knees. What does it mean for a working woman in an unaffordable country facing a climate disaster to commit to a partner, let alone the future of a child? How do you react when your best friend announces that she is pregnant? Is yours a different path? What if your partner doesn't want children? What if they want children but just not yet, not now, not like this? Is this the time to move to a new country, change careers, buy an insanely expensive coat, fuck it all up, and sleep with somebody's brother, buy a house somewhere cheap and go freelance? Should you buy a dog?

Like your teeth being cracked out of your jaw so the cold wind can rush over your every exposed nerve, you realize that you have lost control again. Your body is held, suspended by contraception in a state of false infertility, while your mind races through the futures being lost. You may be on the train, but you forgot, somehow, to check the destination, and now, fists clenched and eyes burning, the world is sliding past you in a liquid blur. Love cannot stem the flow of eggs leaving your body, a warm bed doesn't help you decide what you want to do for a career, a partner doesn't end the civil war between brain and womb, a plus-one doesn't necessarily make you feel whole. Three years after leaving my last relationship I realized once again something painful and something true: the Panic Years do not end with sex or shared towels; they aren't simply quieted by the weight of another body in your bed.

As I careened around my life, ending relationships, trying to earn more money, sharing my rented flat with friends I loved, going to therapy, strengthening my body, and having sex with increasingly kind people, I saw absolutely nothing tying those decisions together. As I move into my mid-thirties and away from all the dust and drama that blinded me to the long view, I see that the prospect of motherhood had been hovering over me all along. It had been my engine, preparing me for launch. Of course. Throughout the Panic Years, my body and my mind were unconsciously breaking up my old life in order to pave the way for a new one, one in which I could decide, if I wanted, to try for a baby. As Luke Turner writes, in his beautiful memoir *Out of the Woods*: "The decision to dynamite the foundations of a life will always throw rubble in unexpected directions." Because, as reluctant as I have been to recognize it, and admit it to the people who mattered, I probably always wanted a baby.

As I sit here, typing on a laptop balanced on my baby's changing table, I know that in many ways, I am writing this book for the Nell at twenty-eight, who stood in that kitchen in Liverpool, in her silver dress, beside another woman's urn and felt sick with panic at what might happen. But really, I'm writing this book for everyone: those embarking on their Flux, those in the midst of the disorientation, those who are curious about motherhood whether they see themselves doing it or not, those who have been through it all and are looking for recognition, and for the men and women who just want to know what the Panic Years are like. I am not pretending to be a gin-swilling party mess, I am not writing an academic treatise, I am not using experimental literary forms to prove that mothers can be creative too. I am simply showing, as honestly and as meaningfully as I can, what this time can be like: why a thirtieth birthday party can seem like a one-woman wedding, what it's like to be the only single person at a dinner party, how to cope with being sexually rejected in a very small tent, why you might start accidentally crying when your boss asks where you see yourself in five years' time, how it feels to get your period after wondering if you're pregnant, the fever that descends when you decide you want to try for a baby, what it's like to imagine throwing that baby against the wall.

This book will celebrate the thundering libido of the thirty-year-old as she drags herself up a mountain with a conspiracy theorist and his receding hairline. What it's like to wade through your own ambivalence about what might be the biggest decision of your life. To describe the lace-edged hell of other people's baby showers. To relate how it feels to piss on a stick in a dripping toilet and hold your entire future in four centimeters of acidic paper. It will stand on the shoulders of those moments to ask: Where are we and how did we get here? How do we liberate ourselves from our social conditioning, why do relationships end, why do people still get married, when does a fetus become a baby, what is the right salary, what is a family, how significant is turning thirty-five, and how should we allocate the responsibility for contraception? As the weight of all these questions, and more, come crashing down on the shoulders of women in their twenties, thirties, and forties, it's time to start looking for answers.

1

SUDDENLY SINGLE

I am lying in my grandmother's bed, listening to church bells and Noel Edmonds.

Of course, it's not really my grandmother's bed. It's not the place where I unwrapped my stocking on Christmas mornings—the stocking that was, in fact, a pair of my grandmother's old support tights, in a shade of "mink" or "bamboo."

No, this is another bed—a single bed the color of prosthetic limbs, tucked away in a small room in the attic of the her nursing home. After decades of farming, livestock, Labradors, apple trees, and open streams, my grandmother has come to live in a single room, overlooking slate roofs, surrounded by bricks. She is spending the last few years of her life in a town—something she has never done in all her ninety-four years of existence. It's great for me: I can come on the train, have lunch in a market café, and pop out to Savers to buy her yet more Nivea talcum powder. Not that I am doing any of these things today.

Today, I am lying in her bed. I am lying, curled on my side, staring at her white wardrobe full of tweed pleated skirts, cream satin blouses, and fluffy, discarded slippers. *Deal or No Deal* blasts out of the small corner television like a boiling kettle. There is a bowl full of clementines on a tray, beside a pile of unread *Shropshire Stars*, weekend newspaper supplements and a book about the royal family. In the room below me, a man the shape of a deck chair is wheezing to the door, his tracksuit bottoms sagging down withered buttocks to expose white, infantile underwear. In the kitchen, the cook is spooning out mashed potato beside an egg and cress salad, listening to Magic FM. In the drawing room, two women in cardigans and tapered trousers doze in front of the television as a cookery show transforms, magically, into an old black-and-white musical. In the garden, one of the younger residents smokes a cigarette the length of a drinking straw and watches a robin pecking at a fat ball.

I am not crying. I have entered that hollow state of pure numbness where you can simply stare, like a stagnant pond, at nothing. I shall lie here, I think, forever. My muscles will atrophy, I will grow whiskers, someone will come from time to time and put me in a clean nightie, I will eat custard and drink sherry. I will lie in my grandmother's bedroom like the layer of talc and tissues that lines the inside of her handbag. I will stay here until it's all better, all over, all finished.

Two weeks earlier, I lay in bed with my boyfriend of six years while he gently and thoroughly broke through my denial about the state of our relationship like a handful of sticks.

"If we weren't going out, I don't know how much time we'd actually spend together anymore," he says.

Snap.

"You're always busy."

Snap.

"I don't think you want to be with me."

Snap.

The night holds its breath as I lie, awake, feeling as exposed as if all my skin had been peeled off. Suddenly touching this man, this bear in a human suit, feels illicit, like a violation, like putting your hand in someone else's pocket. So I lie still. After six years of looking after me, here he is, helping me again. Only this time, he's helping me to break up with him. He tells me to take a couple of days, not to worry, that it'll be all right, but to think about whether I want to break up with him. In the morning, I cling to him like a life raft, crying, terrified, promising that I don't want anything to change. All the while, a small voice inside is spreading out like a drop of ink in a glass of water, telling me that it already has. In those next two days we are closer than we have been for months: talking, sitting together, eating the same meals, folding each other's washing. I look at his back—the size of a mattress—as he washes up.

I tell him that I love him, but I'm not excited. I think I want something but I don't know what.

He looks down. "Of course I'm not exciting," he says. "I'm the man you bought a washing machine with. Nobody's excited by that guy."

My heart falls apart like a dandelion in the rain.

And so we break up. Of course we do. I have never yet met a "are we breaking up?" conversation that doesn't end with yes. Without knowing it, I was falling through a rip in the fabric of what was suddenly my old life and entering headlong and high speed into something new: the Flux. Like so many thousands of children after a breakup, I go to stay with my mother while he packs up his things. In my case, that means three stops down the 48 bus route to the other side of the River Lea. On my way in to work, I actually cycle past our flat and see that he has taken down all his pictures and piled them up on the floor. The flat looks ripped bare, impersonal, and unbearably sad.

When you have spent your entire twenties with another person— first as friends, then as lovers, then as companions—it can come as a bit of a shock to realize that you have absolutely no idea who you actually are without them. What you eat, when you sleep, whom you know, what you own, how you talk, what you watch, where the vacuum lives, what time you wake up, what you'll do for your birthday, what you find funny, whether you like your cutlery, if you can fix your bike, how you do your job, how you dress, whom you trust, what you listen to, what you remember, even just what you like—you don't know any of it anymore. You have no idea who you are because, for the greater part of your adult life, you have been with another person. Their tastes became your tastes became theirs became yours became you became them. I had been an independent, working woman for all of about six months before I got together with my boyfriend. I was unbaked clay. So when, smack bang on my twenty-eighth birthday, we broke up, I had little to no adult self to return to, to draw on, or to take comfort in. I was years behind, years out of touch. No wonder I felt paralyzed, stunned, and untethered: I was lost.

But it wasn't just me that I'd lost. Oh no. I'd lost his family—his elderly aunt with her mantelpiece full of birds and his wonder-knitting mother with her taste for sixties Motown—I'd lost his friends, I'd lost his skills, his help, his tools and towels and foot massages, I'd lost his version of me and I'd lost all the futures we'd laid out together. In breaking up with the man I assumed I'd have a family with, I'd lost my potential children too. When you're a twenty-eight-year-old woman whose mother went through menopause at forty you know, better than most, in both your body and in your brain, that there is a finite window in which to have children. That is bearable when you have a partner because, even if they're not quite ready yet, or you're not quite sure, at least you can tell yourself that you have all the equipment ready for when it comes to decision time. You can wait. For a bit. But if you're a twenty-eight-year-old woman pulling herself through the burning metal of heart-break into the great empty plains of single life, then that finite time suddenly becomes a very different prospect. It can feel daunting. It can feel deadly. And the math that lies across the horizon becomes incredibly important.

If, like my mother, I was going to go through menopause at forty, then my fertility might start to notably decrease from any time in my mid-thirties. That meant I probably needed to start trying for a baby—to find out if I was even fertile—before I was thirty-five. If I had problems, that still gave me a couple of years to try the alternatives. But, wait, if I wanted to start trying for a baby before I turned thirty-five, then that meant I needed to meet someone, specifically someone who would fall in love with me and want to start a family with me, by the time I was, what, thirty-two? That would give us a few years to enjoy together as a couple before we started shagging with intent. It would give us some memories to harvest later when we were sleep-deprived, stretched, and full of resentment. But wait, it had taken me seventeen years to get my first boyfriend and three and a half years to meet my second. If that was anything to go by then I had at least three years of being single ahead of me. That brought me to, what, twenty-nine? But, hold on, almost everyone had at least a couple of years living independently, sleeping with people, concentrating on work before they started "dating" dating. The math told me I should have broken up with my boyfriend at twenty-seven. I was going to have to grieve a six-year relationship when I was already a year behind. Somehow I needed to be able to live my life, be independent, have sex with someone without crying into their mouth, fall in love, and wait for them to be ready to try for a family, and I needed to do it all right now or I would run out of time and never have the choice: my body and its finite eggs would take the decision away from me before I'd even had a chance to try.

Since that weekend, it has been my strong belief that all heartbroken women, but particularly those entering their Flux, should get a week's stay in an institution where everyone else is simply too old and too jaded to talk about babies, love, or heartbreak. We should immediately be checked into a large, semimunicipal building where the proximity of death makes a mockery of heartache and where the gentle rhythm of soap, pads, meals, naps, and bed can take us over completely. During breakups there is a time for analysis and a time for paralysis: those first few weeks belong almost entirely to the latter. You are not yet ready to pick over the bones of what went wrong: all you can really do is hold your seams together and listen to your pulse. There is time enough to digest, discuss, and disassemble the end of a relationship later, with friends, family, perhaps even with a professional listener. You cannot swallow the thing whole, so in the beginning why not just lick your wounds? Why not take some time to escape your real life? And where better to take care of yourself than a nursing home?

You may wonder why I, a newly single, London-living woman, would take such comfort in the pastel curtains, bathroom disinfectant, hair curlers, local radio, paperbacks, pleated skirts, grandfather clocks, and surgical stockings of a provincial care home. Why I was so ready to succumb to the steady, slow schedule of mealtimes, nap times, singalongs, and pill dispensing. Why I felt such profound calm as I sunk into the boil-washed bedding of my indefatigable grandmother or looked out across the unwalked lawn. The answer is simple: for everyone else in that great redbrick house on the hill, the dreadful, urgent pulse of possibility and fertility had been silenced. Their biological clocks had stopped. They no longer had the option. Their work had been retired. Their friends were falling away. Their Flux was long since spent. Those women had either had their children or they had not. They had loved, bled, sweated, leaked, and lost, and now they were coming into their final age. Their bodies were drying, turning pale, thinning to nothing. Their crepe-like skin, white hair, thick toenails, and crumbling teeth were the tangible manifestations of time, inarguable and unstoppable. I may have felt a rising tide of hopelessness against my ribs as I thought of the future, the family, and the theoretical life I had just lost, but it was nothing these people had not been able to manage. My heartbreak was not unique, not unprecedented, not world-changing. I was simply following along the broken path of so many people before me, trying to step from love to love without too much mud along the way.

Which is not to say those women were unkind or unsympathetic. Some of them were wonderful. During a weekend visit a few months later, as I passed through the dining room between sherry time and lunch, a ninety-two-year-old Latvian woman called Elsa suddenly grabbed me by the waist.

"My dear!" she exclaimed, her dark blue eyes fixing me like pins. "You remind me of the gypsy women I used to draw naked at art school!"

I was flattered. Elsa, I later found out, had been a fine art student in 1920s Paris—a time when it was considered unseemly for respectable women to pose naked. In her long life she had been a food writer, had been married, had given birth to two sons, had made dresses, spoke three languages, and held great dinner parties. Her body may have been collapsing like a soufflé, but this woman was absolutely stiff with life, with humor, and with joy at the world. To look into her animated cinnamon bun of a face and try to explain that I felt hollowed out by the loss of love, security, and my twenties felt like trying to whinge at a cliff face about the wind.

In a certain kind of film, pop song, or novel—"I Will Survive," *Muriel's Wedding*—breaking up with an unsuitable partner is where the narrative ends. Single life, freedom, and independence is the happy ending for everyone, from twentysomething graduates to sixty-eight-year-old divorcées. We strive for a life untethered. But for women in the Flux, a breakup is often just the beginning of the story, and freedom is just another word for nothing left to lose. As my friend the author Amy Liptrot once put it to me in a brilliantly caps-heavy text: "I remember when I broke up with my Berlin boyfriend and a (younger) friend tried to console me by saying, 'You're not weighed down any more.' I was like, 'I WANT TO BE WEIGHED DOWN. BRING ME THE WEIGHTS. I'M READY.'"

I knew exactly what she meant. As I slid toward my early thirties like mud off a trowel, I wasn't single because I wasn't ready for commitment. I had ended an imperfect relationship precisely because I wanted to find the person who would commit to me and my intentions entirely. However deeply I had repressed it in the name of self-protection, I wanted to be weighed down by love, plans for the future, co-ownership, and someone else's dysfunctional family. I wanted to buy a sofa together, to walk in the mountains together, to put my passport in a box file bought specifically for the purpose. I wanted a grown-up relationship with someone who felt ready to be a grown-up. Of course, at the time all I thought I wanted was to date someone who drank tea, did the crossword, had a pneumatic sex drive, and worked in a full-time job. In hindsight, those characteristics are still a pretty good pencil sketch of my ideal life partner and co-parent.

While my mind may have been sifting through the chaff of heart-break, loneliness, and female panic, my body and my unconscious were cooking up a kind of master plan.

"I remember thinking, 'I don't want to get to thirty-four and still be having really dysfunctional relationships," says Dolly Alderton, one warm July morning as I sit in her perfect flat, like something out of a French New Wave film, and lightly grill her about the year in which she stopped having sex. Dolly's bestselling book, *Everything I Know About Love*, was an honest, lyrical, and funny look at life, love, friend-ship, and your twenties. She has also written, with wit and wisdom, about her decision, at twenty-nine, to stop dating, stop having sex, stop texting men, even—wherever possible—stop masturbating. Who better to ask about sex, heartbreak, and the beginning of the Flux?

"Until I changed my attitude to sex and men, I wasn't going to be in a place where I could have a loving, working partnership and create a family," she says, biting into one of the bagels I'd turned up with, as a peace-offering-cum-bribe. "It was like that room had been so disproportionately busy and glaring with light that I just needed to close the door, put the key in my pocket, and know I could revisit it later."

When she turned twenty-eight—a fundamental year in so many women's Panic Years—Dolly had just come out of a relationship, was in therapy, stopped dating, stopped having sex, wrote her book, moved out of flat-shares, and started living on her own. All in six months.

"I thought it was a breakdown," she laughs. "I did a lot of reading about sex addiction, made amends with exes, spent a lot of time with the women I loved, and rebuilt a relationship with my family. It was my way of rebuilding a sense of self, really," she explains.

How much of that work was, I wonder, directly related to the desire to become a mother?

"I definitely was thinking of babies, in the sense that I knew I had to get this sorted before the next stage," she says, articulating with frightening accuracy a feeling I have only recently come to understand. "Lots of women I know basically treated their late twenties as a sort of convalescence between their twenties and the next period of their life."

It may seem counterintuitive to stop having sex because you want babies, and yet, as Dolly argues, in order to form the kind of solid relationship you need in order to survive those early years of having a kid, you might need to stop having the kind of sex you've previously been, ahem, hammering away at. Was she ever worried about running out of time?

"No. Not then," she says, looking me straight in the eye. "But I'm really worried about it now. Fertility is such a difficult feminist issue because our biology hasn't caught up with our politics. I would love to be able to say, 'I don't need a man, I don't need to date, I can just focus on myself, click my fingers when I'm forty, and have a baby then!' But it just doesn't work like that."

Alas, it does not.

Of course, not every Flux begins with a breakup. For many women, the Flux is ushered in midway through a relationship or during their single years by some other significant event—moving to a new country, changing or losing your job, watching a colleague get promoted, getting engaged, discovering you have endometriosis, watching your best friends have babies or buy a house, to name just the big-ticket items. But, of course, very often people do break up with a long-term partner at the end of their twenties. A survey carried out by Nationwide Building Society, of all people, showed that the average relationship in your twenties lasts 4.2 years—a statistic I read in 2017 and have carried around ever since like the NHS number and sexual health center appointment card folded into my purse.

During that late-twenties crunch time when jobs become careers, renting becomes buying, lovers become partners, and friends become parents, there is often a mini-earthquake of breakups, as people roll the dice one last time before making a big commitment. We may drift apart, we may argue or cheat; we may despair over snoring, drinking, socks in the kitchen, buying toilet paper, sulking at dinner, making plans, not making plans, hating to make plans. But sometimes all we're really doing is standing in front of another person and realizing, with a cold, blank, and unavoidable sadness, that we were wrong. That we both made a bad call. Under those circumstances, ending a relationship isn't just healthy, timely, and brave—it could be genuinely lifesaving. But what comes next? How do you mend a broken heart? How long does it take to meet the right person? When will you get over it? Will you ever love again? What do you actually want from life? Solving that question brings the priest and the doctor in their long coats, running over the fields.

2

LET'S GO OUTSIDE

I never wanted to get dumped at a train station.

Sometimes dating is like a damp log: it smolders, smokes, and spits, but never really catches. When it ends, your heartbreak isn't so much for a person as for something that never really was: an opportunity ripped away, a trick of hope you played on yourself. This was one of those heartbreaks. And here I was, twenty-eight, standing on platform four of Crewe train station, in a Pumpkin Café, trying to decide between a £2.99 pot of ice-cold, day-old bircher muesli and a £1.29 grab bag of salt-and-vinegar crisps. As the delayed trains and platform alterations rolled above my head like so much amber rain, I held the foil-topped pot of yogurt-soaked oats in my hands and felt my resolve crumble.

Just forty minutes earlier, a man with whom I'd been camping told me that while he did want to be a father, he didn't want to have a girlfriend. We had been sitting on a Virgin train pulling into Stafford, on our way back from a weekend in the mountains, when he decided that now was the time to tell me the good news. He had kissed my lips, picked up his bag, and got off the train. At the window, he winked, smiled, and watched me pull away. From Stafford to Crewe, I stared into the dirty two-pence sun as it lowered against the ground, my heart pushing against my throat like an angle grinder, and tried not to cry. He had kissed me. He had winked at me. He didn't want me. I looked at the people in my train car and burned with shame; they had seen it all. They had watched me, like a wet garbage bag, be politely but firmly dropped. I was tousled, I was in leggings, I had my feet propped on a bag the weight of a corpse, and I was a fool. An utter fool.

Although I'd known this man for nearly two years, this was almost the first proper time I'd ever spent with him alone. I know. Look, I *know*. Going from acquaintance to sweaty, rural lover is a strange move, but it became something of my signature. You see, I never managed to quite get a grasp on low-key hookups. I never downloaded any apps, never swiped right, rarely even asked people out for a drink or dinner. Instead, almost out of nowhere, I would ask a man I barely knew if he wanted to come and spend a weekend with me in the middle of nowhere, sweating beneath two stretched sheets of polyester. You'd be genuinely amazed how often they said yes.

Anyway, because I hardly knew this man I hadn't really talked to him about the future; I hadn't dared. I've never been particularly interested in weddings, and I didn't care about being popped "the question," but I had still imagined waking up in a bed beside him and seeing his armpit hair in the morning sun. I had hoped for clinging kisses, text messages, and private jokes. I had dared to imagine baking him bread, balancing a jam jar of cigarette ends on a windowsill, having a shared bookshelf, and, because it was always something I imagined in my future, a baby. It may sound ridiculous, like the culmination of every commitment-phobic's worst fears, that after just two nights in a two-man tent in the middle of nowhere I was already plotting out a life of total interdependence and parenthood with a man I barely knew. But it's not quite as simple as that.

For me, and for many other people in the Flux, imagining what it might be like to bear somebody else's baby, to trust them with your womb, to entwine your life inextricably with theirs, is a way of testing how you feel—how you really feel—about them. It's like watching someone dance and imagining if you could have sex with them; it's like picturing yourself behind the desk of another office to see if you could do that job; it's like looking in the windows of a ground-floor flat and wondering if you could live with that wallpaper. I thought about having people's babies as a way to test myself, my level of attraction, commitment, and intention. If the idea made me recoil, I knew the thing was a nonstarter. If I felt protective over an imagined child because of that person's temper, habits, recreational drug use, job, or family, it was a pretty good sign I should stay away (whether I did or not is another question—but the signs at least were there for me to ignore at my will). If I could happily imagine them carrying our newborn baby around the house while singing Stevie Wonder, then I knew at least on some level that I felt comfortable about a future together. And when you're dating after the fallout of a long or significant relationship, if you're dating during the Panic Years, if you're dating while those around you start to settle down, then the future becomes a rather real and immediate thing. The shape of things to come is being molded as you speak. Therefore a baby isn't just something that might happen someday; it's something that could actually happen one day rather soon. Imagining someone I'd just slept with as a father was my way of both getting in touch with an inner, childlike emotional self, while simultaneously drawing up a sketch of a potential future.

So when in those few words he proved himself a willing father but not a partner, he hadn't just shamed my hope and embarrassed my affection, but had whipped away yet another unlived life. He had deleted a potential version of Nell, as well as the children she may have borne. Without necessarily knowing or meaning to, he had pulled back the gums of my affected indifference to reveal a raw nerve of longing. But instead of cherishing that longing, he had walked away, with a wink.

Because I am as technically incapable as I am spendthrift, I had only about seven songs downloaded on my phone. So, as I thundered through Cheshire, my heart aching, I had the choice of listening to either a cover of "It's All Over Now, Baby Blue" by Them or a seventeen-minute version of "Love to Love You Baby" by Donna

Summer. I chose the former. I wish now it had been the latter. With my headphones on, my face against the window, I felt blank. I was a ping-pong ball, puckered and split, sitting in the dust of a barn floor. I was a drystone wall, kicked down. I was an empty, age-smelling Tupperware. I was crying like a fire in the sun.

Of course, there is no good place to break up with someone. The act of breaking up has ruined far too many canal-side walks, much-loved cafés, quiet woods, and foggy pubs already. Which gives me an idea: the state should provide specially designated breakup zones. A sort of twin project to my heartbreak care homes. There should be government-funded, municipal spaces where tear-weary, lustless couples can go to untie the knot. Instead of polluting a restaurant, a nearby park or, worse still, your own home, with that conversation about all the ways they no longer long for you, how much better to get a faceless, automated, no-reply email to your Outlook inbox inviting you to a conference center off the M6. To step into a totally neutral, hideously impersonal room above a platform waiting area, where your partner will sit opposite you, on a molded plastic chair, their elbows resting on a laminated MDF table stained with other people's tears, and slowly crush your heart. To walk, your spirits sinking, into a meeting room on an industrial estate beside a gravel pit, to see your boyfriend standing on carpet tiles, under a fluores-cent strip bulb, and know for sure that you're about to get dumped. You will never have to go back there, you'll never be reminded of it during a pub lunch or long walk, it will never catch you by chance three months later as you take your cousin for a cup of tea. It will remain, forever, a remote, bureaucratic nightmare that was endured and then can be ignored. That is how breakups should work.

I suppose, in many ways, this was the closest I ever got to that hal-cyon dream. Standing in Crewe station, a Siberian wind coming off the shit-splattered train tracks beneath my feet, trying to buy some-thing for less than five pounds that might stop the gnawing of my insides, before getting on a slow train back to London. The rucksack hung on my shoulders like guilt and the fridge lights of the café's display stand shone blindly against my gray hairs. I still wonder if it was what I deserved. I still wish he had done it better.

At that point, I should probably have stopped camping. I should have taken my own advice and seen that eating packet noodles in an anorak is unlikely to lead to lifelong love. I should have considered how struggling into a pair of underwear while doubled over like a shrimp, trying to have sex under a dome of mold-smelling canvas or sleeping in two pairs of men's socks might affect my chances for devotion. But, instead, I camped harder. My friends, I camped like a woman possessed. Over the next two years, I crossed the country like an Ordinance Survey map; I became the Baden-Powell of outdoor boning. I had finally grated together enough self-confidence to understand that what was important to me was landscape, being outdoors, people who said yes, sex, and adventure. I wanted a man who smelled of woodsmoke, who owned a decent sweater, and who could order a train ticket in advance. What I hadn't yet grown to admit was that, as well as romance and adventure, I wanted—and deserved—affection and commitment, too. Still, I had some good walks and plenty of fresh air. You know, like a dog.

There is a myth that permeates our culture so assiduously that it took me years to realize it wasn't always true. The myth is that all men are ravenous sexual beings who spend their entire lives in a state of agitated lust that is either condemned or consented to by those around them. This, I am pleased to tell you, is bullshit. Some men have high libidos. So do some women. Most men will have a high libido at certain times in their life and in particular circumstances. As will most women. Some men have low libidos. Some women have low libidos. In his book *What Do Women Want?* the author Daniel Bergner argues that any differences between the sexes isn't so much biological as one of conditioning: while female sexuality is as raw and bestial as male sexuality, women are taught that the expression of animalistic desire is somehow unseemly or unfeminine. Therefore, when that urgent, animal lust finally surfaces, it may be seem shameful or unnatural in women, and can be quickly suppressed. But it's there; it was always there. After all, as Zoe Williams pointed out in one of her most excellent articles, *Fifty Shades of Grey* became the single biggest-selling book since UK records began precisely because it was bought by horny women in droves—the very same women too often dismissed as "frigid" or "past it" by uncomprehending or underperforming partners. It is an uncomfortable joke of biology, for heterosexual couples at least, that while men often enjoy a high libido at eighteen, women tend to thrust into their high libido at thirty, which is a circle I have never successfully squared. But away from social conditioning, in our very sexual essence and appetite, men, women, and nonbinary people are in many ways the same.

All of which is to say that the fable that all men are hungry and willing for sex at all times is stupid and dangerous. Firstly, it subtly affirms the misheld belief that sexual assault is an act of sex, rather than violence and power. It tells us that men cannot help themselves: that sometimes their lust becomes too powerful to resist and so they must enact sex on someone, anyone, regardless of that person's feelings. Sexual assault has everything to do with gaining power over a person, hurting them, ignoring their humanity, hurting their feelings, and very little to do with sex. Secondly, it means that whenever a straight man and a straight woman come together, they both carry with them an unspoken set of assumptions about what will be wanted and by whom. He will want sex, we are told, and it's on her whether or not to give it to him. I spent far too much of my life feeling like a failure, a harridan, every time a man with ample opportunity did not jump my bones. I felt shameful of the fact that I would have happily chewed through denim to get an orgasm, while the men lying beside me seemed more interested in, well, almost anything else. Which brings me, with dreadful inevitability, to a field in Whitby.

I am sitting in a hot orange tent, alone, in my underwear, in a field overlooking the curving coastline of North Yorkshire, wondering what precisely is going on. It was the summer of 2014 and I had met a man, let's call him Max (mainly because I've never slept with a man called Max), at a party some weeks beforehand in Manchester. Somehow, leaving London to go north always gave me a hint of that heady holiday feeling of being less well-known, less easily judged, and therefore more able to grab every opportunity for fun. Anyway, I had gone home with Max and, despite wearing a handmade velour jumpsuit that made access to my erogenous zones all but impossible, had had one of the best sleepless nights of my life. Encouraged by this, and the fact that he had a car and said he could light a fire, I suggested we go camping one weekend in Yorkshire. What I hadn't quite realized at the time was that Max was also something of a conspiracy theorist with a serious appetite for watching YouTube videos.

Earlier that day, as we sat on a tree-lined bank beside a small rippling stream, he had asked, out of nowhere, if I believed in dragons. I was feeling charitable, so explained that I believed that medieval people may have likened the bite of a large poisonous lizard to fire, and that such lizards may have once wandered over from Europe.

There was a short pause before he turned to me, brushed once more at his hairline with his spider-like fingers, and said, "I don't know. I just think there must be more to it, you know? You don't get so many stories without something going on."

Like food poisoning, the inevitable followed: how 9/11 was an inside job, that Jesus hadn't really been crucified at all, that Parliament was designed on the crossing point of ancient ley lines. The works. My absolute favorite came as we drove through the sunlit hills of North Yorkshire and he started speaking very fast and increasingly loudly about the bus shelters along the side of the road.

"Here, man, just look, all these bus shelters—each one's different, each one has its own thing. They're like little homes."

I agreed that they were, indeed, nice bus shelters.

"But in Manchester, you'd never get that. The city, the state—it controls everyone, everyone's thoughts, your behavior. You're literally manipulated by them into behaving how they want."

I wasn't exactly following, partly as I'd been distracted by a field of hay bales, partly because I was trying to tune this whole fiasco out. Who was "they"? Did he mean the council?

"Yeah, sure. I mean, you must have noticed. All the bus stops in Manchester are red."

He left a significant, almost pregnant pause, as if such a statement spoke for itself.

"Red?" I ventured, with the grim acceptance of a cow sliding down a polished slope.

"Oh, come on, babe, don't tell me you don't know about red," he answered. "Everyone knows that red is a warning color, it sets off a chemical reaction in your hippocampus that sends people into fight or flight. They make everything red—the bus stops, the parking meters, the bins—to make us afraid. To keep us locked down. Out here, where the bus shelters are . . ."

I turned my head to the window and tried to pretend this wasn't happening.

Despite all this, despite the theories and the music snobbery and the endless explanations of things I already knew, I was still determined to make the most of my weekend away with this maniac. Which is how I found myself there, in that tent, reclining attractively across a blue nylon sleeping bag, waiting for something to happen. I'd tried smiling coquettishly as he smoked outside the tent. I'd tried asking softly what he was doing, with no reply. In the end, I'd stuck my head out of the entrance flap and had said, as seductively as I could, "Come and have sex with me."

And then I waited.

And waited.

I read my book. I waited a little longer. I checked my phone. I waited again. Feeling a little crestfallen, I finally looked out, to see Max sitting in his car. I crawled over, in just my underwear, and asked him what he was doing.

"I'm rearranging my CDs," he answered, looking away. "And playing with this cool key ring I bought earlier."

I'm not sure if I've ever felt so sexually rejected in my entire life. Crouching on the damp grass of a Yorkshire campsite wearing less fabric than your average cushion cover, peering through a half-open window at a man who would rather alphabetize his compilation albums than go to bed with me, it was tempting to just roll into a ball and spend the rest of my life living in a hedge. I didn't know this man, didn't particularly like him, but I was willing to share my body with him, give him pleasure, to—in the words of Millie Jackson—make the best of a bad situation. Instead, covered in a hot flush of shame and anger that had become too familiar to me, I crawled back to the tent, pulled on my pajamas, and waited for sleep.

In the cold light of day, and over a Tupperware of even colder soaked oats, I drew together every ounce of my remaining courage to ask him why he hadn't wanted to sleep with me.

He said, fairly casually, that in asking for sex I'd sounded "like an angry teacher" and it had put him off entirely. Forget the fact that teacher-pupil dalliances are one of the oldest hallmarks of erotica; when I had shown him that I was a proactive, apparently confident, and sexual person, he had immediately cast me in the role of an angry, aged, and remote figure of authority to be rebelled against. Because I'd been told throughout my formative years, by advertising, popular culture, and banter alike, that all men are horny all the time, I couldn't see this man's perfectly reasonable disinterest in sex as anything other than a painful and personal rejection. And because he'd been told, throughout his formative years, that "real" men were horny all the time, he couldn't simply accept the fact that he hadn't wanted to have sex, but had somehow to cast me as the villain, the crone, the bully—and the whole episode as my fault. Too eager and you're disgusting, not eager enough and you're a cocktease, too hungry for commitment and you get dumped. As I say, I should have stopped camping.

Not that a life of urban sophistication can protect you from terrible dates; far from it. I've had friends who were asked how much their tongue weighed, if their clitoris "looks Chinese" and had the date's ex-wife's postpartum vagina described with cartographical detail all while sitting in normal, urban settings. I've known people who have been asked to look after someone's pet lizard after a one-night stand, catch a night bus home after realizing their date looked exactly like their cousin, or find out after a year (and one significant holiday to meet his parents) that their boyfriend was actually married and living with his wife. I've known Tinder dates that led to being the plus-one at a wedding full of strangers that very evening; people who have been matched with their own brother on OkCupid; and friends who have been asked for visa marriages on Guardian Soulmates. I wasn't having terrible dates because I'm outdoorsy; I was having terrible dates because a lot of the time dating is terrible.

The question, of course, is why I tried to forge something with these two eminently unsuitable men. Why give my weekends to a raging commitment-phobe and a paranoid fantasist? Why was I drawn to people whose age, geographical location, lifestyle, and beliefs made it impossible for me to ever become their girlfriend? Why spend so much energy on something doomed to fail? Ah, now, solving that question cost me literally hundreds of pounds and several years in a cream room, staring at a venetian blind, talking to a therapist. With that informed hindsight I can tell you: the reason I so single-mindedly tried to make incompatible men fall in love with me was because, deep down, I didn't feel worthy of, or ready for, real commitment.

Sometimes, chasing after people you can't have is a way of protecting yourself against the vulnerability of a real relationship with the people you can. And real relationships do make you feel vulnerable: for them to work, you have to show the other person your faults, your weaknesses, your desires, your private fears, and your true intentions. You have to unpick the armor that surrounds your heart and trust somebody else to hold it, even if that means they might break it. All of which is extremely hard to do when, thanks to a period of upheaval involving breakups, career changes, loss of friendships, or changes in your body, you have lost your sense of who you are and what you want.

Thanks to a big breakup, some fairly unsuccessful dating, the professional successes of my peers, my own financial stagnation, and the long-ignored dysfunction of my childhood, my self-worth and self-esteem had been rendered a damp dishcloth, moldering under the sink. Unchecked, my natural inclination for self-criticism had turned into a roaring flame of self-loathing, like a Zippo lighter with the clip ripped off. As a result, subconsciously, I had begun to feel unworthy of love. And when you feel unworthy of love—either as a result of rejection, trauma, a tricky childhood, whatever—it is amazing how forensically you can sniff out people who will not love you back. Age gaps, distance, addicts, people already in relationships, clashing sexualities: there is a cornucopia of ways to sabotage your own attempts at love and commitment, while still bearing all the hallmarks of someone genuinely looking for a relationship. By dating unsuitable people, you can still sit around pub tables with your friends and scream about wanting a partner, revealing the wounds of your latest rejection, complaining about the unsuitability of everyone you ever meet, appealing for introductions, moaning about what a good girlfriend you'd be, but without actually letting anyone suitable get close. It's like filling your fridge with manure and then complaining that you can't fit in any vegetables; it's like eating shit. And those of us in the Flux can do it for years.

The funny thing is that, during this al fresco rejection fiesta, many of my happy and committed friends saw my life as somehow enviable. Here I was, living the single life; traveling around the country, having sex with glamorous strangers, sleeping under the stars, and stacking up hilarious anecdotes like casino chips. Being both the entertainment and the warning for the couples around me. For people already in the together-forever camp—the people who had bought houses together, gotten married, were trying for a baby, had already become parents—my life was a perfect encapsulation of everything they had traded in. I had freedom, I had variety, I had a healthy disregard for my own security. While they planned a babysitter and an evening of bottle-feeds two weeks in advance just so they could spend three hours out of the house eating a dinner they hadn't cooked, I was rampaging up a dew-wet meadow with someone who might try to undo my bra with his teeth. It was only later, as I sat on their sofas, ashen-faced and nails-bitten, telling them how I'd faked an orgasm or risked an STI or how I'd cried in the night because I'd felt so lonely, that I would catch them looking over at their partner with something like relief.

By the autumn of that year, I'd seen enough of my friends find love to know that I wanted a partner. I knew that, although time was against me, and although I might not yet be ready to admit it out loud, I wanted to one day have a baby. I also knew that, if I was lucky enough to get pregnant, I wanted that baby to have a father, but somehow in the parachute lines of my life, the messages had gotten confused. Until I built up enough self-esteem to ask someone for true intimacy, real interdependence, and total commitment, I wasn't ready to have a relationship, let alone someone's baby.

As a couple, you are far more likely to become good parents if you both have the self-confidence and self-worth to ask for help, show weakness, trust each other, allow conflict, be honest, and bear uncertainty. I wasn't yet strong enough to even ask someone not to sleep with other people, let alone to ask for lifelong commitment and children. I was so scared of being rejected that I kept every potential partner at arm's length, showing only what I considered my good side, affecting ambivalence and pretending to care less than I did. I was so scared of opening myself up to heartbreak that I found myself drawn toward people who would never let me in far enough to love them. I was so reluctant to admit what I really wanted (because it would make not getting it so much harder in the long run) that I pretended to want nothing.

And so, equipped with a meteoric sex drive, a sociable job, an adequate income, and subterranean self-esteem, I had crossed countries, marched up mountains, swum through oceans, and wept through cotton fields, all trying, and failing, to make people who couldn't love me, love me. It was a delaying tactic, I suppose, until I got my shit together. It was a way to satiate desire, without looking too closely at my longing. It was a form of self-protection, even when it looked like self-sabotage. The real work had to be done on myself: with a therapist, on my own, at my pace. By choosing unsuitable people I was, unconsciously, keeping myself single. And by keeping myself single, I was forcing myself to get my shit together. The camping, it turns out, was just a canvas-covered symptom, not the cause.

A few weeks after the Whitby debacle, I was lying in my therapist's office, staring at the slivers of blue sky visible on either side of his window blinds, playing with a chain around my neck and shivering from the cold swim I'd just had on Hampstead Heath. By then, I'd been going to therapy for nearly a year. I was spurred into it after I broke up with my boyfriend and realized that absolutely nobody in my immediate family was any longer in a successful, long-term relationship. My mother, father, sister, and me: we were all single and had all broken up with a significant partner fairly recently. As a result, I began to worry that we were all somehow pathologically, genetically, or intrinsically unable to sustain healthy, lasting relationships. I was scared that something deep within us was broken, and I wanted to fix it.

That day I was telling my therapist about something, something so tiny that I felt almost embarrassed to mention it. But it was also, I knew, something so powerful and so significant that it had seemed to pull my entire life inside out. I had been cleaning out the cupboard under my kitchen sink, putting all the dishcloths in one bucket, throwing away the packets of grass seed, tying up a ball of string.

As I wrestled with years of detritus, I thought of that weekend I'd spent up a mountain, sleeping beside a rushing stream, wondering if the man beside me was falling in love. I thought about his wink on the train as my heart hollowed out. I thought about the messages I'd sent since that all went unanswered. Under an old hot water bottle, I had found some white cable ties and a tin of Kiwi shoe polish. Twisting the lid off, to see if the polish had gone dry, I was hit by the smell like an oar to my stomach. Petrol, leather, dust, age, time, paraffin, the past. I had been momentarily transported back to my grandmother's old boot room: the large red bag she took market shopping, my granddad's waxed jackets, the long-abandoned cleaning gadgets ordered from the *Innovations* catalog, the two-dish bowl of dog food and water with thin blond Labrador hairs floating on the surface, the green quilted coats, the stand full of walking sticks, his caps, her scarves. Somehow that smell seemed to wash through me, filling me up like milk poured onto a bowl of sugar.

As I knelt on my kitchen floor, surrounded by J-cloths and jam jars, one clear thought came up into my mind: *I am worth more than this.* That was it. That was all. I was a person. I'd had a childhood, had a grandmother who poached eggs in butter, had once pushed my arm into a water bucket to feel the ripples, had ridden Welsh ponies with backs like big dippers, had a grandfather who wore braces and kept two wooden hairbrushes by his bathroom window, had been squirted with water from the hose as I ran naked around the backyard in summer, had hidden in a coal shed, had kicked a football against their garage doors, had eaten cooking apples off the tree so sour they made my face twist like a sinkhole, had gone to sleep looking at the cracks on my bedroom wall, had skidded down the banisters in my pajamas. I was a whole person, with a whole past. And, as a result, I was worth more than a bit part in somebody else's sex life.

I pause. My therapist says nothing. Doesn't even move. Like a cartoon of Sigmund Freud, he sits behind me during our sessions, and I can smell his aftershave but can't see his face.

I carry on staring up at the window blind. I wait. He still says nothing.

So I push on. "I just thought—I've had a whole history, my own entire life. That means I have innate worth. I'm not the most beautiful, most intelligent, most successful. But I am worth more than the way all those men treated me."

There is another pause. I hold my necklace in my hand. I stare up at the ceiling. Thousands of pounds, hours of talking, and, at last, I have said something that will eventually make a difference.

3

A FRIEND IN TROUBLE

There is a type of hangover that seems to exist entirely as a texture: the fine grit that lies across your eyeballs, the sheen of sunflower oil that ripens across your forehead, the carpet tile ripped up from the floor of a working men's club and laid across your tongue. It was the grit that was getting to me this time.

As I sat in a café, in Liverpool watching people walk up and down Bold Street on a bright Sunday morning, I tried desperately to rub a little moisture back into my eye sockets. My friend across the table chatted about her new flatmate as I pushed, rolled, and squeezed the bulges beneath my lids like someone kneading pizza dough. The sun was that particular shade of hazy white that only seems to happen if you've spent the preceding night drinking gin, by a fire, surrounded by people in glitter, smoking. I felt, ostensibly, fine. Bright. Breezy, even. Just a little brittle, a tad dry around the edges. Rather too gritty across the old eyeballs. At one point, before my coffee arrived, I considered lying down on the floor and asking a passing waiter if he could just pour my glass of tap water directly into my irises, but three gulps in I was doing okay. I had a voice like road works, skin like cream cheese, a blister on my heel like a waterbed, and a coating of spackling paste across my teeth. But I was rather enjoying looking at the world as though through Tupperware. The previous night had also featured me dancing with a team of male cheerleaders, dressed in a midnight blue jumpsuit with a huge pink collar I'd whipped up on my kitchen floor the week before. I had been single for over a year now; I was wearing a lot of Lycra jumpsuits.

Idly, I wondered why my friend was buying a cake at ten o'clock in the morning, why she'd gone home early the night before, why she was drinking juice, not tea. Tuning back in to what she was saying, cracking my back against the wooden slats of my chair, I asked if she'd had a nice time.

She pulled a piece of hair from behind her ear, curled it around her finger, and started to stroke her cheek with it, absentmindedly. "Yeah, sure. I just got a bit tired."

There was a pause. Her words seemed to run aground like a boat on gravel. My heart hit a double.

"Because I'm pregnant."

My face turned to sand and immediately slid right off my head.

Unless you have the mixed blessing of becoming the first person you've ever met to get pregnant (in which case, congratulations, commiserations, better luck next time), one of the unequivocal hallmarks of the Panic Years is the day you find out that one of your good friends is pregnant. I say "good friends" because, of course, other people get pregnant all the time. That daughter of your mum's friend who wears all the necklaces—she'll get pregnant while you're still at college. That person who used to bring their lunch to work wrapped in a square of cloth and drank bouillon powder as a "hot drink" rather than tea—you'll find out they're pregnant on a night out. That old boss of yours who used to keep sachets of mustard and mayonnaise in her desk drawer—she'll get pregnant just after your first year of going freelance. That girl who you once loaned your deodorant to after PE—she'll be up the duff before sixth form is out. The niece of someone your dad plays guitar with who once tried to make a spliff out of banana skins—she's pregnant too.

These pregnancies mean about as much or as little to you as somebody else's new shed. But when it's one of your best friends, one of the women who can be traced through your bone marrow like stem cells, one of the women who knew your grandparents, with whom you shared your first cigarette, and whose clothes you used to borrow for years at a time: when they tell you they're having a baby, it's like opening a whole new chamber in your heart. It hurts, it stops your breath, your whole life flashes before your eyes, you get a pounding in your chest, and you need to sit down. Of course it's wonderful. But it can be other things, too.

I have known Alice since we were teenagers. I first saw her at a fifteen-person party in someone's back garden in about 1997. She had walked up the path in a pair of white corduroy trousers and the most god-awful patchwork high-heeled boots I'd ever seen, a glass of white wine in her hand. She'd paused by a fish pond the size of a bath mat, thrown her head back, and called out, "Anyone fancy a swim?"

It was love at first sight.

She lived behind a police station, there was a running joke about her boyfriend being called Sebastien Le Camel, and she was utterly unflappable, incredibly kind, and impossibly funny. As the middle child of four siblings, Alice seemed to live her life completely immune to teenage angst. She didn't long for attention, or give a shit if everybody was looking at her. If you needed somewhere to sleep, a snack, someone to safety pin your top back together, or a five-hour chat about what you liked in a pasta sauce, Alice was your woman. One of the greatest moments of pure joy I have ever experienced was, aged seventeen, traveling down to Dorset with Alice behind the wheel of the worst car Japan ever dared to make, with the sun shining, wearing one of her homemade boob tubes. Suddenly Apache Indian's "Boom Shack-A-Lak" came on the stereo and, out of nowhere, Alice recited the entire opening rap, perfectly in time, from memory. Who knew?

In the intervening seventeen years since Alice and I first met, we'd not only lived together but, at one point, spent every single day in each other's company for more than twelve consecutive months, bar a fortnight. We lived together at university, we traveled back home together, we went on holiday together, we went to parties together, shared single beds, drove out to the countryside for picnics, went to the launderette together, bought our food together; everything. I have never before or since met anyone I could so happily and easily coexist with. For a few years in my twenties, she was as intrinsic to my life as my own breath and blood. I called her my wife. She called me wifey.

So that day, when she told me that she was having a baby, I think it's fair to say I handled it the way any twelfth-century peasant handled news of the Black Death. I wept. I lifted her top to look at her skin. I asked how, despite the fact that I had been coming into fairly regular contact with semen for at least a decade. I felt my rectum flutter in panic. I suddenly got a vision of lying in my garden, aged sixteen, studying for my GCSE psychology exam with Alice while listening to Marvin Gaye, and realized it was all over. I felt my armpits go slick. I wanted to hold her up into the sky and scream in her honor. I wanted her to become unpregnant. I wanted to be pregnant too. I wanted to empty my veins out and start again.

We stood on the sidewalk outside. I was going one way, to the train station, back to London, back to writing freelance articles at five A.M. before going to my office job, back to an empty bed and humming laptop, back to my hamstrung life. She was driving home, to her husband, her attic extension, her folic acid tablets, and oven chips.

"Next time I see you, you'll be somebody's mother," I said, my voice catching like thread on a nail. Never mind the fact that this was patently incorrect: that I seemed to have confused her pregnancy with that of a gerbil (I was seeing her again in about three weeks), that she was already on her way to becoming somebody's mother, and that because it was still very early she may, tragically, lose the baby: in my mind, in that moment, I was saying goodbye to my friend, to our old relationship, and to a whole era. Instead of going to the train station I ran round to another friend's flat, a woman who I knew would know already.

As soon as she opened the door she said, "She told you, didn't she?"

Sitting on her little terrace, overlooking the roofs of Roscoe Street and the Radio City Tower, I smoked five cigarettes end to end, twisting the leaves of her plants in my fingers and asking, over and over again, what this meant.

"I feel weird," I said, leaning into my friend's shoulder. "I feel like she doesn't belong to us anymore."

She knew what I meant, of course. Both of us had, at different times, lived with Alice, acted out our happiest domestic moments with her, used her as a surrogate for romance, considered her as close as family. And now, she was somebody's wife, due to be somebody's mother. In the hierarchy of her heart, there would always be at least two people above us. Some lucky heartbeat, an about-to-be-person living in her womb, was going to have the greatest mother I could imagine. I was jealous of her baby, and jealous that she was having a baby. I was sad that our party had ended but suddenly aware of quite how much I wanted to have what she had. I wanted the total expression of somebody's love and commitment to take hold in my own body and create something incredible. If she was in the club, then I wanted to join. But, also, I just wanted one more afternoon with her, drinking wine and smoking fags, up here, looking over the city, weaving jokes out of hot air and innuendo, open-hearted, available, and irresponsible. I wanted my old friend back; I hadn't realized she was going.

Women are taught (by popular culture and convention) that pregnancy should be a source of joy. When a friend reveals her news, we are meant to swell with pride and excitement. We are meant to throw ourselves into knitting, baby showers, and, of course, shopping. And yet, ask any real-life woman how she reacted when one of her best friends first admitted they were pregnant and it soon becomes quite clear that the announcement is, in fact, a focal point of panic, nostalgia, grief, longing, uncertainty, and confusion, too. Of course, you feel happy for your friend. Or, most of the time you do. But it would be inconceivable for such an enormous change in a loved one's life not to have at least some impact on how you feel in the world.

"I felt immediately like I'd missed the grown-up lecture and was flailing through life," one woman tells me, via Twitter. "I went to get my first tattoo that weekend, feeling that if I wasn't in the settled-with-baby group, I had to somehow appear wild and free."

Another woman describes how "I crawled into my wardrobe, shut the door, and cried in the dark" after learning, two and a half years into trying to get pregnant herself, that her friend was having a baby.

"I am genuinely over the moon for my friends, especially those that have struggled for years," adds another, "but it doesn't take away the sadness that I'm becoming this kind of strange Peter Pan figure as I still go to gigs, go on holiday, and don't have as much in common with everyone in the group. I also remember one night, on hearing the news from a friend, getting really pissed and angrily telling my boyfriend everyone is moving on and he was keeping me from doing the same. Even though it wasn't his fault, and we both had decided kids weren't for us."

After finding out that Alice was pregnant, I went home and howled into my pillow for nearly an hour. I was a snapped twig of self-pity, fear, maternal hunger, jealousy, and rage. My happiness for her was temporarily gone. Suddenly ambivalence about children seemed like cruelty. Why did none of the men I'd been with understand what pregnancy meant to me? Alice's husband loved her so much that he wanted to bind his actual DNA to hers. He wanted to create a future life, an entire person, within her body. He wanted her to be tied to him, to rely on him, to be his family forever. I screamed and sobbed into that bedding for my lost twenties, for envy, for my failure ever to find a man who wanted a family, for terror at how fast life was happening all around me, for the weight of this decision I was going to have to lug around behind me forever.

Looking back, I can see that, yet again, I was using "a baby" as a catchall for a lifetime's desire for stability, love, security, the ability to rely on a man without driving him away, the chance to right the wrongs of my childhood, affection, and permission to be vulnerable. But beyond that, I was also, genuinely, hungry for the weight of a child in my body, to give birth, to confront the blood and pain of that transformation and come out with something magical, to give myself over utterly to something and somebody else, to breastfeed, to be called "mum," to hold someone's arms, at knee height, as they walked through a garden, to kiss the underside of their chubby cheeks, to be swollen with milk and pride and oxytocin and purpose, to change nappies, to feel a baby kick beneath my ribs, to look down at a sleeping face and know that it had come from my body and my partner's body and our love.

Apart from the gear-change of maternal hunger that a friend's pregnancy can evoke, "the announcement" can also feel like a robbery. Another person's pregnancy can feel like the loss of yours—however theoretical your own pregnancy may have been. You may feel jealous, wrong-footed, betrayed, that someone you loved and trusted has jumped ahead.

"I'd recently lost one and couldn't [get pregnant] again," one woman tells me, over email. "I was unfairly angry with [my friend]. I cried on the phone when she told me and didn't really talk to her again throughout her pregnancy. I was quite selfish; I only realized how selfish once I got pregnant with my little girl. But it's so hard to control your emotions in that scenario."

To react to a newly impregnated womb with tears, shouting, anger, and envy is uncomfortable and upsetting for everybody involved, but it is also really not your fault. Under our old friend capitalism, we are conditioned to view the allocation of all resources as a competition. If you want apples, you have to beat all the other people who want apples in order to get them. If you want a house, you have to see off the sneaky counterbidding rats who want that house too. If you want a job, you might well have to get somebody fired in order to move in on their patch. This dog-eat-dog mentality is what keeps us wanting more, buying more, producing more, borrowing more, believing we can purchase our way out of, into, and around every human experience. In so doing, we keep the economy rolling on.

Even when the resources are intangible and immaterial, the capitalist instinct remains: we go through life feeling in competition for love, relationships, respect, approval, health, fertility, a sense of belonging. We may know, rationally, that love, commitment, and babies are not a finite resource to be doled out on a first-come-first-served basis. But to know it emotionally is another matter. Of course, when humans lived in the sort of 150-person tribes for which we were designed, it was quite possible that one person's pregnancy would genuinely mean that those around her would have to survive on less, in order that she and her baby be catered to But even then, in our prehistoric and largely speculative past, the pregnancy of a peer did not somehow suck up all the fertile sperm available. Just because your friend is having a baby doesn't mean you're less likely to do the same. The competition between women for pregnancy is the effect of perceived competition, not real resource allocation.

It is also true that there is a proportion of the population who never will have kids. According to the Office for National Statistics, of women born in the UK in 1971, 18 percent were childless when they turned forty-five. Firstly, I know that deeming forty-five years old as the cutoff point for women to have children may seem arbitrary, but in order to collect these kind of statistics you need to put the margins somewhere. It is also worth pointing out that, while this statistic is nationally representative, it doesn't mean those figures will apply to your friendship group directly—it is unlikely that exactly 18 percent of your friendship group will remain child-free all their life. The pattern of pregnancy and baby-making is a patchwork, with huge variation across communities, locations, economic groups, and physical types. For every thirty-eight-year-old single woman clenching her fists at another "Baby on Board" badge, there is a twenty-four-year-old seven hundred miles away who will, out of choice, never have a baby. While 18 percent of British women may never have a baby, it is still absolutely possible that every single woman from your primary school may have at least one baby by the time she is thirty-five. Statistical observation is not diagnostic fact. And yet, the more of your friends who have kids, the more likely it feels (if not becomes) that you will be the one who doesn't. Somebody, you tell yourself, has to be the 18 percent, after all.

"For me, it's gone from, 'Shit, are you going to keep it?' ten years ago, to now: smiling through gritted teeth and saying congratulations and offering to babysit while simultaneously feeling I will break with sadness," one woman tells me anonymously on Twitter. "And oddly enough it's not so much the fact of a baby on the way or the years of toil and joy that I envy so much as the certainty and security of a couple deciding together to share something so momentous. Being single and without children, and not welcoming either of these situations, means pregnancy announcements create even more distance between me and my closest friends."

I know that distance. I have poured my envy into that distance. I have wailed into that distance. You may have too.

Some women, of course, are more sanguine about the prospect of a best friend's pregnancy than others. I absolutely love this response from a fellow journalist who contacted me by email after hearing I was writing this book.

"My best friend told us with a 'bun in the oven'–style prank," she said. "We were at Center Parcs and she actually put a paper bag in the oven. I felt total overwhelming joy. It did mean she couldn't do a lot of things over the holiday—drink, go on the rapids, etc.—but in terms of my happiness for her it was a hundred percent sincere. I think it probably is because it's not something I want at the moment, so I felt no envy or comparison to my own life."

But even in these circumstances, a best friend's pregnancy can still bring the question of babies bobbing, unwanted, back up to the surface. As she put it herself, "Obviously, it started me and my partner talking about it more and more. We had a very long car journey home talking about the logistics of parenthood . . . Still, I will be taking the pill for a little while yet please and thank you."

Another friend texted me in response to my discussion on Twitter to say, simply, "I laughed hard: it was the same week I stood in Boots, puzzled that people would need multiple pregnancy tests in one packet."

If the average age for a British woman to have her first child is 28.8 years old, it is, I suppose, faintly ridiculous that I was shocked to learn that my thirty-one-year-old friend was having a baby. This wasn't a teenage pregnancy; I already had a couple of gray pubes. But the fact that we were slap-bang in the middle of the British baby-making window didn't alter the fact that, somewhere in my heart, we were all still the group of seventeen-year-olds who drew heavy unibrows across our faces to go to an eighties party dressed as Madonna. In my head, we were still all just playing at grown-ups, talking about it speculatively, testing the water before "really" settling down. But once one of your contemporaries has a baby, the truth is harder to ignore. Time is passing, chapters in your life come to an end, and your twenties are a decade, rather than a way of life. Don't reproach yourself if that realization elicits panic, nostalgia, fury, disappointment, *hiraeth,* or confusion; your feelings are your feelings and the only way to deal with them is to accept they are real and temporary. But do try to remember that nobody ever got pregnant just to make their best friend feel like shit. The chances are, they weren't even thinking of you at all.

Of all the responses I've heard from women reacting to a friend's pregnancy, one of my favorites is this, of pure, unadulterated shock: "When I called to tell my sister, she was at our best friend's house" said one woman over email. "She started screaming, then everything got quiet. Her friend picked up the phone and said she had run to take a shower. I still don't know if that was a good or a bad reaction."

A study from the Bocconi University in Italy and University of Groningen in the Netherlands using the data of 1,170 women, of whom 820 became parents during the study period, found that after one of the women in each friendship pair had a baby, the likelihood that her friend would also have her first baby went up for about two years, and then declined. In short, once one of you gets "in trouble," there is a temporary spike in friends following suit.

The two researchers leading the study put this down to a combination of factors: social influence, also known as good old-fashioned peer pressure; social learning, i.e., once you've seen someone close to you wrestle with sleep deprivation, mastitis, croup, and crawling, you feel more able to embark on them yourself; and finally cost-sharing—if you're going to have a baby, why not do it while those around you can share the burden of childcare, get their children's secondhand clothes and old toys?

To this list, I would also add the matter of emotional permission. When Alice told me that she was pregnant, it suddenly seemed that I was being given license to want the same thing. I was no longer the secretly broody outlier in the group—my desire had aligned to that of at least one of my friends, not to mention her partner. If she could do it—could put her career on hold, take the hit to her relationship, stop going out, and start spending her evenings googling rashes—then surely I could too?

As the renowned professor of philosophy and cognitive science at Yale University, L. A. Paul argues, you cannot know what the experience of having your own child will be like until you experience it. You cannot judge accurately whether the experience will be positive, negative, or somewhere in between; it is impossible to judge as a hypothetical. And so into that vacuum and onto the pregnancies of your closest friends, you pour all your anxieties, hopes, and disquiet. Their experience becomes a yardstick against which you can speculate about your own decision. That might mean a hardening against the prospect of babies, an acceleration in your plans to start trying or, simply, downing a bottle of wine and screaming into the abyss until the panic starts to fade.

The greater part of how you react to a friend's pregnancy will depend on your own circumstances. When I was single, friends' pregnancies turned them temporarily into strangers, embarking on a life that shared little with my own. When I was in an established relationship, the pregnancy of a peer acted as an emergency flare, burning in the sky above my head for days, forcing the baby question into my immediate field of attention, blinding me to rational argument, lending the prospect a kind of urgency that I internalized while my partner simply pushed it from his mind. When my son was small, I greeted each friend's new pregnancy with joy and a deep-felt sense of sisterhood unlike anything I'd really known before. Now that I have a baby, have my period back, and am frequently being asked if I'm going to have another child, I've started to feel the same old creeping envy, sadness, and anger whenever I hear that one of my contemporaries is up the duff. How can we stop seeing other women's lives as a comment upon our own? How can we learn not to compare ourselves to others around us? How do we take the sense of competition out of the sisterhood? If I knew that, my friends, then believe me, I would tell you. I certainly wouldn't be sitting here, today, in a caravan in Essex, with a child of my own, writing this and staring at a photo of my friend's twelve-week ultrasound with a boulder in my chest.

4

GLASS BABY

Here's a thing I don't often admit to: during my more vulnerable moments, I sometimes like to imagine my funeral. I'm no goth and—having watched two people die in front of me—have no glamorous misconception about death. But the funeral fantasy is one that I will return to again and again. Somehow, as part of my will, it is dictated that every single person who ever dumped me, dismissed me, put me down after sleeping with me, described me unkindly, ghosted me, embarrassed my attempts at seduction, or belittled me in public is forced to sit in the very front rows of my funeral. In this scenario I am, obviously, an incredibly successful and much-loved writer, broadcaster, author, and, what the hell, philanthropist. My funeral will be screened across the nation, and every time another luminary stands up to give a tear-jerking eulogy about my wit, my beauty, and my phenomenal success, the cameras will do a hard zoom in on the faces of all those pathetic little flaccid people who sought to hurt me. They will be shamed before a nation for the way they treated me; they will beg for my posthumous forgiveness.

Like I say, I don't often admit to this and am perfectly aware that the fantasy paints me as both a narcissist and, possibly, a psychopath. But I don't doubt for a moment that the majority of you have your very own version of such a fantasy. The version of a future in which your professional accomplishments provide a salve for your personal failures. A revenge fantasy based not in violence or cruelty but merely your superiority. As that inexplicably popular *Desert Island Discs* favorite Frank Sinatra said, the best form of revenge is massive success. And I want both.

Clearly for me—and probably many other women of my generation—work, sex, identity, self-esteem, money, and status are intermingled in a way that is far more complex than I might like to admit. How many people have met a significant romantic partner through work? How many of us have used hard work as a tool in processing grief? How many of your friends have you made at work? How often have you gotten to the end of a holiday and realized that without the structure, discipline, and company of work, you might actually spiral into nocturnal, ice-cream-fueled, drink-addled loneliness? How often have you gone out for drinks after work rather than going home to an empty flat? How many of us would be quite depressed if we didn't have work dragging us out of bed most mornings? The line between work and "life" is perhaps unhealthily, perhaps unavoidably, as blurred as a bus window on a frosty January morning. Which is why, for many of us, work plays an enormous role in the Panic Years, driving us forward, shaping our identity, enabling our activity, as we try to hash out a future in which we can flourish.

A few months after Alice dropped her bun-shaped bombshell, sitting at a long wooden dining table in my friend Raphi's house, my teeth turning black with red wine, I am regaling her flatmates with an account of the exhibition I'd visited for a *Guardian* article that day. It's not often that a hypercolor Freudian nightmare strolls into your work life and punches you squarely in the uterus. And yet today—it seemed—was that day. I had entered the first room of the show to find a young male gallery assistant gliding over to me, a hollow, handblown glass baby the size of a six-month-old cradled in his arms. Without so much as a word, he had passed the baby into my arms. Due to turn thirty at my next birthday, this was, I'll be honest, a bit much.

As the glass sculpture settled into my grasp, I had let out an inaudible sigh before finally, tentatively, looking down into the baby's tiny, upturned face. I saw the floor. Just the hard, black floor beneath me. There was no baby here, just some transparent glass and a very clean floor. And yet I was somehow flooded with all the fear, longing, joy, and desire a real baby can evoke. I wondered about kissing it; I imagined dropping it. As my heart thumped and my neck began to stiffen, I thought of watching this precious and probably highly valuable creation smash into a thousand pieces at my feet.

"My hands got so sweaty I was worried they might dry ice me, or wrap me in a fire blanket," I say to one of Raphi's housemates, biting back the memory and refilling my own glass.

Once I had finally relinquished my hold on the glass baby, passing it to another young female journalist with a mixture of regret and relief, I had walked into the next room to find a long shelf of eggcups with hard-boiled eggs inside. A finite number of eggs. Of course. As visitors, we were encouraged to break open and eat one of the hard-boiled eggs right there in the gallery; an act of creative expression that suddenly felt like cannibalism. The artist had even provided little salt and pepper shakers—the everlasting partnerships of complementary condiments standing vigil over this finite quantity of eggs. That day, that gallery had been stiffer with symbolism than a Catholic church, and I had been rubble in the artist's hands.

I'd walked around the show scratching into my little red notebook, my face fixed in the sort of smile usually seen in public information films about cervical screening, trying not to choke on the hot ball of panic in my throat. This is my job, I'd told myself. I am a cerebral person, a professional intellect; I am guided by reason and language and theory. I'm not some hot-skinned beast crawling through London on a tide of sweat and the albumen of so many unfertilized eggs. It's just work—nothing personal.

Safely back at Raphi's, we eat salty pasta and smoke roll-ups under a giant map of the world. We talk, tell jokes, share gossip, check our phones, and illustrate each anecdote with an iPhone photo, passed around the group like a joint. I talk of a man I recently slept with who described my legs as "pencils;" a friend calculates how much shortbread he has to eat to make up for the twenty-seven-mile bike ride to and from his film job in the suburbs; we compare war wounds from our workplaces and speculate about our survival in an apocalypse. All very normal stuff. Suddenly, in the midst of so much chat, I hear Raphi say to the woman next to her that if she's ever going to take time off work—probably to have a baby—then she somehow has to get promoted now, "because who wants to hire a thirty-year-old assistant." She says it with doubt in her voice, as though hoping we'll argue otherwise.

Her words go through me like ice. Nobody wants to hire a thirty-year-old assistant. I am a twenty-nine-year-old assistant editor working for a small online arts magazine, charity, and networking site. I have been writing anything and everything I can wring out of my few university contacts, in and around a full-time job that pays me just enough to afford a room in a shared flat. I have been emailing pitches into the great silent void of newspaper and magazine commissioning desks and rarely even getting the courtesy of a rejection. I love writing, love journalism, am desperate to get noticed, and so will do pretty much anything for a hundred pounds. I have no pension, cannot pay off the interest on my student loan, let alone the full debt, and have no idea if my contract even covers maternity leave. I may be nearing thirty, but somehow I feel no closer to really establishing myself in my field than I did at twenty-five, or even twenty-two. Nobody wants to hire a thirty-year-old assistant. Of course. And it goes much further than just reputation and perceived potential. Get pregnant while you're still just an assistant and you might not be earning enough to cover the cost of childcare after your maternity leave. If you're lucky enough to even get maternity leave. Which means you might have to come back to work part time. But a lot of workplaces won't want a part-time assistant. Then add to that the fact that you'll now be reentering your industry as a thirtysomething parent, competing against a host of hungry young twentysomethings who will all want your job and are all able to do it for less money because they have almost none of your responsibilities but all the same work experience. Get pregnant while you're still an assistant and you might be unable to afford the break in earning, but not earn enough to afford returning to work either. It's a classic double bind.

Perhaps it's because of my glass-baby encounter earlier in the day, but suddenly the conflict at the heart of my existence comes roaring to the surface. If I want to have the kind of career enjoyed by my male and child-free contemporaries, as well as the kind of independence I always imagined for myself, then I have to get to the top of my ladder now, before ever considering a family. But, as today's left-on-the-shelf boiled-egg crisis reminded me, if I want to have a baby then I'll have to start trying soon, maybe even now, or I might run out of time and, well, eggs.

Because of the way we organize work; the way we pay people on parental leave; the physical demands of pregnancy, birth, and breast-feeding; the unaffordable cost of childcare and the competitive nature of modern employment, it seems simply impossible for many of us to take a year out and start a family. Because it wouldn't just be a year, would it? Unless you earn enough to pay the grand a month or more it can cost to send a child to full-time daycare while you go back to work—that's after taxes, on top of all your existing bills, mortgage, and living expenses—then suddenly you're looking at five years at home, until that child (and that's if you only have one) goes to school and they can be looked after for free.

In those five years, anyone who hasn't had to give birth, raise an infant, provide childcare, or be physically close to their baby in order for them to be fed and stay alive can suddenly race ahead of you at work. Promotions, experience, training, contacts: you lose out on them all. And yet, choose to spend those five years working—building up your career, proving your worth, earning money, climbing the ladder—and suddenly your store of eggs, your chances to get pregnant, and your possibility of a healthy baby may have dropped away, immeasurably, permanently.

All at once, the contradiction that has been drawing in around me like a cage is unavoidable, undeniable, all too clear. I need to work now, or I'll miss my chance at a career completely. I need to get a boy-friend now, or I'll miss my chance at a family completely. Who knows how the truth of this situation had eluded me until now, but suddenly, under the weight of Raphi's words, my state of innocence crumbled like a service station scone. I am thirty. My mum got menopause at forty. I may have only ten fertile years left. I am still just working as an assistant. I am fucked.

In 1970, Ruskin College in Oxford held the founding conference of the Women's Liberation Movement, known, catchily, as the Na-tional Women's Liberation Conference. I remember learning about the conference when I worked at the Women's Library; I'd stood in the basement archives of the former Victorian washhouse and stared at photographs of bearded men in thick-necked jumpers running the conference's day care center, while their partners discussed, debated, and agitated in the room next door. I'd heard an audio recording of a Welsh woman describing how, as a newly married twentysomething, she'd climbed into a coach and traveled down to Oxford for the first time in her life to attend the conference, after cooking her husband's dinner and tea and leaving a note by the fridge. I'd read the list of demands drawn up during that first conference:

- Equal pay
- Equal educational and job opportunities
- Free contraception and abortion on demand
- Free twenty-four-hour nurseries

When I'd looked at those photos and read those accounts from the Ruskin conference, I'd felt something pulse through me. Not just pride, not just wonder, but triumph. This must be what it's like for football fans to watch Bobby Moore raise the 1966 World Cup. This must be what it's like for soldiers to hear their national anthem while riding into battle. These were my people, these were my women, and they were coming together, doing something incredible in order that I may live in a way that they could not. During later conferences—held across the United Kingdom—three more demands were added to the list:

- Legal and financial independence for all women
- The right to a self-defined sexuality. An end to discrimination against lesbians.
- Freedom for all women from intimidation by the threat or use of violence or sexual coercion regardless of marital status; and an end to the laws, assumption, and institutions which perpetuate male dominance and aggression to women.

They are demands that speak to their time, but also the centuries that came before and the decades that we've lived in since. They speak to me today as they would have spoken to my mother nearly half a century ago. I wonder if anybody could read through such a list and not, in their blood and their bones, feel them to be right. Sex, money, children, power: the four corners within which women are held and live. Suddenly, there was a way to push those corners out, stretch out against the sides, redefine what we'll accept as normal. And yet, here I was, forty-five years later, punching my knuckles against the blood-smeared glass walls that still separated me from my male peers. Without universal childcare, equal pay, and equal opportunity, it was impossible for me to approach my career, my fertility, and my future like a man. I may have had access to free contraception, but abortion on demand? Round-the-clock nurseries? An end to the laws, assumptions, and institutions that perpetuate male dominance? Are you kidding me?

If I worked, I would almost certainly earn less than a man in an equivalent position. (In 2015, as I sat, staring at Raphi with a cigarette burning down into my fist, the gender pay gap in the UK was 17.5 percent.) If I wanted to have a child, I'd have to somehow conjure up an entire second income just to pay for childcare or leave work entirely for five years until they went to school. My local authority nursery charges forty-three pounds or fifty-seven dollars a day minimum for any child between birth and age two. If your household income is above thirty-five thousand pounds or forty-six thousand dollars (although ours certainly wasn't) then it rises to fifty pounds, or sixty-six dollars a day. That means that to send my baby to a nursery round the corner and return to work full time, I would have needed a secure and regular income of at least £215 ($284) a week or £860 ($1,136) a month just to cover the childcare for when I was working, let alone earning money for food, travel, rent, heating, and all those other luxuries parents like to throw their money at. In the UK, the average cost of sending a child under two to nursery is £127 or $168 per week if you work part time (twenty-five hours) and £242 or $319 per week full time (fifty hours), and the average wage in the UK for someone working full time is £569 or $751 a week (or approximately £29,500 or $38,953 a year). Meaning that, once you've taken away the cost of childcare (for just one child under two) you are left with, on average, £327 a week to live on; every other bill, everything you eat, every bus ticket and student loan payment. That's 43 percent of your income going straight to childcare. Even with the financial support of a partner this is bad; for single parents the situation seems nigh on impossible.

Unless you make considerably more than the national average wage, it would be a huge struggle to earn enough to pay the bills, feed, clothe, and care for yourself and a baby, let alone the childcare that would allow you to actually earn that salary. We may have a certain degree of reproductive choice and a certain freedom to work, but it is not a true choice or true freedom if the cost of childcare and the inflexibility of the workplace make it impossible for so many women to afford both a family and a career. Similarly, we may now have the freedom to pursue careers in more high-status, high-visibility jobs like the media or the arts, but it's not true freedom if you are also being expected to pay hugely inflated rent to a distant and wealthy landlord while earning minimum wage and being asked to work for free at every turn because it might "raise your profile." For women in the Panic Years, security, opportunity, and freedom are by no means guaranteed by reproductive choice and access to employment. And I say this, let us not forget, as one of the inordinately lucky ones: a white, middle-class woman living in an economically developed country with a high-status job.

For people of color, people in low-income jobs, people without qualifications or access to higher education, people with disabilities, and people living in the developing world, the possibility of those demands being met in your everyday life is even more remote. If, like so many girls from my own school, I had left formal education at sixteen, got a part-time job as a cleaner, met a man who didn't like using condoms, didn't want to put him off by being "frigid" or "difficult," had fancied him so much I took the chance, had got pregnant, wasn't part of a union, didn't have sympathetic parents, didn't have any savings, didn't have the right to maternity leave, couldn't afford nursery fees, then what actually would I have done? In what way would I have had equal opportunity, financial independence, or freedom from male dominance?

Five decades on from the National Women's Liberation Conference in Oxford, we have failed utterly to create a society in which a career and a child are not, somehow, in opposition. I was still trapped between the egg timer of my body and the teetering ladder of my career. I loved working, loved my job, loved the independence and confidence it gave me. If I'm honest, I loved the cruel sense of superiority my work gave me over all those happy, contented people who seemed to be able to sustain a long-term relationship with an adoring partner. I loved the idea that every person who had ever spurned or dismissed me would, one day, have to open up a newspaper or turn on the radio and be confronted with my success. And yet, in order to have a child I might have to compromise or even abandon that career, at least temporarily. Back in 1970, women weren't demanding equal opportunity, equal pay, and liberation from childcare simply in order to make money (although as centuries of slavery, workhouses, serfdom, and chattelism can attest, financial independence is a pretty bulletproof motive in itself) but because of all the other things that work can provide: security, a sense of self, public recognition, purpose, an occupation away from the mindless drudgery of a certain kind of domestic life, colleagues, physical space, something to talk about to your friends, equality, an opportunity to prove your skill at something, distraction, camaraderie, and simply the ability to be considered "normal" by the majority of the working world.

For many people, the question of how to solve the opposition between career and parenthood is answered by simply not having children at all. As the editor, writer, and broadcaster Terri White put it to me: "The biggest myth our generation was told was that we could have it all. I've definitely felt like I couldn't have the career I wanted if I had a kid." And so, for decades, Terri chose her work. She dedicated her attention to writing, networking, traveling, and managing huge teams of people, all in order to get the kind of career, the sort of life, she'd dreamed of. She spoke honestly and brilliantly about being child-free; she defended the right of women to choose; she fought back against biological determinism. Then, six months after our interview, a few months into her forties, and just weeks after I thought I'd finished this book, Terri announced on Instagram that she was pregnant.

Which just goes to show that the Panic Years and the Flux often extend well past our thirties and that everyone is apt to have a change of heart as well as a change in circumstance. Anyway, despite choosing a slightly different path, I agree with Terri. I'll never know what I might have achieved if I hadn't taken the time out to have a child, if I hadn't had my sense of ambition and priority permanently rearranged by parenthood, if I hadn't created a lifelong dependent. By telling people, particularly women, that they could have it all if they just tried hard enough, we somehow took the onus off our employers to create workplaces in which that was actually possible. Because of this, for many people the compromise to their income, lifestyle, intention, and responsibility that parenthood would cause is simply too great, the sacrifice too significant. I remember being at my friend's thirtieth birthday barbecue as her leopard print–clad aunt gently interrogated me over a grilled sausage.

"Do you have children?" she asked.

"No," I answered, dislodging a piece of charcoal with my teeth.

"Oh, I see," she said, with a knowing smile. "You're a career girl."

I remember wanting to scream in her face that this shouldn't be our only choice. That mothers should be allowed to be ambitious too. That career girls should be able to have babies. Instead I not-so-accidentally dropped some ketchup on her shoes.

Ironically, just a few months after the glass-baby incident and my post-pasta wake-up call about my own career prospects as an assistant editor, I did get a sort of promotion. The meeting was noteworthy for two reasons: firstly, I nearly cried when my boss asked me where I saw myself in five years. That question, let me say, belongs in a therapy session, not a professional meeting. As I sat at a small, white-topped table, looking out at the Shard beneath a partially extended roller blind, the sheer uncertainty of my future seemed to come at me like a tsunami in response to his question.

In five years' time, would I still be single? Have a job? Be living in London? Would I have hit menopause? Would I have a column in a national newspaper? Would I be married? Would I be managing my own team at work? Would I still be drinking three bottles of white wine before cycling home over London Bridge, pretending I was invincible? Would I have a baby? Would I be living in a small rented flat beside a river with my last still-single friend? Would I be on Radio 4? Would I be happy? Would anybody love me?

My poor boss saw the tide of panic flood my face and, quickly, moved on to less weighty matters like the state of my desk and my travel expenses.

The second noteworthy moment came a little later, when I brought up my job title. I explained that before I turned thirty I would like to graduate from being "assistant" editor to something with a little more status. I explained that, if I were to ever take time off work to have a baby, I would probably have to reenter the industry, maybe two or three years later, with the same title I left with. If I could do that with something like "commissioning editor" or "deputy editor" on my CV, it could make all difference between total rejection and even just getting an interview. I explained that, if I was ever to be able to have a family, I needed to get out of the assistant editor pool beforehand or I'd never have a seagull fart's chance of getting a job that could support a family when I came back to work. I needed to reach the next rung of the ladder now. I needed a promotion, even if it was just a change in title. He sat listening, making notes, and nodding.

Two weeks later, my deskmate and I had become commissioning editors. He had heard me, understood me, and, like all the best bosses, done something to improve a situation that he hadn't, until then, been consciously aware of. I did do some work, of course, to earn the new title, but sometimes all it takes to change a situation is identifying the problem in a public space. That's what the attendees of the 1970 Ruskin Women's Liberation Conference believed. And that's what those men at the conference's crèche believed too. There are allies out there. But sometimes you have to ask for help in order to get it.

That strange September day, as I stood in the gallery, holding that glass baby, and felt the rush of violence, shame, and longing wash through me, I was doing my job: I was reacting to some stimulus in the world in order that I could communicate the experience to others in writing. I was being a journalist and a critic. But, more than that, I was being myself: a warm-blooded, intelligent, hormonal, biological person held in flux. The Flux. I was confronted with a physical manifestation of all the decisions I felt unable to make, I was looking at a future not quite realized, but tangible and on the horizon. I was in the world of work, looking at motherhood and panicking at the apparent contradiction, compromise, and confusion that lay before me. The Panic Years is a reckoning of sex, money, biology, and power. You can survive it, but to do so will take action, armor, and allies.

5

BIG THREE-OH

In a silent room above a pub in Hackney, my ex-boyfriend behind me on the record decks, a man I fancy standing beside my dad's ex-wife, some old school friends at the back in a haze, I stare in amazement as my mother walks toward me with a plate of fire. Everybody starts to sing "Happy Birthday," the fire becomes candles on a cake, and I wonder—for the eighty-seventh time that night—if I've got a front wedgie and who might be looking at it.

My thirtieth birthday was, effectively, my own one-woman wedding. I invited university friends, most of my office, my sisters, my godmothers, my cousins, friends from school, old housemates, my ex-boyfriend, his friends, people I'd met through swimming, famous people I'd interviewed for work, people who had invited me to their weddings, former colleagues, family friends, and, in a move of extreme bravado, both of my parents. My parents had barely been in a room together for about twelve years, and the last time they did communicate, it was a bitter email exchange about an Npower bill that turned from acrimonious into apocalyptic in less than three moves. I invited four men I was hoping to sleep with, a few people I hadn't seen for nearly a decade, and a handful of acquaintances I dearly hoped would become friends.

I made the invitation myself—three photos of me as a tiny child, with three re-creations of those same photos by me now, aged twenty-nine. There was me in a pink cardigan running at the camera in a high wind—re-created on the marshes by my house; me cleaning the table in a train wearing more excellent knitwear—re-created at my dining room table; and my first school photo—re-created in my mother's attic wearing a pink polyester jumper from a market stall. On the invitation I wrote, "I'd really like you to be there. I think you're great" in big white letters. Under this I added, "There will be booze. And food. And dancing. You know, a party." Even smaller again, under this I wrote, "Bring pals. No gifts." Funny, sincere, light-hearted, I thought. Not too begging? No. Not too self-aggrandizing? Hopefully not. Would anybody come? Who knew.

The realization, a few months earlier, that I was going to be facing this birthday entirely single dawned a little like the calm, quiet way you watch a mobile phone slowly drift down to the bottom of a river: it was done and there was nothing I could do to change it. Just two years earlier, I had assumed I'd be strolling into my thirties beside my boyfriend: the man I had first kissed on my twenty-second birthday, the man who had helped me dump him not two years before and who had come that night to help me (again) by bringing along some of the records that had once lined the walls of our flat.

But here I was. And perhaps I didn't really mind being single. As is so often the case during the Flux, knowing that something wasn't going to happen was as much a relief as knowing it was. I had spent almost the entire year I was twenty-nine being asked what I wanted to achieve "by the time you're thirty." Such a question is obviously fetid and should be outlawed, but I'm sure we've all been asked, and are guilty of asking, something similar. It's a question that has also spawned some absolutely terrible lists, manifestos, and intentions among my contemporaries, including the one friend who so panicked while drawing up her "30 things to do before I'm 30" list that she discovered she had written down "ride a horse" three times. To finally have gotten there—to be turning thirty—would mean not just the end to those intentions but an end to any feelings of guilt, shame, panic, or disgust at my failure to achieve them. Like so many people around me, I simply had no option to turn thirty in a cottage on the coast with my boyfriend and a log fire. There was no possibility of spending my thirtieth birthday in a camper van at the foot of a mountain with the father of my child. There was no chance I'd be turning thirty pregnant, engaged, in my own home, or staring into the eyes of someone who wanted to spend the rest of their life entwined in romantic love with me.

In the absence of all the hallmarks of adult, emotional, and material success I found I could still throw a party. A proper party. I would invite all the people who brought joy and excitement to my life and thank them for loving me.

I didn't wear a dress. Instead I found an old, shiny black jumpsuit among my underwear that I had bought from a lingerie shop down an alleyway off Petticoat Lane in Whitechapel two years earlier. It was to wear to a Grace Jones gig that night and I'd become convinced that none of my clothes would be right. When I'd bought it, the small woman in cardigan and sari who ran the shop had asked, perfectly calmly, if I wanted a fishnet body stocking too. I thanked her politely but said this would do me fine, thanks.

The night before my thirtieth birthday party, I had cleared a space on my kitchen floor and methodically cut out twenty-one silver letters to spell out "Well Done Mum" across the front of the jumpsuit and my birth date and birth weight across the back. I sewed them on, by hand, over the course of about three hours. I also sewed a huge swathe of white netting around the neck like a sort of Elizabethan cloud. As this was my one-woman wedding, I wanted to look both sexy and adorable; striking and celebratory; intimidating and glamorous. I would look, I imagined, like a mixture between David Bowie and a middleweight boxer. In the event, my mother spent the entire evening walking up to anybody within elbow distance and hissing, in a theatrical whisper, "She's put the 'mum' right over her you-know-what."

Intending to give my father a role, and therefore remind him that as a parent he was expected to help and support me in some way, I'd asked him to decorate the room. He and his soon-to-be-ex-wife were in one of their many and increasingly frequent breakups, but his whole family came along, nevertheless, with a car full of velvet, gold, sequins, and drapes that turned the whole thing into a kind of drag queen dressing room. By that point, I was entirely beyond caring, but looking back it was a kind gesture during what must have been a time of acute stress for them all. Because this was a one-woman wedding, I had also been sure to provide plenty of food, including about four trays of burgers, salads, and what felt like about eighty-seven bowls of chips. The whole place probably smelled like a mobile burger van. My long-suffering and saintly mother also baked a cake big enough to feed an army.

Now, in my speech (yes, of course there were speeches—this was, as I think I keep saying, my one-woman wedding), I did not do my mother justice. Not even close. My mother is a still point in a turning world, my greatest ally, a generous, kinetic, brave, indefatigable, intelligent, beautiful, kind, and genuinely hilarious person to whom I owe my entire life. I should have stood at the front of that room and told everybody who would listen that she was the light of my life, that I loved her like water and that I needed her as intrinsically as the bones in my body. I should have thanked her for my every success and for her unwavering support in the face of my every failure. I should have mentioned the years she spent selflessly feeding, teaching, holding, nurturing, and entertaining me at the expense of her own freedom and her own comfort. I should have mentioned the time, aged six, I went to her in a heaving panic about the Tudors homework I hadn't done and she had wordlessly held my face in her hands and stared into my eyes with such a look of love and empathy for so long that I stopped crying, steadied my heartbeat, and pulled the world into focus once again. I should have told them that during a picnic when I was barely taller than her knee, she had stood, unflinching, between me and a crowd of whinnying horses, stared down their stamping feet and their steaming nostrils, until they fled in retreat. I should have forced everyone in attendance to hold her above their heads like a queen. Not just because she is great but because, as I realized with palpable intensity the year after my son was born, birthdays should be a celebration of the person who gave birth, not the person changing age.

There can be no greater love than that of she who risks her life to create that of another. According to the latest UN global estimates for 2017, 295,000 women died from preventable causes related to pregnancy and childbirth. That equates to about 810 people every day. Roughly one every two minutes. In all the wars, all the pioneering voyages, all the mountain ascents, all the scientific experiments, all the acts of terrorism, and all the great leaps of mankind, men have never put themselves at such significant and sustained risk of death as women simply trying to give birth to the next generation. Every person who dies heroically was birthed by a person who risked her life in order to do so. So, no, I did not do my mother justice at that birthday party. I will never repay the debt I owe to her, nor thank her adequately. That also, I now realize, is a mother's lot.

Like most brides, I failed entirely to have sex that night. Rather than seeing in a new year entwined in the limbs of a tall, dark-haired, dark-eyed man with soft lips and a deep laugh, I woke up on the morning of my thirtieth birthday in bed with my best friend Alice. She was pregnant and deep in the midst of all the nausea, fatigue, and emotional unpredictability that entails. Although the material division between us that morning was undeniable, from the ring on her finger to the swelling in her belly, I cannot think of anyone I would have been happier to wake up beside. So many nights in our twenties, Alice and I had slept together: curled up on the floors of warehouses in Birmingham smelling of cheap cider and cheese toasties, in our student flat when I had scared myself sleepless with a horror film, in the shed her parents had built in the garden after accidentally downsizing to a house with too few rooms, in the small seaside cottage where we had cooked risotto and drunk whiskey and re-created music videos on the stone wall coastal defenses. I may not have been in love, but I was loved and it was a love that had already stood the test of time, distance, change, heartbreak, pregnancy, work, and mental illness (on my part—Alice is resolutely and sometimes infuriatingly steadfast).

The first thought that passed through me on that dry-eyed, hangover-bright morning was that at last I could stop worrying about turning thirty. I cannot express how profoundly turning thirty had built up in my mind as a deadline: a numerically specific judgment day on which you either survive or die according to your material success. Make it to thirty with a mortgage, a baby, or at the very least a partner, and you will be allowed to live on. Pass Go. Collect your £200. Fail to make the grade in time and, like a battery hen facing yet another eggless morning, you will be taken away and disposed of. So, that morning, as the sun rose, the electricity still flowed, my body still breathed, I felt relief. In fact, I felt something a little like joy: I was thirty. I was still here.

There was another side to this relief of course. As someone who is, at heart, pessimistic, I was also quite relieved to find myself, at such an apparently pivotal staging post, completely crapped out. The milestones of turning thirty were, I now realized, mere symbols, and I had none of them. But if I was alone and untethered then at least I was also invulnerable to disappointment. Much of the panic that characterized the Flux for me was, in fact, fear of loss. I panicked at the idea of losing love, losing an assumed future, losing money, losing status, losing friends, and, as time went on, losing a partner, losing a baby, and losing my mind. So, to be turning thirty with no boyfriend, no job (thanks to a recent and not entirely unexpected layoff when the charity I'd been working for finally closed due to lack of funds), no mortgage, and no family of my own meant that, really, I had very little left to lose. I was on the floor and there wasn't any farther I could fall. If this sounds a little melodramatic, then yes, it almost certainly was. After all, I was healthy, I had savings, I had amazing friends, parents who cared about me, I had a huge amount of freedom, and I could make a piece of toast any time of day or night despite the fact that I knew almost nothing about how electricity works.

My father, a man who is not known for his wisdom or his sensitivity, gave me one of the most useful pieces of advice during that birthday. Turning to me under flashing pink lights, his tattoos and earrings and dirty trousers fading into the background, he said, "Ah well, you know, it's only because we count in a decimal system. If we counted around a factor of eight, you'd all just be freaking out about turning twenty-four, or thirty-two."

Much as I loathe to admit it, he was to some extent right. Thirty is no more significant in our biology or destiny than thirty-one or twenty-eight or thirty-three. Sometimes age really is just a number. And yet, I also know that giving ourselves deadlines and rituals, marking points and anniversaries is part of how we spur ourselves on in life. It is part of how we, as a society, build up a common language and set of expectations that push us into forward progression. Sometimes that progress is difficult and sometimes it is extremely patchy, but without it, you may well end up with a man in flip-flops and a bucket hat, dancing alone at a festival, off your face on pills, to music you don't recognize and with nobody to help you back to your tent. It is also worth mentioning that many people will turn thirty married, in love, with a mortgage, planning a baby, only to lose it all by the time they turn thirty-three. These deadlines may feel significant, irreversible, eternal at the time, but they are all, essentially, arbitrary. An individual life will weave through dates and ages as unpredictably as the weather—the secret is how you prepare, adjust, and adapt.

The real kicker of a deadline—the one that has been misunderstood, disseminated, and weaponized to the detriment of almost every woman I know—is thirty-five. Boy oh boy do we have a problem with the number thirty-five. Thanks to a confluence of sloppy newspaper headlines, panicked hearsay, medical terminology, and my mother's early menopause, I grew up believing that the moment I blew out the candles on my thirty-fifth birthday cake, what few remaining eggs I had left in the dark and lonely corners of my ovaries would immediately and spontaneously roll over and die like bloated carnival goldfish. A very lucky few may have missed these thirty-five-specific warnings, but I certainly came to believe that my fertility would nosedive off a cliff, my body would go into retreat, and, were I to get miraculously pregnant, I would be officially deemed a "geriatric mother," beset by health difficulties and a stratospheric chance of miscarriage. If I wanted to have a baby—and I was pretty sure I did—then I needed to start trying way before such a dangerous and depressing deadline.

All of which, I now realize, was scientifically unreliable if not actually inaccurate. Writing in the *Atlantic* in 2013, the psychology researcher Jean M. Twenge wrote that:

> *The widely cited statistic that one in three women ages 35 to 39 will not be pregnant after a year of trying, for instance, is based on an article published in 2004 in the journal* Human Reproduction. *Rarely mentioned is the source of the data: French birth records from 1670 to 1830. The chance of remaining childless—30 percent—was also calculated based on historical populations.*
>
> *In other words, millions of women are being told when to get pregnant based on statistics from a time before electricity, antibiotics, or fertility treatment.*

It's like looking for advice on how to fix your car from a manual on a Victorian steam engine.

Of course, fertility does decrease with age, but perhaps not with as much drama or speed as we have been led to believe. A study published in the American journal *Obstetrics and Gynecology* in 2004 found that, using data from 782 couples recruited from seven

European centers for natural family planning, "the percentage of infertility was estimated at 8 percent for women aged 19–26 years, 13–14 percent for women aged 27–34 years, and 18 percent for women aged 35–39 years." However, that decline is not nearly as dramatic as you may suspect. The report's authors also add that "many infertile couples will conceive if they try for an additional year." With enough sex and health on your side, some people can get pregnant at forty and even forty-five. It is worth noting that male fertility also declines with age, a part of the puzzle often overlooked by the hand-wringing articles about your post-thirty-five "cliff edge." To quote a cheerful little study called "Fertility and the Aging Male," published by the journal *Reviews in Urology* in 2011:

> *The idea that robust fertility for a man will continue well past a woman's decline in fertility is untrue. Although the female ovarian reserve is perhaps the most crucial component of a couple's per cycle fecundity, the age of the male partner also has significant impact on reproduction. Beyond the fact that older men tend to have older female partners, increasing male age is associated with increased time to conception. This reflects the age-related increase in acquired medical conditions, decreases in semen quality, and increasing rates of DNA fragmentation seen in sperm. In addition, there is an association between age of the male partner and the incidence of birth defects and chromosomal abnormalities.*

As always, the true nature of fertility is complicated and varies more between different individuals than you can ever really cover in an article, or even this book. While you may be able to get pregnant into your late thirties and forties, rates of miscarriage increase with age—about 10 percent of people will miscarry at age twenty, compared with 90 percent or more at forty-five years of age or older—as do chances of delivering underweight and premature babies. IVF and other fertility treatments are also less likely to be successful the older you get. According to the NHS, between 2014 and 2016, the percentage of IVF treatments that resulted in a live birth was 29 percent for women under thirty-five; 23 percent for women aged thirty-five to thirty-seven; 15 percent for women aged thirty-eight to thirty-nine; 9 percent for women aged forty to forty-two; 3 percent for women aged forty-three to forty-four; and 2 percent for women aged over forty-four.

Because all women are born with a finite but unknowable number of eggs, it is currently impossible to predict how an individual's fertility will decline, at what speed, or at what time in her life. Even testing the anti-Müllerian hormone (AMH) level in your ovaries—as many women who are worried about their fertility or are considering IVF pay to do—is only really a useful indication of suitability for IVF, not a diagnostic tool for an individual's fertility. As modern humans, we are so used to being able to nudge, pay, pressure, and cheat our way out of biological unpleasantness—through antibiotics, anesthetics, surgery, equipment, circumstantial change, and all the other wonders of science, medicine, and capitalism—that we have risked losing sight of the fact that certain parts of our physiology are finite, irreversible, and beyond our control. At some point, a body will no longer be able to conceive and bear children. That point is different for everybody, of course, but it's there in all of us. Holding the number thirty-five above us like a fertility guillotine is going to induce panic in most people—panic that in some cases is unmerited, panic that may well be the unconscious spur for the Flux. But having some sense of your fertility as finite, just like having some sense that your whole existence is finite, is necessary. We are human. We are not immortal.

During one of my occasional fertility freak-outs a few years earlier, this time while sitting on some wooden decking outside a New Zealand bungalow, eating mussel fritters, my cousin Hana stamped her foot, threw back her head, and shouted, "For fuck's sake, Nell—I've had three kids since I turned thirty-five! Stop worrying and drink wine while you still can."

Hana, I should point out, is not a trained medical scientist. But she may have had a point. To consume women with an anxiety that their bodies may fail them, that their possible futures might be lost, and that the time for decision making is running out, just at the time when they could be reaching the pinnacle of their career and personal potential, seems a cruel trick. I'm not quite cynical enough to argue that this is yet another means by which the patriarchy can dominate women. But I'm not *not* arguing that either. It suits a certain kind of capitalist, fear-driven sexism to spread a simplistic version of fertility where women must compromise early, invest heavily, or lose out completely. To talk solely in terms of women's bodies, egg reserves, ovarian hormones, and menopause leaves little room for the parallel but necessary discussion about sperm count, male hormone imbalance, testicular damage and temperature, semen quality, the amount of sex you're having, stress, how much you smoke and drink—all the other myriad things that affect someone's chances of getting pregnant. In painting male fertility, age, health, medicine, and sexual activity out of the picture almost completely, we can too easily fall into a situation where a thirty-year-old woman will do almost anything to get pregnant, with anyone, before it's too late; meanwhile men can dick their way into middle age shrugging off commitment like an ill-fitting anorak.

When I stood in that room, blowing out my candles, worrying about my gusset, and doing my best to avoid a major diplomatic incident between my parents, the silver numbers I had carefully stitched across my back indicated what I had taken to be the facts of my birth: my weight and the date. What they didn't say, what I didn't really put together then but can see now, was that at the time of my birth, my mother had been thirty-four years old. Four years older than I was then. Another six years away from menopause. So, even if I followed my mother on her more extreme timeline, I had ten years. It's a massive shift in perspective that at the time I was unable to make, but if time was running out, that was—in part, at least— because I felt it to be so. The reality was that I was standing in a pub, not trapped in an egg timer.

6

PARENT TRAP

There is a particular, chili-in-the-eye thrill about delivering incredibly bad news to your own parents. It's like swearing at a retiree, or flushing a child's pencil case down the loo: a devilish power pulses through your veins, making you stronger, crueler, more audacious than you ever dared imagine.

Standing on the exposed beams of a kitchen roof, in a pair of his old jeans and a free T-shirt from a builder's merchant, nailing down tiles and measuring angles, I tell my father that I need to explain something. That I'm sorry. But I may never make him a grandfather. It's not a lament, a cry for pity, or a burst of anger; I don't want him to find a solution or dribble out platitudes. It's just time he realized that I'm thirty, single, and facing early menopause, and the math is stacked against me. I'm fine with it. He should be too. I take a nail from the box sitting between us. I line it up to the hole I'd drilled earlier in the top left-hand corner of the slate. As a man who played some form of father to four daughters and is the youngest of six siblings, my father starts to cry. I don't look at him. I pinch the nail between my thumb and forefingers and carry on hammering.

By the summer of 2015, I'd been single for a year and a half and had gone fully freelance. Which is the middle-class way of saying I had been laid off and was trying to see if I could make it as a proper journalist and writer without the security and structure of an office job to pay my bills. I'd listened to a lot of Joan Baez and Joni Mitchell, I'd stopped eating meat, and I'd moved out of my mum's and back into my flat with an old university friend who'd also just nosedived out of a long-term relationship, her home, her job, and her imagined future. I'd decided that I would say yes to absolutely every work invitation and request I was sent: every commission, every party, every press trip, every favor, every cover shift, every task. As a result, I was busier than ever. In every area of my life I was pushing it. I was running ten kilometers at least three times a week, I was cycling across London every day, I started performing comedy, I was sewing myself entire outfits most weeks from fabric bought for eighty pence a yard from Ridley Road Market. I got a new hairdresser, a middle-aged Iraqi barber in London Bridge (on one memorable occasion I walked in to find him polishing a man's bald head with a tea towel, while his colleague trimmed the customer's beard with an electric razor). I had muscles, I was getting published in national newspapers, I was turning my face into farce with a blog in which I re-created famous portraits using junk around my house. I swam in freezing rivers, I sought the affirmation of strangers on the internet, I was spending time with my old school friends, I did push-ups at dawn on the marshes near my house, I listened to Radio 4 while making dinner, I was smoking rolls-ups and drinking tea instead of eating. I went on holiday with other single friends—ones with cars and freelance jobs and no plus-one. I liked life at this pace; before I'd been made redundant from my job at the arts charity I would often write an article at five A.M., then go to the office for eight hours, come home, and pitch for more work. Without a full-time job to work around, I now had even more time to fill. I would use my work to try to impress people, in the hope that they would then sleep with me. I ran a half marathon, I took selfies, I turned up alone at birthday parties, I slept with someone eight years younger than me (I didn't realize at the time and only found out because I noticed there were maths textbooks on his bookshelves), I planted cauliflowers and strawberries in my tiny garden, I cycled drunk, I claimed travel expenses,

I did a comedy gig in South Kensington wearing trainers and a romper and then decided to walk the twelve miles home, alone. Three separate men took me on dates to Beachy Head. Three. I got a new flatmate, a brilliant comedian I'd loved, admired, and magically befriended in the year after my breakup. I stopped wearing makeup, I spent hours typing on g-chat when I was supposed to be working, I had dalliances with people in different cities, I watched *Poirot* at my mum's house on a Sunday. I felt like a hybrid, an interperson, a midpoint. I was simultaneously the old, pre-relationship Nell and the new, post-breakup Nell; I was physically strong and emotionally vulnerable; I was building a career and earning less than most of my friends; I wanted everyone to fancy me and had lost faith in relationships. I was thirty. I was molten.

On that day, as I stood on a roof, half a mile from the house where I'd grown up, and listened to my father crying, my initial reaction was anger. How dare he cry? Why wasn't he following my script? Here I was, a single, accomplished, strong woman, telling him that I might not have children, might not need children to be fulfilled. He should have been impressed, been on my side. The second feeling was a sort of sadistic pleasure. I had made my father cry. My lifestyle, the potential hopelessness of my love life, my apparent inability to find security had crushed his spirit. The straight-A student, natural musician, accomplished graduate, and published journalist that he'd been able to show off about had finally delivered a body blow. I wouldn't make him happy, wouldn't give him grandchildren, would deny him the pleasure of seeing a new generation bearing his blood. After years of frustration and disappointment at my parents' behavior, I was finally getting in a jab in of my own. I was taking control.

Of course, that control was—and always will be—nothing more than an illusion. To live in a human body is to exist in a state of uncertainty. As I ran around the world, carving out a life of professional success, personal drama, and physical strength, I was also locked in a civil war with my own womb. It was forcing me to make a decision about something that I felt I had no control over—and it was threatening to take that decision away if I left it too long. As Terri White put it, that day as we sat together and chewed over the sexual injustice of the modern world, long before her path changed direction and she got pregnant: it is the unknown.

"I'm still pretty sure I don't want to have kids," said Terri, "but I think it's really rare not to question it. There is nothing I can do to simulate that experience, I can't try it out. The clarity I've always sought, and had, over every other area of my life is impossible with this. I can make big decisions. But this has always been a question in my mind I can't resolve. I still think I've got the right answer; I don't think I should or would have kids, but the fact that I still could is what keeps pecking away at me."

Peck, peck, peck. On and on and on. It is exhausting.

For some people, the hammering panic of finite fertility is eventually silenced by the decision to do it alone. People like my friend Freddy—a fellow journalist whom I first met on the steps of Melbourne Town Hall during the Comedy Festival back in 2015. At the time, Freddy was already a few years into his transition from female to male and had been taking testosterone for two years. At the time, I thought very little about his gender or long-term plans but a lot about the fact that here was another person, in this strange hemisphere, who would understand immediately what I meant if I mentioned WHSmith, Twiglets, Radio 4, White Lightning, Highbury and Islington, CBBC, or PG Tips. We were both, I suspect, a little homesick. Today, we are both parents, have both been pregnant, both been in labor and both given birth to sons.

"I always saw myself as having children," says Freddy as we talk via WhatsApp video, just weeks before his extraordinary documentary, *Seahorse*, is released. "I wasn't thinking of myself as a mum or a dad—I couldn't visualize the sort of person I would be—but I did think about the children I'd have. In that way, wanting children was very separate for me to the question of *how* I would have children."

Despite our somewhat divergent lives—me, a cisgender straight woman in a long-term relationship, him a trans man raising his son as a single father—there is one significant point on which Freddy and I have a quite remarkable affinity: how the fear of finite fertility spurred us on to make a decision that changed our lives entirely. Freddy was, incorrectly, told before transitioning that taking testosterone would make him infertile. And yet, as time went on, he became increasingly aware of other trans men who were having or had children. People like Trystan Reese and Thomas Beatie were showing the community that testosterone didn't necessarily take away the opportunity to carry a child. There are in fact hundreds of trans men who have had children, some in relationships but some as single parents too. According to figures compiled by Medicare for Australia, fifty-four people who identified as male gave birth naturally or via C-section in Australia in 2016 alone. But these things are, as we know, never simple.

"At that point, I still thought testosterone would damage my fertility," explains Freddy. "I now realize there's no evidence for that either—it would really help if doctors started giving us clear and unbiased advice about this stuff—but for a few years in my twenties I definitely thought I was on the clock."

This notion of being on the clock is all too familiar.

"I don't know how similar that is to what you're describing," Freddy says, as my face breaks open in a smile. "But I literally didn't know, from day to day, if I was going to become infertile."

And so he made the decision: to come home from Australia, come back to the seaside town where he'd grown up, get a house, and have a baby. Was he apprehensive about doing it on his own? About becoming a single father, albeit one who had given birth?

"I did think about whether I, as a man, could provide what a baby needs," Freddy replies, sitting in front of a fantastic kitchen play set, a bookcase full of picture books, and a rack of washing. "Was I nurturing enough? Was I going to have those instincts? These are things that women mostly think about but also men have to deprogram in order to give themselves space to consider."

Freddy could not have done this, he says, without the phenomenal support of his family. Thanks to them, he can dedicate himself to parenthood in a way that many men do not.

"Every baby needs a primary carer," explains Freddy. "They need somebody whose main job is looking after them. And beyond that, every child needs lots of love and security. I know people in all different setups and of all different identities who play that role and the child doesn't care. I had to realize that for myself, but I wish other people could realize it too."

Would he recommend single parenthood to other people in their Panic Years?

"Being a parent feels like part of my purpose; that's just my internal makeup," he explains, smiling. "But if you don't have that urge? If you can imagine your life and future, happily, without kids, then don't do it. It is *hard*," he says.

We both laugh. And then sigh.

In telling my father that I might not have a baby, I was drawing a battle line: I was setting up camp in the child-free territory as a form of defense. I'm not for a moment saying that people who don't want to have children are doing so out of aggressive or mistaken intentions. Quite the contrary: I believe that people who know in their bones that they won't have babies and don't want to be parents are absolutely right. They should be respected, protected, and celebrated. God knows, the world doesn't need a growing population or more unwanted children. But that doesn't mean that their decision won't be just as tricky, as turbulent, or as occasionally contradictory as my own has been.

Parenthood is one of the few utterly irrevocable decisions a person can make. Even if you give your child away, have them adopted or taken into care, leave the country, or your child dies, you will still be, in some way, a parent. Confronted with the reality of that, it is utterly rational to decide you don't want to do it. It is sensible, reasonable, maybe even altruistic, considering the huge poisonous burden the human population has become on our one habitable planet. But I wasn't being rational, or reasonable, or altruistic that day I told my father to give up hope. I was testing the waters of being willfully child-free because I was scared it was going to happen anyway, against my will. If I was going to run out of time and opportunity, I thought I might as well try to own it.

In a café on the top of a hill, overlooking a reservoir and a treatment works, I tell my mother that I'm sorry. But I may never make her a grandmother. She smiles sadly at me. She strokes my hair. Suddenly I bubble up with tears and watch them fall onto the plastic garden table between us. Anger and cruelty give way to sadness. Perhaps because my mother seeks to reassure me that she doesn't mind, I feel a weight of guilt and loss in my stomach that slides inevitably into self-pity. She tells me that as a teacher her life has been full of little children, that she doesn't care what her friends think, that she doesn't mind how I live my life as long as I'm happy. I am so grateful to her and so relieved by her kindness. But, at the same time, without the wooden beams of someone else's opinion to bang, hammer, and fight against, I am forced to confront the fact that I am uncertain, maybe even unhappy, about the prospect of a childless future.

It is easy to see such a swing in attitude as inconsistent or unreliable, to write off both extremes as "just feelings." In truth, that shifting, uncertain, precarious experience is absolutely innate to the

Flux. It is the very nature of the beast. When you are forced by time, circumstances, and biology to ask yourself what you want from your future, you are being forced to confront the unpredictability of life. We cannot know what will happen and so cannot say what we want. Because our circumstances are always transient, so our feelings will fluctuate. Human life is uncertain. To come down squarely on one side or the other of any decision might look like strength, but it is, in fact, a position as fragile as a dandelion. And, let's be honest, a baby is one hell of a decision.

As Terri put it, "The more I live, the more I think the decision to have a baby is not a binary thing; I think we move in and out of it more than we admit."

So yes, I told one parent I wasn't having a baby and felt sure it was my choice. I told another parent I wasn't having a baby and felt it wasn't my choice. That's not a contradiction: it was the truth.

The interesting question is why I felt the need to have this conversation with my parents at all. Why did I feel I owed them an explanation? Why did I consider it my duty to provide them with descendants? Both of them chose to have children with other people, both spread the nuclear family across the walls like so much ketchup, so why did I still feel that I was letting them down by not making a "proper family" of my own? Despite living for seventeen years alongside their disastrous relationship; despite begging them on the stairs, aged nine, to break up; despite the fantastic examples of single motherhood, child-free adulthood, and unconventional co-parenthood I had around me, I still somehow felt I owed my parents an apology for not yet settling down with a nice man and having a baby. I still felt panicked that I was running out of time to do it the "right way." I still wanted to have a partner, before I had a baby.

That summer, after breaking my bad news, I had the very strange experience of going for a walk with both my parents. That might not sound particularly radical to you, but at the time, my parents had barely spoken to each other in nearly fifteen years. Even at my birthday party. But at the time, my father was rolling off the rear exit of a second divorce and, as so many people do, was taking the opportunity to put things right with the last person he broke up with. Namely, my mother.

There was certainly a lot of muck to be raked over. For nearly two decades, theirs was the most incompatible, most unpleasant, and occasionally most violent relationship I have ever witnessed. In every muscle and organ in my body, I can still remember the stiff, corrosive stress that would fill me as I sat at a dinner table, in my bedroom, in the car, on the stairs, or in front of the sofa and listened to the screaming, grinding, hissing, thudding, relentless juggernaut of their arguments roll on for hours. They would follow each other into the garden, brandishing some sock, or piece of paper or half-empty jar that, for that moment, acted as the focal point for all their mutual loathing, disappointment, frustration, and self-pity. They broke chairs. They punched holes in walls. They argued about everything from mayonnaise to music, from biology to life after death. Never in my life have I ever known two people so locked in mutual unhappiness, yet so unable and unwilling to climb out of it. Finally, three weeks before my A-Levels, they broke up. The timing was so phenomenally shit, so apparently designed to specifically fuck me over, that I told them both if they ever got back together after this, I would never speak to either of them ever again. For seventeen years I had watched them scream, scratch, tear apart, waver, falter, panic, get back together, make nice, wear thin, lose it, fight, argue, hate, separate, get lonely, panic, sleep together, forgive, try again, then act like nothing had ever happened. I, for one, had had enough. In each instance I had been expected to play along with their bullshit. When they were together, I was supposed to believe in their union completely. When they were apart, I was supposed to stay utterly partisan. One day I would come downstairs to a silent, broken house full of unspoken irritation and barely suppressed rage; the next morning I'd come down to find them kissing in the kitchen and asking if I wanted to make pikelets. It was like being insane. I had no idea what was real. I could trust nothing.

When people say they are staying together for the sake of the children, they are telling themselves a lie so dangerous and so vicious it makes my veins burn. People stay together because of financial interdependence, fear of being alone, illness, the unaffordability of housing, religious belief, social pressure, conditioning, complacency, or cowardice, not because it's what's best for their children. The idea that you are somehow protecting, nurturing, or caring for your family while also exposing them, daily, to the most harmful, poisonous, or depressing elements of human behavior and interaction is almost laughable. Because children are aware. They can read body language, catch subtext, and taste tension in the air as well as any adult. And, if you're not careful, one day they will write a book and tell the world all about you.

During the Panic Years I suppose I developed three parallel but contradictory responses to the question of having a baby. Sometimes I told myself I didn't want one anyway—self-protection; sometimes I told myself it would happen with the right person—optimism; sometimes I told myself it would never happen and I had to learn to be okay with that—pessimism. All three, in their different ways and at different times, got me through those early years of the Flux. Because the fact was, having a baby was never really an option available to me until I got together with my current partner. Putting my own unconscious baggage to the side for just a moment, the stark truth was that, from the moment I lost my virginity at seventeen until the day I wept on my boyfriend's lap at thirty-three, no man had ever wanted to start a family with me. Not in that moment, perhaps not ever. Was this because my parents' unhappiness had bred in me a deep and fungal distrust of love, interdependence, pregnancy, and commitment that radiated out of me, to be picked up by any potential partner? Was it because I was unconsciously drawn to men who echoed my own father's adolescent emotional intelligence? Was it because, as Rob Delaney once argued, "Men in their twenties are the worst thing happening on our planet"? Who's to say.

It seems like a not-unreasonable stretch to say that your own experience of being parented is highly likely to influence how you feel about becoming a parent yourself. As Terri put it, with her unique mix of crushing honesty and Cheeto-light humor: "I'm very conscious that my mum was an alcoholic and a drug addict and a terrible mother; my dad is violent, a psychopath, and also—you won't be surprised to hear—a terrible parent. I had a real concern about becoming like them and passing those sins on to further generations; I didn't want to bring up someone who would become damaged or hurt in some way." As that leather-headed commitment-phobe and poet laureate of neurotics Philip Larkin once famously wrote, "They fuck you up, your mum and dad. / They may not mean to, but they do. / They fill you with the faults they had / And add some extra, just for you."

And yet. And yet. For as long as I can remember, I pictured a baby in my future. Sometimes I wanted it in the way I wanted to be happy, good-looking, or clever—as an abstract idea, as a solution to my own current unhappiness or as a product of social conditioning. Sometimes I disregarded it as a confidence trick—a way to keep women distracted, oppressed, and disabled in a world designed to ensure the eminence of men. But sometimes I imagined it in a way that seemed primal, animal, night-scented: to feel an unborn person push against my ribs, to hold a neck as thin as a banana in the crook of my elbow, to dry a tiny belly after a bath, to smell my own young's milky breath in the pale dawn. When I stood on that roof beside my father, or wept in that café opposite my mother, I may have been talking about having babies, but I was also trying desperately to wrestle control over my body, my finite womb, my unknown future, my bruised heart, my past, my present, and my future. At the time, it seemed unbearably unfair that my own body was pushing me into the panic of such a monumental decision, while my male contemporaries felt protected by their biology from ever thinking about this shit. In retrospect, I understand that without that pressure, that panic, and that pursuit of love, there would be no such thing as parents—we would all keep wanting children "one day" until suddenly that day had passed, and we were all too old to do it. How you feel about that idea, of course, is entirely up to you.

7

DING-DONG

Halfway up the ladder, the wire flex gritted between my teeth, my fingernails scraping on wood, the metal at my feet starts to tilt. I hear a scrape. My foot kicks through thin air. I teeter.

It is the autumn of 2015 and I am at the 276th wedding of the season. Where once my friends and I danced in thudding basements, ate toast six ways, or compared bruises, these days my weekends are taken up almost entirely with either weddings or bachelorette parties. Those weekends now spent in a cottage drinking supermarket prosecco and playing "guess how predictable my partner is" games of Mr. and Mrs., or finding your name on a chipboard seating plan and wondering which spare cousin you will be expected to get off with are, in my case, spent working wildly to earn the literally thousands of pounds other people getting married seems to cost.

When I was thirty and single, I went to a lot of weddings alone. That is fine. I would far rather turn up to a wedding solo than with a man I've known for a month, slept with four times, who makes tea the color of false teeth, and who uses the word "myself" when he just means "me." One of my favorite wedding attendances was when I cycled twenty miles out of London to the stately home where two friends were getting married. I wore a black-and-white trouser suit and orange stiletto heels, chained my bike to a fence by the generator, listened to two of the speeches while having a cigarette on the lawn outside the marquee, danced for two hours, and then cycled home, completely sober and entirely, gloriously alone. To the 98 percent of the wedding guests who didn't know who I was, I can only assume they thought someone's licentious bachelor aunt had turned up as part of the world's least likely attempt at a Duke of Edinburgh Award.

And so, when Raphi, one of my oldest and closest friends in all the world—a woman whose chimney I could see from my childhood bedroom—was getting married, it never so much as occurred to me to bring someone. In retrospect this probably made things like accommodation, seating, and transport an absolute shit fight for the people organizing the wedding, but I genuinely had no idea at the time. I was there, or so I thought, to support my friend, make a speech, crack jokes during times of tension, and lend my shoulder to any bit of manual, emotional or logistical labor going. Which is how I found myself, one Dorito sunset evening before the wedding, standing up a ladder in bare feet, nailing a string of outdoor lights to the wooden exterior of a French barn as a cow lowed like a stuck saw in a neighboring field. Now, I was taught by my father, who was taught by the same Irish laborer who crossed my palm with silver when I was just a few days old, that when you're painting up a ladder, you reach out to your arm's length and then paint inward, toward your body. That way, you're not tempted to stretch, overextend, and, well, teeter. I knew this. But I was, like Icarus in a betting shop, overreaching. As the ladder tilted, I quickly flicked my eyes up to the wide blue sky above my head and wondered—is this how I die? Stringing up lights at yet another wedding? Killed by my own need to thumb my nose at tradition and gender stereotypes? My life ended barefoot, unwashed, and conspicuously single? Luckily, before smashing to the floor in a blaze of electrical wiring, I grabbed a roofing joist. The ladder settled, and I hooked the flex over the last nail and shamefacedly climbed down to where the groom's brother was watching, his foot on the bottom rung, his face betraying nothing of his amusement.

In truth, I have never enjoyed weddings. No, wait. That is too simplistic, sounds too settled in disinterest or mellow in misanthropy. In fact, I am scared of weddings. Like an arachnophobe standing at the door to a dusty shed, I enter weddings with my shoulders tight, my skin prickled, and my heart racing. The fruitcake and forgotten speeches, the strained smiles and pinched toes, the sugared almonds and shifting anxiety, the pantomime formality, admin-heavy ceremony, group photographs, cold starters, unspoken indiscretions, endless small talk, first dance, toilet weeping, contract signing, blister Band-Aids, red wine teeth, drunk uncle, "I now pronounce you," thrown bouquet, head table, pastel bunting, pocket square nightmare of the thing has set my teeth on edge ever since I can remember. Is that really true? Not quite. Peel back the scab a little further and I can tell you: I have hated weddings since my father got married. Twice.

My parents, in just the kind of unfathomable move I'd come to expect of two people who once laid an entire patio using crockery they'd broken during just a year's worth of arguments, decided to get married after spending the previous year not just separated but living in entirely different houses. I was nine. I was to be a bridesmaid. My aunt would make me a blue dress in whatever shape I wanted. I asked for puffy shoulders and if I could wear trainers with sparkly laces. On the morning of the wedding I accidentally sat on a plate of butter (how, we'll never know) and had a grease mark right across my arse throughout. During the enormous picnic after the city hall affair, all the kids found a set of gravel heaps to roll in, off, and over for at least an hour before a park warden came over and warned us that these were what the peacocks used as a toilet. My father had a thin, graying ponytail and sang The Platters to the accompaniment of a tiny white portable cassette player; my mother wore an enormous hat covered in fabric mushrooms and sang "The House of the Rising Sun" at the evening karaoke; my maternal grandmother wore a navy blue skirt suit, white court shoes, and matching handbag; my grandfather wore a tie with a diagonal stripe. My parents were married for seven ill-advised years.

By the time of my father's second wedding, I was twenty, at university, and single. Despite the fact, or perhaps because, my own parents' marriage had been such a colossal waste of effort, I was finding the prospect of another wedding hard to swallow. As my father and his new wife danced out of the ceremony to James Brown's "I Feel Good," I was slumped, behind an electricity meter, vomiting against a brick wall. It was as though all the tension, all the sadness, the fear and the inescapable self-consciousness was trying to climb out of my own body, repel itself out of my mouth and onto the floor. Being the daughter from a previous marriage at my father's second wedding made me feel like the grim reaper in a coral pink dress (yes, the wedding had a rainbow theme). Here I was, an uncomfortable physical reminder of quite how tenuous and how meaningless those vows really were. At some point in the afternoon, my dad ordered everyone to get into a huge rainbow semicircle around "the family" for a photo. There they sat, The Family: my father, his new wife, and their two little blond daughters, sitting on a blanket at the front of the photo, smiling at the camera. And where was I? Standing at the back of the orange section, beside a woman I'd never seen before in my life. I didn't belong to The Family that day. I belonged to The Past.

So, yes. No great wedding associations here. Which is probably why I spent so much of my twenties viciously and vociferously denouncing marriage and particularly weddings to anyone who had the misfortune to listen. I would spit out acidic little diatribes about the meaningless gestures, the hypocrisy of undertaking a religious service in full knowledge you have no faith in god, the nonsense of promising to act in a certain way fifty-seven years into the future despite the fact that you can't be certain how you'll act in a week, of the heteronormative bigotry of it (this was long before the Equal Marriage Act). Give me long enough and I would also start to lash out at the pantomime pretense of virginity with all those white dresses and wedding-night gags; the gross, laddish tradition of a best man's speech; the colossal expense everyone has to go to buying a train ticket, a hotel room, a present, an outfit.

Give me a little more rope and I'd scream at you about the license it gives strangers to ask you if you want to get married, the acrid tang of warm white wine, the creaking shame of first dances between two people who never dance, the pitying whispers about any recently divorced guest who made it along anyway, the awkward half chuckle of the vicar as he (and it's always a he) announces that it's nice to see the church so full for a change, the top table of divorced parents all trying to make small talk over stuffed mushrooms, the heavy, damp, thrumming weight of thousands of years of unhappy women trapped, stripped bare, and killed by bad marriages, the crushing, unspoken subtext that it'll be babies next.

If you had told me at twelve that by 2020 nobody would get married anymore, I would have absolutely believed you. If you'd told me that public attitudes about euthanasia and legalized marijuana would change quicker than attitudes about marriage, I would have laughed in your face. If you'd told me that by 2016, 50.9 percent of British people aged sixteen and over would be married, I would have covered my face with despair.

None of which I was going to mention at this wedding, with its carefully arranged outdoor lights. I had learned, through several deeply uncomfortable and ill-advised experiences in my twenties (including the time I had to go and lock myself into a car, alone, and cry for half an hour midway through my housemate's wedding before getting so pissed I heckled the vows and threw up in front of the groom's parents), that the best way for me to get through a friend's wedding was to drink nothing, say as little as possible, and keep it light. By staying sober and being surrounded by people with exactly my sense of humor, I actually managed to have a rather wonderful time that day. The sun shone, my handmade pale blue jumpsuit didn't explode at the seams, and, because another friend had recently given birth to a delicious baby son, I could occupy myself by jiggling, rocking, and bouncing him around while people around me talked about the weather, the flowers, the music, the flooring—whatever it is that people find to fill the eight or nine straight hours a modern wedding often lasts.

It was only that evening, after I'd given a speech (and hooray, by the way, for all couples who ask women to speak at their weddings), that I allowed myself to home in on some of the booze and to reminisce about the old days: when I'd walked to school each day with the bride, wearing our little Puffa jackets and record bags; when we'd gone on holiday to her grandparents' caravan; when we'd spent hours recording strange improvised radio documentaries about two Welsh hairdressers called Stella and Wella on our cassette players; when we'd gone swimming together every week and bought plastic butterfly clips for our hair at the weekends. Suddenly, there she was—tall and beautiful and vowing to love someone else for the rest of her life. A feeling that had been welling up behind my heart for years suddenly spilled over and I realized I was never, ever going to get that back. I was never again going to be the closest, most important, most intimate person in her life.

Although I was still single, still full of recesses that another person could fill, she had fitted herself to somebody else now. She had found someone who would make her laugh, make her tea, join her on trips to the supermarket, watch telly on her sofa, give an opinion on her hair, throw her a birthday party, talk late into the night and drink too much, help her remember the words to a song she was humming, do silly voices. But more, more than this: he could give her love. Proper, adult, romantic love. And a family. He could make her a mother, if she wanted. They could own a house together, perhaps. They could share a life. I wanted all that for her, of course. I was absolutely thrilled that the man she was marrying was the best of men in every single way—funny, intelligent, curious about the world, beautiful, devoted, mature, and kind. And yet.

When I watched my oldest friend walk onto the dance floor with her new husband, I started to cry so hard that one of the groom's best men had to physically pick me up and carry me out of the barn.

"She's gone, she's gone," I was saying, sobbing into his shoulder. "She's a wife now and she's gone."

If you think this sounds like the mad raving of a drunk and frustrated lesbian, then I'm afraid I have to disappoint you. I wasn't drunk, not really, and I am not gay. I think what happened that night, as I watched my friend whirl around the dance floor in a white dress and the arms of her husband, was threefold. Firstly, I had to finally admit that part of our childhood was over. The formative years we'd spent together, that had etched themselves onto our accents, our sense of humor, our jobs, and our behavior had passed. We were adults now. Secondly, I had to confront the fact that, for a lot of people, marriage isn't about presents and dresses and hen dos and balloons, but about declaring publicly that you want to live in a committed, interdependent relationship with another person. You want to rely on them, to think of their needs before your own, and to sacrifice some of your autonomy in order to be part of something bigger. She had found someone she wanted that with and she had just promised, in front of all of us, to work for it. Finally, I had to admit that I did not feel like that about anyone. Not yet, anyway. To admit to that—that there were tender parts of me that I wanted somebody else to look after—was incredibly painful. To admit that I wanted to love and be loved was also to admit that I was vulnerable, that I could be hurt, that I had to risk my already-on-the-floor security in order to get it. I didn't despise what she'd done and I couldn't blame her for wanting it; I wanted it too.

Luckily for me, the man who carried me out turned out to be, well, the best man. He was as emotionally mature as he was physically strong. And lads, he had great shoulders and biceps to match.

He held me against his enormous shoulder and said calmly, "You've not lost her. I mean, look: my best mate just got married to some woman. That means he's going to live with her and probably have a kid and probably not want to hang out and will stop being much fun. But I'm not crying because I've not lost him. They're not dying, or leaving. They just love each other. We're still their friends."

I may be misquoting him slightly here because I heard some of it through his shirtsleeves and was hiccupping and sniffing like a hand blender. But his point was a good one and he was kind. Our friends don't disappear the moment they become part of a couple, but your relationship with them will change. It's up to you how you react to that. It's about commitment, care, and intention. Just, I suppose, like a marriage.

According to the Office for National Statistics, there were 249,793 marriages in England and Wales in 2016, the year after I stood in that barn and sobbed. That's, what, 999,172 shaking speeches, 4,995,860 packets of pocket tissues, maybe 7,493,790 new outfits? Whatever way you slice it, it's a lot of fuss. But when nearly half of UK marriages end in divorce (43 percent to be precise), why do we still bother? Why go through the pantomime of vows, rings, hand-binding, henna-painting, glass smashing, garland swapping, veil-lifting, and solemnly swearing when, in our heart of hearts, we know that the knot can be untied, the promises undone, the rings handed back? Of those 249,793 marriages, 106,907 are likely to end in divorce.

I used to find it vaguely ridiculous that my gay friends were fighting for the right to something I considered as plainly meaningless as a wedding. I thought it was like fighting for the right to own those knitted toilet roll covers or an Aga: outmoded, wasteful, and expensive relics of the past that all right-thinking people had dismissed years ago. But, of course, weddings do have a role. It's just that, like the explanation behind a magic trick, the truth is almost unbearably prosaic.

The entire function of modern marriage is to make it just that little bit trickier, more embarrassing, and more administratively complicated to break up. That's all. There is no magic in a ring, in a vow, in walking around a firepit or treading on a glass. The priest, rabbi, celebrant, or imam cannot really grace you with a supernatural power to stay in love, keep faithful, and remain happy. There is no great secret behind it all. Despite what we say during weddings, no commitment is absolute. People don't really promise to stay with someone in sickness and health, for richer or poorer; nor would we, as guests, force them to. Your family and friends are not really expected to strong-arm you into staying with someone who just gambled away your house, became a violent alcoholic, or refused to touch you. No amount of cake or dancing, toasts or flowers, swearing or symbolism can save you from that kind of heartbreak. The only reason a married couple should stay together longer than an unmarried couple is because they pumped so much money, attention, time, and energy into actually getting married that they will be slightly more reluctant to throw it under a bus when things go sour. That's it.

Marriages, like all relationships, are uncertain. To commit to another person puts you in a constant state of uncertainty. To live together, have a child together, pool your earnings, make compromises for each other's career, and trust each other makes your life more uncertain. That makes me deeply uneasy and, frankly, scared. It makes me claw at my bouquet in a church, prickle with sweat on a dance floor, and bite the inside of my lip at a registry office. But that I loathe uncertainty is my own problem, not the fault of weddings. I can't lay all the blame on the sugared almonds and white lace.

Throughout the Panic Years, I wrestled with this uncertainty across aisles, in flower-strewn barns, in churches, and, as in this case, up ladders until it drove me almost mad. I want marriage and weddings to mean more than they do; I want them to be absolute and eternal and unbreakable, because then I can finally learn to believe in enduring love. Having seen both my parents back out of unhappy marriages didn't make me just lose faith in marriage, but in love itself. I learned, before I'd ever been in love, that love can end. I learned not to rely on other people, not to trust their loyalty, to question their commitment, and to shy away from interdependence.

When, in the middle of a wedding, I want to stand up and scream, rip the flowers from the walls, smash my chair through the window, and run, it isn't because I am overwhelmed by the commitment they are making; it's because I'm overwhelmed by the fragility of it. I hate the idea that two more people might do what my parents did. I am scared of it all going wrong. The prospect of heartbreak, loss, and separation after so much hope and pomp and promise is almost impossible for me to bear. I feel like a woman in a coral dress, standing in a crowded field; I feel like the nail, poisoning the tree. In the midst of so much happiness, I am a living reminder to everyone at every wedding that love does not last, that marriages can be unpicked, that parents do not stay together, and that vows can be broken. I am proof of failure.

No wonder nobody ever asked me to marry them.

8

MEETING THE MAN

Standing above a ditch, the smell of rot and woodsmoke all round me, the evening sun glancing off the flapping tarpaulin, foot-hardened soil, and plastic bags of the Jungle refugee camp, I hear the engine of our car rev, dust rises, and the wheel spins, hopeless, in midair. Stressed, panicked, without thinking, I grab the coat of the man beside me and bury my head into his chest. We're stuck. That's it. Our car is stuck and we're going to have to spend the night here.

He puts his hand on my shoulder. I look up at his face; his dark hair, twinkling eyes, the small creases around his mouth. A little embarrassed, I let go and stand back, the sun pouring through the opening between our bodies. He smiles and pulls a tiny pad of paper out of his coat pocket, covered in columns of handwritten numbers.

"I've got all the train and ferry times here," he says. "Just in case we can't get the car out tonight."

And just like that, I want him.

A few months earlier, I had been covering for someone at an online women's magazine. Because I felt far from established as a freelance journalist—even though I was getting more work all the time—I had jumped at the chance of being able to charge a day rate, rather than pitch for new work, day in, day out, often ending up with nothing or four things all due on the same date. I was still single, still sleeping with what my friend Jean-Luc affectionately called my small "portfolio" of men, still freelance, still living with my flatmate Chris, still caught between freedom and fear of being left behind. As it had been a while since I'd worked as a full-time commissioning editor, I'd done something a tad rash and tweeted out my temporary work email address asking PRs, writers, and other work-related people to get in touch with ideas. One day, as I sat overlooking Shaftesbury Avenue, counting down the minutes before I could make another cup of tea and wondering why so many of the women in the office were dressed like extras from *The House of Eliott*, an email arrived. I still have it.

> Hi Nell
> Hope you're well. I work in PR and I wondered if you'd be interested in visiting Calais to meet refugees, specifically refugees from Eritrea?

Not only was I excited at such a prospect, I was also flattered to think that someone—a man, even—had read my writing and considered me a good enough journalist to cover something so newsworthy. This could be the shift in my career I'd been looking for. You have to understand: as a woman working in the media, I'd spent my whole career watching my male peers get asked to write about the Big Wide World: politics, news, migration, the economy, emergencies, science, Westminster, and money, while I had, again and again and again, been asked to write about My Life: my body, family, relationships, hair, childhood, friendships, opinions, and sex life. (The irony that you're reading this sentence in a book about my body, family, relationships, hair, childhood, friendships, opinions, and sex life is not, dear reader, lost on me.) In print and digital media alike, the overwhelming message I got back from editors was that while men wrote about the world "out there," we women could write about our lives "in here." Men got elections, we got food. They got wars, we got art. They got the hard-hitting features on global events, we got the thousand-word pieces on our latest heartbreak. They got front covers, we got lifestyle features.

Of course, I was very lucky: I got to write funny columns for national newspapers, interviewed artists whose work I admired, ate in amazing restaurants, explored the new incarnation of feminism, and was often called on to "punch up" some drab or humorless copy. But still, there was a little part of me that rankled at the thought of all those men, my peers and contemporaries, who were being sent abroad, called to Parliament, or managing their own team while I was told, once more, to dig over my autobiography, look a little closer to home, and stick to "women's issues." I grew up as the intellectual equal, often the superior of the men around me and knew, if given the opportunity, I could prove myself a more diverse writer than my portfolio suggested. So, when an unknown man singled me out to write something weighty, political, topical, and potentially risky, I was thrilled. I replied immediately.

> Hello Nick,
> I am so, so pleased to get your email.
> I would absolutely love to. I'm free the first or third weekend of
> September?

I can't quite describe it, but somehow his name seemed familiar. So I did what all right-minded people do and googled him. I found a Twitter account, saw that he'd once worked for the UN, had been to university at Sheffield, and, according to his profile photo, bought his luggage at Sports Direct. Satisfied that he was a real person, that I didn't already know him, and that he did work with refugees, I thought very little more about it. I got an email a few days later suggesting I join the group traveling to Calais that week, at one of their meetings.

Which is how I found myself, one quiet weekday evening, taking a seat in the Comboni nunnery in Hammersmith. I waited, surrounded by crochet-covered easy chairs and women the size of parking meters, wondering what exactly I'd signed up for this time. Had I really been sent to a nunnery? Was my love life that hopeless?

There was a small ceramic jug in the shape of a Madonna and Child on the windowsill and the kind of municipal blue carpeting last seen in my grandmother's care home. I was listening to the clock ticking in the hallway and trying not to look at my phone when the man who'd emailed me walked into the room. He was tall, with a Lego helmet of dark brown hair and spherical nostrils, and he was wearing the male version of my own brown boots.

"Shall I be mother?" the email man asked, holding out a flower-patterned tea tray. This made me snort, out loud; you don't get much opportunity to make nun puns in this life. Once the hot drinks had been handed out, we all moved into the library next door, where a few Eritrean and some white Londoners were already sitting at the large square table. I took out my notebook and Biro, ready to discuss dates, gas costs, shopping lists. Then, without warning, the nun on my left whipped out a magnifying glass, opened her Bible, and started to sing out the words in a high, wavering voice like someone playing a saw. It was like sitting next to a heavy draft. Now, I am not religious. My Church of England school was about a third Muslim and I've never really read the Bible. But, if journalism teaches you anything at all, it's to just go along with whatever's happening. So I looked at the floor and listened to this tiny owl and her strange, fluting voice. At a few points, all the others around the table joined in the singing, repeating the last few words of a verse, their eyes closed. I looked at my knees. I daren't look at the man who'd emailed me. Was this all some complicated way to introduce me to the wonders of Catholicism? Was I having a spiritual intervention? Did they want me to become a nun?

As quickly as she'd started, Sister Marguerite closed her Bible, patted her knee, and sat back on her chair. An Eritrean woman pulled a Tupperware box out from her large leather handbag and started passing around squares of Madeira cake the size and consistency of washing-up sponges. The people at the meeting were wonderful. For some of them, this was to be their eighth or ninth visit to Calais. Every month, they'd been loading their cars up with food, books, clothes, cosmetics, and anything else that might prove the difference between life and mere existence. This is the thing about religious groups; they don't wait for larger organizations to take the lead, they don't ask for permission—they just get on with what they can, immediately. To watch them work this way is inspiring, guilt-inducing, and invigorating in equal measure.

The one-day round trip was planned for September 27, a holy day in the Eritrean Orthodox church known as Meskel. Once the car places had been allocated, I made my excuses and left. The Nell Frizzell Sleep Calculator had gone off and I knew that, once I'd traveled across London, I was going to be lucky to be in bed by midnight. Of course, you can't admit to a room full of adults that you need to leave at nine P.M. because it's bedtime, so instead I mumbled something about last trains, made a sort of curtsy to the huddle of nuns in the hallway, and left.

On the train platform, in the muddy riverside dark, I got an email from Nick Stanton apologizing for it being so late. It was barely nine thirty P.M.—a time when most people I knew would be barely finishing dinner. And yet here he was, this brown-booted, thick-haired activist, apologizing that I might miss my bedtime. *Now why*, I thought, *do I never meet men like him?*

On Sunday, I left London at four A.M., crammed into the back seat of a Toyota Yaris beneath fourteen boxes of sourdough pancakes called *injera*, sitting between Nick and a Slovenian "street counselor." Swimming with nervous excitement, trepidation, and adrenaline, I began to worry about my insubstantial offering of tampons, sanitary towels, toothpaste, and fruit. I turned to Nick. What had he brought?

"I've got a hundred Mars bars and some satsumas," he said.

I laughed so hard that a box of *injira* slid onto the handbrake.

Once we got to Calais, the man driving our car announced that we were all going to go to mass. Right then. A full Catholic mass before heading to the refugee camp. The excitement over what we were doing that day was, slowly, turning into nervous trepidation, a sort of hungry adrenaline. I'd never been to a camp before, nor had

I ever been one of a handful of women surrounded by four thousand exhausted and dispossessed men. I'd watched the flood of people leaving football matches, I'd been to festivals, and I'd seen refugee camps on the news, but none of that would quite prepare me for what I was about to see.

The service was, of course, entirely in French. As my AS French oral exam had centered around how Gauguin spread syphilis through Tahiti in the name of art, I was a little shaky on the vocabulary for your average Catholic service, but the singing was beautiful and I stood quietly for the prayers. Nick was standing beside me, in a wool shirt and brown suede jacket that screamed Blue Harbour. I couldn't tell if he was praying—how can you—but his head was bowed and he seemed engaged. I later found out that Nick was actually having some form of misguided spiritual epiphany at that very moment. He was standing beside one of the younger nuns from our party, and as the music soared and the morning light poured through the stained-glass windows, he remembers thinking, *Am I falling in love? Am I going to fall in love with a nun today?*

I was, I'd like to point out, standing on his other side at the time. Hey ho.

The Jungle was about the size of a service station, hunched against the razor wire and industrial blockades of the coast. *How do you enter a refugee camp?* I wondered *Do you need a pass? ID? A bribe?* The answer, of course, is that you just walk in. Just as so many dispossessed, hungry, traumatized feet have walked in before yours. We parked the car and started to unload. A group of men—largely Eritrean but also Afghani and Sudanese—started to approach the car. For a second I wondered if we were about to get rushed. I am ashamed to admit that now. But at that moment, confronted with a sprawling mass of men, many of them young, sinewy, walking around in groups, in sports gear, my first uneasy thought was that we were vastly outnumbered. But, of course, they were merely offering to help.

As his old job at the United Nations High Commission for Refugees had involved several visits to refugee camps, I felt hugely comforted having Nick with me as we wandered through the packed-mud alleyways and snapping tarpaulin in the midday sun. Two men, one Eritrean, one Afghan, came with us and insisted that we join them for a cup of tea in one of the makeshift cafés, hammered up by just the sort of capable, practical, entrepreneurial migrants our country so desperately needs. Uneasy about the protocol of accepting hospitality from someone surviving on the bare bones of fuck-all, I drank milkless black tea out of an *X Factor* mug and snuck bites of the oatcakes in my pocket while Nick talked to the two men about their attempts to make it to Britain.

The Afghan man, whom I'll call Ahmed, was twenty-one years old, worked as a translator with the Americans for three years, and was willing to be wrapped in plastic (so security dogs wouldn't smell him) and thrown into the freezing bowels of a truck, risking both asphyxiation and freezing to death, just so he could, as he explained, finish his studies in Britain.

The Eritrean man, whom I'll call Gabriel, was gentle, clever, funny, and unerringly positive. In order to flee the life sentence that is Eritrean national service, he had walked across Sudan, been falsely imprisoned, been shot at, had traveled through Turkey, Greece, Albania, Montenegro, Serbia, Hungary, Slovenia, Italy, and France, surviving on nothing but what little money his family could wire to him, his ability to learn languages, and his own resilience. He looked about thirty. He was just nineteen. He is now the godfather to my son.

We continued our loop of the camp, Nick offering little observations, jokes, keeping close beside me in a way that was almost protective, if it hadn't also been strictly professional. A man walked past in a Liverpool Half Marathon T-shirt. Another cycled past with laminated phone cards tucked into his hat like a crown. A chicken pecked the ground outside the volunteer-run French school; a man washed his T-shirt in a bowl of water next to a standpipe. Men charged their phones off petrol-powered generators, and a young guy, barely more than a teenager, sat in a white plastic garden chair getting his eyebrows threaded beside a giant lake of mud. As the sun started to dip, we joined a group of Eritreans in one of the larger shelters for coffee. A woman from our group danced; kids raced around the tables; the man who had driven us was nowhere to be seen. Inevitably, I started to get a little fidgety. I am, I should point out here, the sort of woman who will get to a train station at least an hour before my departure.

Once he had finally herded everyone back into the car—a process that took almost an hour—Emor the driver managed to steer us all immediately into a ditch. It was then that my spine turned to sawdust, my fingernails dug into my thighs, and I instinctively buried my face in Nick's chest. Strangely enough, that duck-and-grind torso assault was almost exactly the same move I pulled during the final hours of labor, when I bit Nick on the stomach. But that, as the romantic novelists say, was all to come.

In the end, it was as simple as it was miraculous. Without so much as a horn beep, a group of at least forty men walked over to our car carrying bits of wood, rocks, and scraps of plastic. Two guys shoveled earth out from under the chassis, ten guys got into the ditch to heave, about twenty people leaned against the hood to give the wheel some traction, and, with no more than a couple of false revs and a fair bit of hollering, the car was out. A disparate group of Eritrean, Syrian, Iraqi, Afghan, Sudanese, Chadian, Ethiopian, and Pakistani men, who had nothing to gain, didn't know us, and were stuck in a holding pen of desperate filth by our governments, stood in the dirt and helped us get back to our warm and dry homes.

On the ferry back to Dover, in the sort of strange, companionable mood that happens when you've just spent fifteen hours together at a site of unspeakable poignancy, Nick and I wandered through the gift shop and played shag, marry, kill with a travel set of Guess Who? I took a chance and asked if he was Catholic (and therefore opposed to a bit of light sex before marriage). He said no. Probably attached, I thought. With all the ease I could muster, I asked if he had a girlfriend. He said no. Something inside me immediately burst open.

Whether it's snogging at the office Christmas party, flirting over a box of printer ink, breathless sweaty eye contact during a weekly statistics meeting, or smiling over a pile of baked potatoes in the canteen, a lot of people meet their partner through work. According to a study by the Trades Union Congress, one out of every five couples who are either married or in a civil partnership met that way. When I still had a full-time job, I had the good fortune to become unprofessionally well-acquainted with several people either through or because of work, both through my office role and the freelance commissions I was juggling on the side, so I can well believe it. Unfortunately for me, since being pushed into going fully freelance, I was more likely to network with my duvet cover than a single, attractive, straight man. But that's my own, self-employed problem. As you head into your late twenties and thirties, the opportunities to meet other single, pleasant, unseedy people away from work become frighteningly scant. Sure, go *out* out and you can meet men who wear jeans like sky-blue plastic wrap, women who collect motivational quotes on bits of driftwood, people who communicate almost entirely in memes, people who Deliveroo themselves mashed potato, people who still sleep on sofa beds, call their friends "geez," believe shampoo marketing, use Febreze, consider cocaine a personality, wear novelty socks, have tattoos of their school nicknames, and talk to you for forty-five minutes without asking a single question.

Go to a dinner party and you can meet men who wear woolen hats indoors, women who have to ask shop assistants what color a jumper is, people who want to open a food van selling lobster pot noodles, people who talk about the "old-school pleasure" of a CD jewel case, people who drop their salary into conversation, wear festival wristbands, were bought flats by their parents, wear those little white ankle socks that look like panty liners, remember everyone from their halls of residence, and ask you if you've ever had sex in a treehouse.

Go online and you can lose hour after finger-numbing hour messaging a hundred people who all, somehow, have exactly the same four profile photos as everybody else: standing by a lake, in a suit at someone's wedding, out partying, holding a baby with the caption "Not mine—my nephew!!" You can scroll through messages calling you a "gorgeous creature" or "rare jewel" followed swiftly by either a foulmouthed whirlwind because you didn't reply within fifteen seconds, or a specific and extremely gynecological description of what they'd like to do to you (note the "to you," never *with* you). You can meet people who turn out to be ten years older than their pictures, still live at home, want to shag their flatmate so are dressing it up as a threesome, hate pets, think commitment "will be extinct before landlines," carry pictures of their parents in their wallet, work six nights a week and want to go out till four A.M. on their one Tuesday night off, do tarot, wear sweater vests, eat raw onion, know your ex, have rashes, lie compulsively, have absolutely no sense of humor, drink protein shakes before sex, or send you photos of their new bike that you only realize, on the third look, have their shaved balls hanging over the saddle.

Of course, you can try these things, all these things. And sometimes have fun doing it. But you can also see why meeting someone at work seems an attractive alternative.

So it was with something very close to excitement that I read an email from Nick the next day asking me if I'd like to go for a drink, to debrief on the visit. During the trip to Calais we'd spent fifteen hours together, including a long drive back from Dover during which I'd idly pointed at the huge, lonely, concrete Frankie and Benny's, Odeon and Travelodge at Greenwich Peninsula and said, "Well, there's the recipe for an ideal date."

So the fact that he thought it might be worth meeting again was reassuring, both personally and professionally. He suggested we meet at Bethnal Green tube station. As he'd grown up in London and gone to school in Bethnal Green, I assumed he'd know of a cool, locals-only bar or pub where we could discuss politics and compare notes. It was only as we walked past the taxicab office and the empty building site and down a dark, damp alleyway that I started to have my doubts. Until we turned the corner and there, in front of us, as unlikely as it was hilarious, was the Bethnal Green Travelodge. Unbeknownst to me, Nick had called ahead and asked to book a table at three separate Travelodges: here, one near my work, and another in central London, just in case I changed the location.

When we revealed to the receptionist that we weren't staying there, that we just wanted a drink, she looked us up and down, frowned like someone who's just pushed their fingers in a cow pat and said, "You do know this is a Travelodge, right?"

Which is how I found myself sitting beside a pyramid display of breakfast cereals, under a fluorescent strip light, meters away from a paper salesman from Newcastle who was watching darts on an enormous television, drinking a glass of wine, and laughing at almost everything Nick said. Later, as he stood at the bar, I stole his diary from his bag and, using an enormous Tower of London novelty pencil I swiped from the hotel reception, wrote my birthday in it. Later still, I got so drunk I managed to lose my handbag in a pub we'd moved on to, and so Nick had to take me home in a cab. Despite some rather lackluster protests, he came inside, where I promptly introduced him to my flatmate Chris by saying, "This is my husband, Chris. Chris, this is Nick."

In the morning, I woke up, rolled over, my legs hairy, in the middle of a heavy period, my bedroom a mess, looked at Nick lying there on my pillow, and said, without thinking, "I think I'm in love with you."

It was the first time I'd ever said it. I had told people I loved them, sure, had said "I love you" countless times, but the phrase "I'm in love with you"? Never. I'd known this man for mere hours. And yet, somehow, I didn't care. I knew. I'd committed myself. Later that day, he secretly booked two train tickets to Berlin on my birthday. We were off.

Why did this relationship succeed where so many before had floundered? Of course, Nick was clever and kind and funny and surprising and articulate and mature and handsome, but so were many others. And I'd never told anyone I was in love with them before. I'd never risked my heart so soon, or cared so little about doing it. But no, what really mattered was that after two years on my own, pressed against the cold, hard truth of my desire, and after much self-investigation in therapy, I was now ready to risk it all and show a man my vulnerability. I was finally able to let go of the toxic myth that all men want is casual sex, freedom from commitment, and surface-level attraction. I was willing to test the theory that some men, if given the opportunity, will want partnership, companionship, even a family. I was willing to be honest. I was finally ready to depend. After years of putting on a brave face, faking insouciance, sleeping with people as an act of self-assurance, asking for nothing for fear of being disappointed, saying I didn't believe in marriage, building crackpot theories about commitment, using sex as a method of self-harm, considering myself worthless, inviting others to treat me as if I were worthless, hiding my fears, silencing my wants, I had finally, eventually, learned that I deserved better.

I came to believe that I was worthy of love and that interdependence was not a dirty word. Therapy isn't a silver bullet. In many ways, it's a dip-dye process: you say and hear the same things over and over and over again for years, but each time they hold a little faster, until eventually the color's different, the dye is fast, and you have changed. I'm not saying that you can only fall in love if you have the money and time for hours of therapy. I wouldn't be so stupid. But I am saying that, in my case, it took the perspective and insight of a professional and a stranger to finally dig out the sedimentary layers of my own unhealthy thinking about relationships and build new foundations. Ones that allowed me to ask for love and offer love in return.

But, of course, the Panic Years are not solved by telling someone you're in love with them. Even if the sentiment is reciprocated. There is always something to throw you off the rails. That night on the ferry, as we had traveled back from Calais, Emor had turned to Nick and me and—like so many happily married men in their forties—asked us each independently if we would one day like to get married and have children. Here it was. The Question. The Big Question. The very question that drove into my imagined future like nails through chalk. The Question, as always, asked as if it were no more trifling than inquiring whether you prefer tea or coffee.

I had been tired and more than a little overwhelmed by the sheer weight of humanity I'd witnessed that day and so had decided to be completely, baldly honest. I'd said I didn't mind too much about marriage but I would like to meet someone and have a baby. Nick had said that he didn't really care about getting married or having children. I'd said nothing, pulled my eyes away from his face, and ran my mind through the smoke whirls of what Nick had just said. Didn't care? Didn't want to? Didn't mind either way? Didn't know?

Last week, while walking home along Regent's Canal with our son asleep in the stroller, I asked Nick if he remembered that conversation.

"I do," he answered. "I was working that day—you were too—so I had to make a good impression. They were Christians; I was probably thinking about not insulting them, but also wanted you to hear a good answer. I was almost looking for a nonanswer; something I could say without actually addressing the question."

What would he have said if he'd been answering completely honestly?

"I'd have said no," he replies. "If someone had said, 'Do you want to be in a happy, loving relationship?' I'd have said yes. But I don't think that's synonymous with getting married and having children. The person asking that question probably thinks they are, but they're not. I'm from a nontraditional family; I know that a loving relationship doesn't necessarily involve marriage and babies."

Back in 2015, of course, I didn't realize any of that. And so I would return to that scene over and over and over again—trying to unearth some clear, honest, unimpeachable truth, untainted by my hopes and my suggestions. I would picture Nick there, under that cornflake-colored light on the ferry, and try to remember how he'd said it, where he'd been looking, how I'd reacted, and, above all, what he'd meant. If I could just get to that kernel, I thought, travel back in time to a pre-Nell version of Nick, get him whole and separate and true, I would understand what to do. Because despite the fact that, in almost every single way that mattered, Nick and I were ideally suited, despite the fact that we were honest with each other from the start, despite the fact that I knew in my bones that he was the one for me, I eventually realized, over the tentative course of the following year, that Nick didn't want a baby. I finally heard the truth of what he'd said on that boat when we first met. He didn't really want a baby. Not with me, not yet, perhaps not ever. Shit.

9

BERLIN WALL

Cycling in the sun can really work up an appetite for roughly dissected pork phallus covered in curry dust and tomato ketchup. Especially when it comes served on a paper tray, handed over by a brusque apron-wearing granddad as bald and porcine as his *wurst*.

On a hot September morning in 2016, Nick and I decided to cycle the entire path of the former Berlin Wall in a single day. By lunchtime, we'd made it to Wannsee—my hair was sweat-streaked, my hands were covered in chain oil, and two perfectly round saddle bruises were forming, unbeknownst to me, across my buttocks. We'd cycled past the Brandenburg Gate, the Tiergarten, a vending machine selling condoms, through hay fields, across motorways, beside a poster warning of wild boar, past former Nazi housing estates, around coffee factories, all the while tracing the border along which hundreds of refugees had died, trying to reach a different life.

I'd drunk two bottles of Club-Mate—a sort of bog water energy drink full of enough sugar and caffeine to make your freckles fizz—eaten a pretzel and an apple, had fixed Nick's bike once already, and was absolutely desperate for some food, any food. As we rolled up to the ferry terminal, ready to follow the border as it had lain through an actual lake, the smell of currywurst hit my saliva glands and, suddenly, my vegetarian childhood disappeared like so much pig hair on the wind.

I genuinely can't remember how we decided to move to Berlin that summer. I'm not sure we really did decide it at all. Somehow, what started as the usual "We should move out of London" party chat with our friends, a couple who had recently relocated from Bristol to Whitechapel, suddenly became serious online flat hunting in Kreuzberg. Without quite knowing how, the four of us had quit our jobs, sublet our flats, kissed goodbye to our mothers, and climbed aboard a Eurostar to experience new flavors of urban gentrification and artisanal coffee. We were on the train. Not the baby train, or the house-buying train, or even the marriage train—but a train of our own. And that, I suppose, was the point.

You see, I might not know how we moved to Berlin, but I certainly know why. I could have told you then and I'll tell you now: Nick and I moved to one of Europe's most beautiful, dynamic, and hedonistic capitals precisely because all our friends with babies couldn't. Their first blooms of parenthood were making me feel panicked and jealous, so I thought I'd do something that made them feel panicked and jealous in return. They couldn't go to Berlin for the summer; in choosing to "settle down" they'd cut off the possibility of running away; their security precluded them from my freedom. Nine months into our admittedly turbo relationship, Nick and I were doing something they couldn't do, to feel better about all the things I hadn't done.

If that sounds cynical and unkind, then it is only because I was probably feeling cynical and unkind about myself at the time. In truth, I didn't wish the people who had taken more conventional steps toward maturity anything but good fortune, happiness, and health. I wanted their marriages to last, their babies to be bonny, and their homes to be cozy. Of course I did—they were my friends. But I also wanted to feel better about my decisions along the way. That meant taking action. That meant changing the narrative from "not having a baby" to "living in Berlin." That meant turning an absence (of children, of marriage, of my own home) into a presence.

And Nick? When I asked him recently why he thought we moved to Berlin, he paused for a moment, ruffled his hair, and said, "I was bored by work, I suppose."

This is one of the major headbutts of your late twenties and early thirties: once the wedding bells start ringing and muslins start hitting the radiators, anyone in a couple will start to be defined either as Parents or Not Parents. You're no longer just Nell and Nick—you're Nell and Nick Who Haven't Had a Baby Yet. People will spring the question on you anywhere and everywhere: "So, do you think you two will have a baby?" Even when they're not actually asking it, the question is still pushed toward you by the slow growth of their bump, their maternity bra, their buggy, their long, sympathetic smiles as you hold their baby, their whispers, their raised eyebrows, the knowing smile every time you turn down an alcoholic drink. In my experience, it is a question that seems to land far more heavily on women than men. It is the one with the womb who is really being asked, you see. You may be gay, you may have expressed no maternal inclinations before in your life, you may be living in a different city from your partner, you may be unwell, you may have polycystic ovary syndrome, endometriosis, a blocked fallopian tube, or an underactive thyroid, you may have depression, anxiety, psychosis, be bipolar or suffering panic attacks, you may have just landed your dream job, you may have just been laid off, you may be training for an utterly overwhelming physical adventure, you may have no money, you may be reeling from the death or illness of a parent, you may be falling out of love with the person you got together with six years ago; nevertheless, if you are in a relationship during the Panic Years (and sometimes even if you're not), people will ask you if you're going to have a baby. Because I met Nick at plum settling-down time, the pressure was almost instant—within two months of us first sleeping together, two of his old flatmates and one of my best friends had announced they were pregnant. I'm not claiming any hand in that, you understand. Even I am not so powerful a love-maker that I can impregnate friends of friends across different counties. But as our peers started to buy houses, get hitched, and become pregnant, we had to do something that all those people with mortgages, wedding debts, and babies couldn't do, in order to prove that we were more than just parents-in-waiting. In order to prove that the child-free life was as valid, and perhaps more pleasant, than the baby-making one. In order to stamp our own ticket.

That headbutt hurts both ways, of course. I now know, from experience, that once you've had a baby you lose hours to scrolling through Instagram, pricked with tears of furious envy as you look at your child-free friends climbing mountains, celebrating promotions, wearing close-cut and stain-free clothes, drinking cold glasses of white wine on sun-kissed beaches, going to gigs, meeting their heroes, making magazine-worthy meals, getting haircuts, sleeping in camper vans beside Welsh waterfalls, running marathons, going to parties, and wearing underwear that doesn't also double up as a surgical stretcher. The fact that you enjoyed very few, if any, of these things before you had a baby is immaterial—the envy is real and it is inescapable and it is fired between parent and nonparent like a missile.

I now understand why my friend Alice, six months into motherhood and so delirious with fatigue that she'd just put her house keys, remote control, and wallet through the washing machine, once rang me just to say that I shouldn't rush into motherhood.

"Don't make Nick have a baby yet," she said, her voice quieter and slower than I remembered. "Give yourselves a year before you get pregnant. Have a nice time. Enjoy each other. Because you'll need nice things to look back on when you're going through absolute shit."

She was right. During our first year of being together, I absolutely loved just being Nick's girlfriend. I loved sitting across from such a beautiful man at dinner. I loved that he wanted to cycle across Ireland with me even though he couldn't actually ride a bike (yes, I taught him). I loved that he went to galleries on his lunch break. I loved that he wanted to come with me when I went to give talks at universities. I loved that he let me have sex with him using a Femidom just so I could write about it for a magazine. I loved that when we went to the Tate Modern to drink wine overlooking the river, he stole a decanter just to prove that he'd also been a great teenage shoplifter. I loved that we could get up when we wanted to, could go camping with four hours' notice, could walk up mountains or just spend an afternoon playing cards. Sure, sometimes I was so overwhelmed with love that I would nearly blurt out the words "Please will you have a baby with me" before throwing my hand across my mouth with horror. But I also knew that we were irresponsible, we were untethered, we were having a lovely time, and that I should make the most of that while it lasted.

Which is how I found myself, at the eastern edge of Germany, cycling along the route of a former border with a man I wanted to spend the rest of my life with, but who didn't want my babies. A man who had brought my life delight and depth and devotion but who, simultaneously, seemed unable or unwilling to recognize a maternal desire that had been pulsing away at the very root of my soul for decades. A man who sighed, pulled at his hair, or stared sadly out of the window every time I brought up the possibility of having children. A man who would greet my tears of longing or frustration with kindness but not understanding; a man with whom I had a relationship that, for the first time, I could imagine bearing the burden of parenthood; a man who seemed so emotionally mature, so thoughtful, so open. And yet, a man who—throughout the months and years during which I wrangled, writhed, and wrestled with the question of how, why, whether, and when to have a baby—seemed genuinely to never consider it. Ignored it, forgot it, dismissed it, or simply overlooked it.

Today, as our son sleeps off his lunch in the room next door and we tidy up the Mount Rushmore of toys, I ask my partner why it was that we had seemed so out of sync, so mutually unintelligible on this fundamental point.

"I just didn't think about babies," he says. "All those years you were thinking about it, I just wasn't. It plays into your argument, I suppose, that men are sort of encouraged not to think about their fertility. I just didn't think about it. Don't think about it."

How I envy that freedom. How it scares me.

"I could see why you wanted a baby when your friends started having them," he continues. "But I just thought you weren't thinking about the practical side. I'd just quit my job and we were living in Berlin with no prospects. I don't mean money. It's like bandwidth: being able to think about enough things at once. If we were going to have a baby, then for years that was where all my energy would be going. So, if I didn't already know what I wanted to do for a job, what my hobbies were, or where I wanted to live, then I'd have been stuck for years where I was, with what I was doing. When I say practicalities, I mean being settled in the other aspects of your life because once you've had the baby, you can't put any energy into them. Babies need to be brought into fairly stable environments. We had a stable emotional environment, but I didn't think at that time we had a stable financial, work, or home environment—all those other things."

It turns out, he had been thinking about babies. Just not in the same way I had been thinking about babies.

Back in Berlin, replenished by my spicy porcine delight, a cup of coffee that tasted like agricultural diesel, and a chocolate wafer so dry it could have doubled as a dehumidifier, Nick and I pushed on to Gross Glienicke, just north of Wannsee. Here stood a low, crumbling brick wall, decorated with faded spray paint and overhung with ivy, running along the edge of someone's garden and down into the lake. Beside this was another wall, this one made of steel mesh, standing between six-foot-high concrete posts. About five meters on, there was a short stretch of three tall, imposing concrete posts, still joined together with huge concrete slabs and topped with a great metal tube, clamped to the wall with bent girders. The whole section dwarfed Nick—it was at least twice his height, and under it all ran the two parallel lines of brick that now denote where the Berlin Wall once stood. Here they were: the three incarnations of that infamous and deadly border between East and West Berlin, between Europe and the Soviet Union. We were standing in front of a time capsule of one of Europe's strangest acts of annexation and political cannibalism.

Did I understand the jealousy, fury, sadness, and regret it might cause when I posted a picture from that bike ride to Instagram? Did I know how my tanned limbs, my sleep-taut eyes, my red nails digging into my slim waist, and my unsubtle crowing about the 170 kilometers I'd just cycled would be seen by all the gray-faced, swollen, claustrophobic new mothers back home? Probably, yes, I'm afraid I probably did.

Did I care? Of course I cared. Did it stop me? Sadly, it did not. Instead of keeping my private life private, I fired photo after photo of azure lakes, Soviet typography, flea markets, beech forests, rooftop bars, and tall Berlin apartments into the online ether, precisely because I wanted to show the world what fun I was having without a baby. I was unconsciously reinforcing the painful divide between the parents and the nonparents by carving out a picture of child-free liberty online. I was undertaking a not-so-subtle war of propaganda against the baby pictures, the fetal scans, the wedding photos, and the nursery pics uploaded onto my timeline by proud and deserving friends. That summer, in a new city with a newish partner, I weaponized my empty womb to fight back against the rising panic other people's happiness was eliciting in me.

At this point, you may be wondering why I was still with Nick at all. After he'd made it so clear that he didn't want a baby now, perhaps ever, why hadn't I pulled my self-esteem together, put my eye to the horizon, and walked away? I was thirty-two, I had never been pregnant, and all my life, in some way or another, I had wanted a baby. So why was I letting someone else's ambivalence stand between me, my body, and my future?

This week, I asked Nick why he thought people who want children stay with people who don't.

"Because those things are so fundamental, you basically don't believe that, deep down, the other person doesn't really feel the same as you," he said.

Perhaps this is also true. How you feel about having a baby is so personal, so profound and pushed so deeply down into your own complicated tapestry of being that you simply cannot believe that anyone you love, really love, doesn't somehow feel the same. Which, instead of an argument you must win, makes having a baby a waiting game you must simply bear out. Perhaps I really did think that, given a year, maybe two, Nick would eventually recognize that, yes, he did want to have a baby with me. Perhaps I thought that, if I could just stick it out long enough, his desires would align with my own. But that's still not all of it.

There is the other possibility, that by committing to somebody who feels differently to you, you are unconsciously forcing yourself to examine, question, and ultimately defend your own position. It forces you to be definite, when you're not actually feeling definite at all. If Nick had blithely said he wanted a baby any time I fancied, then I would have had to confront the reality of having a baby far sooner. I would have had to ask if it *was* really what I wanted right then and there. I may have found that actually, I wasn't quite ready, wasn't quite sure. Without Nick's brick wall to kick against, I may have been forced to confront my own ambivalence, concerns, doubts about motherhood.

As my friend Scarlet recently put it, while leaning on a bench outside London Fields Lido with her head in her hands, "Since my pals have started having babies, my boyfriend's started to say he wants a baby. I'm the one saying 'not yet.' Because I'm the one who's just heard all their terrifying pregnancy stories and I'm not ready for that yet. I know that's going to be an emotional battle. So I think, let's just do one more year and stay on the train and do all the jobs."

Scarlet is doing this with a man who is ready, willing, and hope-fully able to become a parent whenever she is ready. With Nick, I had the perfect foil to fight against, to plot out my rational arguments to, to try and win over with emotional appeals, to try and lure with little practices around other babies or to double-bluff by saying I didn't care either way. He was my backstop: I knew that he would push against my appeals to get pregnant for long enough to force me to prepare for it myself, alone. His opposition was forcing me to realize what a baby meant to me. At times, it made me genuinely wonder if I could and should leave him. Nick's disinterest in being a father gave me a perfect wall to throw my every maternal fear, hope, desire, and anxiety against. Just as I had defended myself against the vulnerability of commitment by trying to make unsuitable men love me, so I defended myself against the uncertainty of parenthood by staying with a man who didn't want children. He slowed me down, forced the issue, and, eventually, made me fight for what I really wanted.

This was not the case for Ellie, the female half of the couple I moved to Berlin with. I first met Ellie one adrenaline-fizzing, spring lunchtime as we slid out of secondary school for a cigarette. I was enthralled and intimidated by her immediately: her messy blond crop, her trousers the perfect width to cover her skate shoes, her fingers like the mechanism of a clock as she rolled a thin, straight cigarette. She was in the year above me and she was hilarious, her sense of humor as dry and light as a salt-and-vinegar Chipstick. She seemed genuinely not to worry about what other people thought and, as a result, was easily the coolest person I'd met for years. If you'd told me then, at thirteen, as I gazed up at her blowing smoke rings into a nearby bush, that in eighteen years' time I would be sharing an apartment with her in Berlin, I would probably have swallowed my own braces with shock.

That summer, as I hurled myself around Brandenburg, jumping in lakes, cycling to Poland, running along train tracks, gathering up new friends like spilled salt, Ellie seemed to slide naturally into Berlin life without a backward glance. She drank sour beer in low-lit bars, she mooched around flea markets, she actually wrestled the bureaucratic mountain lion involved in registering as a resident. Her boyfriend got a studio, she got a job, they ate out, went to gigs, and wore black. One weekend, as Nick and I dodged wild boar and collected tick bites in the Black Forest—a trip during which we were forced to stop in a semi-abandoned hotel in the middle of nowhere and make mutually incomprehensible small talk with the geriatric owner as she gave us stale cake and showed us her original CD single of "Candle in the Wind"—Ellie quietly and calmly proposed to her boyfriend in bed one morning. Upon our return, as we celebrated the happy news with *Sekt auf Eis* in a bar over the road, I realized that Ellie and Robin were building a life here. They belonged here. Nick and I were having a last hoorah, while they were creating something different entirely.

Two years later, as I slid into the sleepless, twitching, milkbeast early months of motherhood, Ellie opened her own illustration gallery—the only one of its kind in the whole city—in a former gambling joint in Neukölln. She had stayed on in Berlin. She had learned a new language. She had become a wife, become the resident of a different country, thrown away the structure and security of her old career, and surrounded herself with beauty, creativity, and choice. We had entered the Flux together, both provoked by the pregnancies of our peers, but had drawn up at quite different destinations.

"If my mates hadn't had children, it's very possible I would not now be in Berlin and would not have a gallery," she tells me over WhatsApp one evening as I browse her online shop and complain about my new crop of white neck hairs. "Seeing the reality of child-rearing knocks the romantic corners off the idea. And so moving abroad was a reaction to do something, anything, when our friends started getting up the duff."

We are, as Ellie admits, in a very privileged position to be able to react this way: freedom of movement, freedom to choose our own work, freedom to use contraception, freedom to not be pregnant unless we want to be.

"I am extremely lucky to have this decision available to me. I am a white woman with savings. I am privileged to have lived in a country that meant I had choices: I had an abortion ten years ago when I was skint, unemployed, and unhappy. God knows how that child would have stuck me fast to one man and one place and I wouldn't have had any of the joyous life I have now."

According to the NHS, one in three British women will have an abortion in their lifetime, while the ONS reports that 197,533 women in England and Wales had abortions in 2017 alone. Those women had a choice. They do not have to have the rest of their life dictated and curtailed by the consequences of sperm meeting egg. Of course, it shouldn't be a case of luck, nationality, and wealth—the decision to have or not have a baby should be a universally acknowledged human right, because having a baby is something that will affect the course of your life forever.

"It's an unknown until it's too late to change your mind," Ellie adds. "If I end up hating this gallery life, I can burn it all down. I draw the line at burning a child to the ground. Also, being abroad means I feel like nothing has quite the same impact as if I were doing this in London or Bristol. I can always Lord Lucan out of here and go back to the mothership if I want to. I think the word is noncommittal."

It is noncommittal. But in that sense, my friend Ellie hasn't committed to being child-free either.

"I'm not sure that I've made a decision whether or not to have children," she explains. "I'm not sure that my gallery precludes having a child, but I just haven't been swept away by the biological imperative yet. I do think about it regularly, though. If my husband turned to me and said he'd like to try and be parents, I'd be into it. I also don't know if I will get to the point where I have the Big Regret and at age fifty start trying to have a baby, how can you know? I just knew I would regret not grabbing this opportunity right fucking now while the stars are aligned."

Two women, two tickets, two trains, and two reactions to the same circumstances: here I am with a baby, and here she is with a gallery. Of course there is a wall between us. As a mother, I will never again be the woman who moved to Berlin with her boyfriend and her best friend to have a summer of sun, fun, and affordable beer; in turn, she will never have a child my child's age, use my hand-me-down breast pads, or be awake at two A.M. feeding her baby while I, doing the same, scroll through my phone looking for company. Luckily for me, our friendship is strong and supple enough that the Flux has not driven a wedge between Ellie and me. The division that runs between us is not concrete but hazy.

Not everyone is so lucky. According to research undertaken by the British Red Cross and the Co-op last year, more than 40 percent of mothers under thirty say they are lonely often or always. When you have a baby, your life changes, your freedom evaporates, your priorities shift, and your very ability to move through the world becomes compromised. The unending manual labor involved in raising a child leaves you little time for friends, conversation, even leaving the house. The obliteration of your memory, vocabulary, and sense of humor by months of sleep deprivation makes it hard to hold a conversation, let alone socialize. The omnipresent risk of death, illness, or catastrophe with a newborn leaves you very little energy or residual empathy to keep up with other people's lives. The endless logistics involved in getting your child to sleep, to eat, and to stop crying make it hard to exist in public spaces as you once did. And so, of course, all too easily you can lose touch with your child-free friends. Resentment can creep in where affection once lay, exhaustion can obliterate interest, self-pity can drive away companionship.

As we continue to message back and forth, Ellie adds a little postscript that brings me up short. "Most importantly though: I don't want to be a weird perfumed childless auntie figure who scares kids with her over-drawn eyebrows and costume jewelry, and I don't want to be a small gray sad woman who can't look into a pram without her eyes brimming with tears. What is the other option? NELL! WHAT IS IT?!"

I know that she's joking, but I also know that under that joke is a kernel of something real: The fear that being child-free will mark you out, forever, from your parent friends. The hunger for aspirational, representative child-free women in culture and in our community. The unease that not having a baby may render you creepy, sad, or ludicrous in the eyes of people who do have children. Under that joke is a nut I long to crack.

There is a solution, of course, a way to avoid the pain, the jeal-ousy, and the panic that so often follows in the wake of parenthood and separates adults into the breeders and the child-free. It will take money, time, and a dismantling of the patriarchy. But hey, doesn't it always? In order to pull down the walls that inhibit our lives, we need to redress the financial, cultural, social, and institutional im-balance that forces parents and the child-free into parallel, mutually incomprehensible silos. To take just a tiny example: imagine if your place of work were to introduce a free, twenty-four-hour crèche. This, believe me, could be revolutionary.

Firstly, it means that new parents could return to work even if they weren't on the sort of high income currently needed to pay those crip-pling nursery fees (where I live, even just the local authority nursery costs £926 per month—entirely unaffordable on my salary). It would mean that people who wished to could carry on breastfeeding longer, that they could work more flexible (perhaps even longer) hours, they could keep up with their professional training and qualifications, they could have lunch with their child and build up a day-to-day, caring, involved relationship with their key workers, or some days choose to have lunch with their colleagues and chat about office gossip, last night's telly, the wildly inappropriate temperature of the air condi-tioning, or somebody's breakup: the very social fabric that makes your colleagues feel like friends.

By this one small change to the modern workplace, we could bring parents back into the social and economic fold without compromising any of the freedoms and benefits held by the child-free. We would put everyone in that workplace in daily contact with babies and toddlers and therefore break the "out of sight, out of mind" culture that some-how allows the first few years of everybody's life to be seen as a private and irrelevant affair. We could give people without children, but who are thinking about it one day, the chance to actually exist alongside a whole load of them, every day, and therefore test their feelings about parenthood in a more tangible, prosaic way. By literally putting small children in our employers' faces, we would also make it far less socially acceptable to introduce and uphold employment practices that discriminate against parents. Telling a woman she has to work through lunch and then sit in the bathroom to use a breast pump is one thing: telling her that she can't go to feed her hungry child just twenty meters away feels, somehow, quite another. Yes, you would have to adapt the adult world to make it more conducive to children, but with current rates of work-related mental illness, is that really such a bad thing? According to the Labor Force Survey and a report by the Health and Safety Executive, last year 602,000 workers were suffering from work-related stress, depression, or anxiety, while 12.8 million working days were lost due to work-related stress, depression, or anxiety. The system, as it is now, simply isn't working. We need to change it, for everybody's benefit, not just those currently holding the shitty end of the stick.

As my friend Lauren, a neuroscientist, put it to me one hot bank holiday as we walked through Epping Forest, in her industry there are a lot of very unhappy women because, in order to progress within a system designed and largely managed by men, they are trying to live like men.

"Because white women get so close to 'winning' the game, we are most at risk of losing sight of the fact that the game itself is broken," says Lauren, passing yet another leaf to my son as we walk along a winding tree-lined path. "We need to pull the whole thing apart and start again."

Lauren, as well as explaining the workings of the retina to me on a fairly regular basis, is one of the women who keeps me sane, keeps me honest, and keeps me fighting. The system is broken, the modern workplace does not work for women (or men either), high-income and high-status jobs are inherently designed to exclude disabled people, people of color, people with special needs, and people from "nontraditional" backgrounds. The fact that people like me only realize this when we are booted out of the inner circle by dint of having a baby speaks of our inherent privilege. But it should also give us the will and the momentum to dismantle the system and rebuild it, stone by jagged stone, until it's fixed.

When Nick and I came to leave Berlin at the end of that summer and return to London, we had both decided to retrain as teachers—just like our mothers once had, just like everyone had always joked we would—and I wanted more than ever to start trying for a baby. We'd had an adventure, I thought. We had lived a life without responsibility and unfettered by thoughts of the future, I thought. But now it was time to go home and become part of something: a community, a school, and a family. People have created far more out of far less.

10

GIFT HORSE

There were about seven of us there, by the time someone noticed the hypodermic needle.

Seven women, in pastel tops and sneakers, sitting on colorful blankets, eyeing up the sweaty cherry tomatoes and sun-warm Kettle Chips. Seven child-free women, sitting in the dappled sunlight of a park, wondering how far their trousers had slid down, what knickers they were wearing that were now on display, if they bought the right present, when they last ate a marshmallow, and where they're going to pee. Seven disparate women brought together to celebrate one of our best friend's happiness/fecundity/betrayal—delete as appropriate. Suddenly, one of the other baby showerers bent down, a paper napkin in her hand, and carefully pulled a spike-tipped syringe out of the grass beside our feet.

"Oh, that's nice!" I say, looking at the needle. "Baby's first heroin!"

Amidst the nervous laughter, I catch one woman staring at me with a look like I'd just used her hair as a handkerchief. I smile apologetically and pretend to be looking in my bag for something important.

I hope I'm not bursting too many pink and blue bubbles when I say that there is a kind of pastel-colored agony to baby showers. Nothing puts your own state of flux into more sharp relief than watching an old drinking buddy sit, bulbous and flushed, on a pale green blanket, opening parcel after parcel of booties, knitted hats, breast pads and bottle sterilizers while you chew for a cigarette and wonder how many days until your next period. It marks the fiercest division between the hedonists and the homemakers and seems to unconsciously encourage criticism of both. Where once you were all traveling together through school, work, bootcut jeans, casual sex, and Argos kitchen starter kits, somehow the baby shower years make every slight point of deviation seem enormous: a mortgage, a partner, a health problem, a heartbreak, an abortion, a savings account, a disability, a fiancé, a redundancy, a change in sexuality. Suddenly you are looking across a tapestry of sofa throws and crochet hats at your friends, wondering if they hate you, pity you, in fact if you have anything in common with these people at all anymore.

When I was growing up, nobody had baby showers. As a term, it was something I'd only ever heard on American television shows, along with "faucet," "pocketbook," and "date" (the latter being a particularly hellish mystery—the British path to true love led, I knew, through a shitfaced one-night stand, an awkward kiss goodbye on your doorstep, perhaps meeting up for a drink a few days later to actually get to know each other and then decide if you wanted to "go out"). I didn't go to any christenings either, as my parents and their friends were of the benevolently ineffective "let them choose what religion they want to follow when they're older" school of thought. Of course, very few of us ever did wake up, aged seventeen, and shout, "I'm going to be Jewish!" or got to twenty-three and announced one Sunday, "It's Roman Catholicism for me!" But, as I say, it was a well-intentioned approach and certainly spared me the tricky, combative relationship with religion that my more formally indoctrinated peers seem to carry around with them.

In an increasingly secular, consumerist society, the baby shower seems to have wedged itself into the gap left behind by more formal, religious ceremonies like Namakarana, baptism, or Brit Milah. Where once we bore witness under stone gables or whispered the baby's name into their ear beside a sacred fire, today's infants are ushered into being on a tide of shop-bought onesies, nipple cream, ventilated blankets, and envelope-neck vests (my friends, take note: these can be pulled down as well as up, so you can undress your

baby without smearing shit through their hair—something my partner and I only discovered four months and several scatological inci-
dents in). Even a hardened, anti-consumerist eco-warrior like myself
can't begrudge people for wanting to buy baby things: they're small,
sweet, and colorful and remind us of our own innocence and childhood infatuations.

You want to buy that friend a copy of *Winnie-the-Pooh* because
you remember it being read to you when you were little, and cared
for, and safe. You want to knit them a baby blanket because you remember your grandmother teaching you to knit, one cozy half-term
holiday in a caravan in Ireland. You want to buy them a little furry
tiger because in all your life, nothing has ever thrilled and excited
you as much as the page in *The Tiger Who Came to Tea* where Sophie's parents take her out for tea in a café and she wears her coat
over her nightie.

To give gifts is, I believe, a natural human inclination. It is an act
of community-building, an emblem of belonging, and part of what
the sociologists Nicoletta Balbo and Nicola Barban call "cost-sharing."
These physical manifestations bind us together in a debt-credit relationship that ensures we stay close. If that sounds cynical, it's honestly
not meant to. In one sense, we come together to give new parents
gifts because it makes it more likely that, if and when we are having
children, they will be there to look after us in return. But, sadly, this
natural inclination has been entirely manipulated by modern capitalism to make us buy thousands of tons of shit we don't need, out of a
feeling of guilt, duty, aspiration, and competition.

Shop displays, hysterical sponsored editorials, those revolting plastic
Bounty packs full of advertising material, promotional freebies, and
scaremongering marketing that are thrust on vulnerable and disoriented women on actual labor wards (a practice that must be stopped
immediately) all trick us into thinking that, in order to be good parents, people, and friends, we must buy things. Lots of things. Lots of
new, plastic, ecologically unsound, ethically appalling things. Things
made in sweatshops, driven thousands of miles, wrapped in plastic

that will not decompose for fifty years and sold in shops that refuse to give their staff sick leave, maternity benefits, or pensions. The piles of tiny unworn clothes, shoes, ignored toys, ridiculous and unnecessary gadgets that are slowly covering the earth's crust with poisonous rubbish is, however you look at it, terrifying. We are shopping ourselves into a humanitarian crisis—using our finite and precious natural resources of oil, wood, coal, and gas to mass-produce things that nobody needs, values, or will remember.

Of course, I would never in a million years use the old "If they got by without it a hundred years ago, we don't need it now" argument. A hundred years ago, thousands of babies—and mothers—died prematurely for want of certain gadgets, tools, medicines, and knowledge. But electric-powered, self-rocking baby hammocks? Disposable breast pads? Plug-in wet-wipe warmers? Single-use spoons? These we absolutely do not need and must stop buying. Please.

Aside from the matter of capitalist-driven ecological and humanitarian disaster, there is also something about buying things for an unborn baby that simply makes me anxious. My boyfriend's Irish Catholic grandmother refuses to buy any baby a thing while it is still in the womb, and I love her for it. At eighty-one, she's seen enough accidents, tragedies, and sadness to understand that counting your children before they've hatched is risky and probably unwise. Many months after the needle picnic incident, when I was pregnant, I became absolutely terrified of miscarriage, stillbirth, infant mortality. Of course I was. They are a prospect so utterly sad, unfair, and unfathomable that I still feel unqualified to talk about them in any detail. I was haunted almost every day by a vision of coming home from the hospital, my heart broken, my body changed utterly, only to find a house full of baby clothes, an empty cot, an un-pushed buggy, sterilized bottles, teddy bears, unopened boxes of nappies, blankets, wallpaper, mobiles. The deep, aching sense of loss, triggered by the sight of so much stuff with no life to animate it, would have been unbearable. And so out of fear, as well as rational thought, I determined not to buy things, not to shower my unborn baby, to try and avoid that particular element of potential pain. It made me determined to move the focus away from prebirth shopping and onto caring for women, however and wherever their pregnancies take them.

A baby shower also seems specifically designed to pit each woman against some idealized and ubiquitous version of the future, and in doing so, induce a state of panic, self-reflection, and unease among anyone not yet there. Maybe you've had a baby already and being reminded of those first few precious months makes you ache for a new child you can neither afford nor care for but want all the same. Perhaps you're single, have always wanted children, but have no means of getting pregnant, and so sitting in the early afternoon sun beside a pile of carefully unwrapped crib sheets beside the woman who introduced you to your ex-boyfriend makes you feel like you're running out of chances at happiness. Maybe you have known all your life that you have a physical or mental health condition that precludes you from having children, even if you wanted to. Perhaps you have a new partner, are euphoric with love, had sex twice that morning, and can still feel their thumbprints on your buttocks, and the idea of having a baby seems like nothing but a massive drag. Maybe you've been with your partner for two years, are still attracted to other people, have never spoken to them about children, don't really like their parents, and don't want to move in together because you actually prefer the company of your flatmate, and so every month cross your fingers that you're not pregnant. Perhaps you loudly and jokingly tell people that you hate "snotty little kids" but remember, with some pain, the abortion you had at seventeen that you couldn't tell your parents about and that ruined your exams that summer. Maybe you've missed a period and are too afraid to do a pregnancy test in case it comes out positive and you have to give up smoking and drinking and eating sushi. Maybe you have been trying to get pregnant for three years, have done all the tests, have found no biological reason you shouldn't conceive, take your temperature every morning, chart your ovulation on the calendar on the fridge, and love your partner a little less every time they smile and say, "Oh well, it was fun trying!" Maybe you'll go home from this baby shower and sob so hard that you retch. Maybe you'll go home from this baby shower and drink a pint of wine while dancing in your kitchen to Robyn. Maybe you don't go home after this baby shower and wake up in bed with someone who smells like peach flesh and sweat.

For the women who attend baby showers—and in my experience, baby showers are more exclusively attended by women than even hen dos, where for some reason gay men are now considered "basically women" by the rules of woke wedding engagement and are invited along too—each one acts as a sort of mini-reckoning, forcing them to take stock of their life, pan across the landscape of their social circle, and see how they fit in.

After the cherry-tomato-and-hypodermic-needle baby shower, I remember lying in my therapist's office and howling about this strange ritual that seemed designed to make me feel like a failure, an outsider, a maverick. How did we get here? A gift-wrapped twentieth-century incarnation of the great sorting match: the fecund and the child-free suddenly made strangers by a packet of nipple cream? Why was I spending my money on another woman's life choice? Why must she be remunerated, rewarded for her own fertility? Why are we throwing belongings at something that has never breathed air or tasted water? And, most of all, why do I want to scream into the earth at the sight of another woman becoming a mother?

As usual, my therapist sat, in silence, for some minutes as I poured out a confused stream of envy, regret, second-wave-feminist rhetoric, anger, and self-pity. Eventually, after much gentle questioning, insightful repetition, and reframing of my own words, he explained that, surely, the homogeneity of it all was the point. Hasn't society created these rituals—weddings, baby showers, christenings—to make us act collectively? If there is a codified practice around birth—giving presents, writing cards, making toasts, knitting blankets—it forces the rest of us to go away and agitate our lives in reaction to it. It might make us ask our partner if they want to have children and when. It might make us look into artificial insemination and embryo freezing. It might make us admit to our parents that we don't want to make them grandparents. But collective customs make us all, as individuals, take stock and take action. Or so the theory goes. Perhaps that function can one day be served without it becoming a giant gifting exercise.

When the first few people within a group start to have children, they are outliers within that larger community—open to criticism, isolation, and regret. But, by a process of repeated ritual, time, and pressure—the engagement parties, weddings, baby showers, christenings—the core philosophy of that group gradually starts to move. What was once remarkable is now entirely acceptable. The fun sponges are now the valued mentors.

In my case, the group dynamic seems to move toward career progression (birthday drinks are now awash with talk of office politics, funding applications, promotions, and "big projects") and family life (who's pregnant, who's trying, who accidentally got pregnant with twins the second time round). If you agree with the direction of movement you stay in the group, and move with it. If you dislike or disagree with the direction of movement you leave and find another group more aligned to your interests. By this subtle process, five years after the first few people were scoffed at for having a baby while most of their friends were doing lines of coke off football magazines and having sex with strangers for the sake of an anecdote, that first couple are now part of the majority, looking with confusion, even pity at the few friends who are still sleeping with their interns, calling marriage "a life sentence," and occasionally getting mugged while trying to buy drugs off someone half their age. This is not to say that there is a moral superiority to being at either end of the spectrum, but that the job of peer pressure is to make everyone act alike and so confirm one another's life choices. That way, ideally, you all start to creak toward a predictable, hopefully enjoyable destination together.

For people who choose to live child-free, the codified celebration of the mothering life can seem at odds with their very existence. They will never have a baby shower, never have this lace-strewn and unguent-smeared element of their femininity celebrated, never recoup the money and effort they have spent on others, never be admitted, fully, into that new group. We already know that, according to the Office for National Statistics, 18 percent of women in England and Wales in 2017 ended their childbearing years childless. Nearly twice as many women are turning forty-five without children as did thirty years ago. And yet, women in their thirties, particularly cis women in heterosexual relationships, are still defined as being either mothers or "not mothers."

A large part of what spurred Ellie and me to move to Berlin was a discomfort with this tacit labeling of us as "non-mothers," particularly as members of our close social group started to reproduce. In Berlin, Ellie tells me, that pressure seems less intense.

"All of our friends in Berlin are child-free, and it's just not a facet of our lives, other than nieces and nephews," she explains via email. "Everyone I know is mid- to late thirties and we're all getting wrinkly from the beer, smoke, sun, biting cold, and schnitzel. We go to dirty little bars to talk about Marvel films and food trends and makeup; there's a significant chunk of my spiteful little heart that is pleased that I'm free to do that shit and enjoy the thought that my friends with children might be a little jealous. It's exactly all the stuff that makes people want to fucking murder DINKs [Double Income No Kids]. When I balance the scales of my heart, I think I like that more than I like the idea of having a kid."

This is not a person we can easily categorize as a "non-mother." Despite the fact that she is still a decade away from the Office for National Statistics' cutting-off point of forty-five, Ellie is also part of a large and growing group of women who simply haven't made a hard-and-fast decision either way, who are well into their thirties. In 2017, according to the ONS, more women were pregnant in their thirties than their twenties, and the number of pregnant women in their forties had more than doubled since 1990, while there was an all-time low in pregnancy rates for women aged twenty-five and under. Nobody is completely sure why—as with all sociological trends, the picture is too variable and too nuanced to claim any definite conclusions—but as Natika H. Halil, the chief executive of sexual health charity the Family Planning Association, was quoted in the *Guardian* as saying, the figures "could show that women are waiting longer to have children, which might be due to a number of reasons, including but not limited to: higher costs of living, fewer young people able to afford mortgages, or perhaps feeling less pressure or desire to start a family."

When talking of babies, social pressure, choice, freedom, rituals, the future, and feminism: those women who choose not to have children should never be undermined, disregarded, or criticized for that decision. Those women who cannot or do not, for any number of reasons, get pregnant should not be made to feel left out, less valuable, less female, or more socially conspicuous because of those circumstances. Those women who choose to get pregnant and wish to mark that life-changing decision with some collective celebration among the people who mean the most to them should never be made to feel selfish, old-fashioned, smug, or irrational for doing so. We can only thrive as individuals if we are supported by our peers; we can only benefit our community if we are acknowledged by that community as an individual; we can only offer support to our contemporaries if we can be honest about our own personal desires and disappointments. It can be painful, scary, intimidating, and nerve-racking to admit what you want, of course, because in admitting our hopes, we leave ourselves open to the possibility of disappointment. In telling someone how you see your future, it can feel like you're inviting their judgment, criticism, or pity if it doesn't quite turn out that way. But perhaps the best way to avoid being judged or pitied is to be genuine and honest with yourself and others about your thinking, your aspiration, and your desire.

Inside each of us, there is a struggle going on between the hedonist and the homemaker, all the time. We simultaneously want to let rip, take care, be in the world, stay home, run free, nurture, wreak havoc, and create safety. At various times, one or other of those urges will take precedence. That is exactly as it should be. At various times, one or other of those urges will be reflected in those around you. That is precisely as you should want it.

Before I became a mother, baby showers made me jealous, because I wanted a baby. But baby showers also made me feel sad, because they felt like the end of my youth. The prospect of coming off contraception, trying for a baby, and getting pregnant both thrilled and terrified me. It made this little fertility dance under the trees somehow much more agitating. As Margaret Atwood wrote in *The Handmaid's Tale*, "You can only be jealous of someone who has something you think you ought to have yourself."

11

NEW YEAR'S IRRESOLUTION

Standing on a Greek rooftop, a chipped mug of red wine in my hand, I watch fireworks explode over ice-dry hills, orange trees, sagging electricity cables, and a beach covered in snow and tents. A woman to my left is trying to light a cigarette off a sparkler; a short man so proud of his A-frame that he's wearing a tank top in January is flirting unsuccessfully with a ballet dancer from Paris; a tall guy with long blond hair is proposing a toast; and a Syrian man with a beard like velvet is taking a selfie with a bottle of raki.

It is New Year's Eve, 2017. Nick and I are on the island of Chios, volunteering at a school for refugees. After the 2016 EU-Turkey deal, Chios became a sort of island-wide holding pen for thousands of people trying to reach the safety of Europe via the Turkish route. According to the agreement, anyone found trying to cross from Turkey to Greece (and therefore Europe) could be sent straight back to Turkey, back to their war-torn homeland, or to prison. If those desperate young men, women, and their children did manage to stay in Greece, they could be stuck for years on a tiny island that had little water and the kind of medieval plumbing that turns even toilet paper into a weapon of mass destruction: stuck with no money, living in tents, with no hope of work or ever reaching Athens, let alone London. They were trapped in a wind-blown limbo for the crime of escaping war, famine, disease, bombing, state-sanctioned terror, or death. It's an obvious place to ring in the new year.

Another firework screeches up from a neighboring roof and we all cheer. It is freezing; I'm wearing a coat that makes me look like a football manager; the sort of up-tempo reggae only white mainland Europeans like is blasting out of a Bluetooth speaker balanced on a plant pot; a lecturer from Newcastle is, unaccountably, drinking sherry out of a pint glass; Nick has his arm around my waist. A Swiss-German woman who has been in Chios for two years turns to me and, smiling innocently, asks a question that is about to tear my heart wide open: "What do you want to do this year?"

A pulse runs through my muscles like I'm about to dive off a bridge. My breath catches in my chest. My bowels quiver. *Oh shit*, I think. *Oh shit. I'm going to say it. I'm going to say it out loud.*

"I want to have a baby," I say, the words falling out of my mouth like stones. "I'd like to have a baby this year."

Studiously avoiding Nick's eye, I stare off at the horizon, at the rocky hills and crumbling city walls. He and I haven't spoken about babies for a while. I had been trying to give him space to think about it. He has been using that space to think about other things. I have been crying every time I get my period. He has been unaware of exactly why.

That week I had been volunteering in the high school. Some of my students looked older than sixteen. Some had crepe-like skin, stooped shoulders, rasping voices. These people were still young: children and teenagers. But, physically, they had experienced the kind of trauma, exhaustion, punishment, and fear that desiccates youth. As it was the week of Christmas and New Year's, I'd decided to spend one of our lessons cutting out about fifty paper leaves, and to ask the students that same innocent question: What do you want to do this year?

The students wrote down their new year's hopes and resolutions, and then we made a big tree display with them at the front of the room. Very *Blue Peter*. Very happy primary school. Very Mrs.-Tatton-with-her-Laura-Ashley-blouse-and-bottle-of-Elizabeth-Arden-in-a-desk-drawer.

My favorite student, a young man called Ali, who had the dark eyes and pale skin of northern Syria, never chatted in class, made tiny neat notes in the exercise book he never forgot, and once drew me a rose, wrote: "In 2017 I want peace for all country, and I want go London."

His classmate, a young woman from Afghanistan who looked like someone straight from a Shirley Hughes illustration, wrote, "My dream for 2017 is to go to England, because I would like to be a policewoman."

Another girl, Maanah, wearing spray-textured jeans and second-hand silver shoes, wrote, "I want to go to Germany by bus."

Nour, a loud and confident girl who challenged the boys at football every lunchtime, wrote, "My wish for 2017 is play guitar concert at school."

An Arabic-speaking girl called Saima, with hair like treacle, wrote, "My dream for 2017 is go back to Sirya and I see my cousin."

Manir, who borrowed one of the felt-tip pens in the entrance hall to draw on an earring every day before school, wrote that in 2017 he wanted "to come to England and meet Cristiano Ronaldo."

Khalida, a slim girl dressed in a sweatshirt designed for a grown man, and who shared a hotel room with her baby brother, mother, and older sister, wrote that "My dream for 2017 is to watch a film on television."

Was it this that made me finally choke out the words that reared up inside me with newfound urgency? Confronted with such simple hope and shameful injustice, did I see the world stripped back to the bare bones of birth, life, and death? Or, when faced with the sheer mundane horror of a family of six living in a tent with little heating, no toys, wet shoes, and crumbling teeth from malnutrition, did I slip into a temporary nihilism where I felt that what I said didn't matter, so I might as well lay it all out like a dirty towel anyway? I don't know. Perhaps it was just the cheap red wine and being far from home. But for whatever reason, up on that roof, surrounded by people I didn't know, I said it. I said it out loud, with witnesses, that I wanted to start trying for a baby. I said it in front of Nick, knowing that he could hear me. I said it like throwing a brick at a window. I remember feeling like I'd just lifted up my skirt and showed the world my pubes. I was as exposed as I'd ever been. But here's the amazing thing: nobody panicked. Nobody even seemed surprised. After all, here we were: a couple in their thirties, who lived together and were about to start training as teachers. That one of us was ready to start trying for a baby was about as surprising as the fact that kids ate jam.

After a quick "Ah, nice!" the Swiss woman moved on to the man next to me and asked him the same question. I had just loosed the volcano of my maternal longing, with these people as my witness, and not one of them seemed in the least alarmed. Even Nick hadn't taken the opportunity to throw himself off the roof.

As the night wore on, spurred on by a not-insignificant quantity of booze, I told about twelve different strangers that I wanted to have a baby. I told the Syrian man who worked as a translator and teaching assistant at the school, I told an American woman who was dressed like Liam Gallagher, I told the two British women who we were sharing a flat with, told an Italian Ph.D. student who kept trying to get everyone to listen to him on the guitar. I was daring myself. I knew that the more people I told, the harder it would be to deny my feelings later. I was trying it out in public, making myself accountable for what I wanted. I was also baiting Nick, trying to get a reaction—any reaction—out of him.

About two hours after going to bed, in the biting cold of the apartment that accommodated all voluntary teachers, lying in our sleeping bags, Nick started to shiver. He seemed to get colder and more agitated until, finally, he threw up all over the floor on his side of the bed. Worrying that this was some sort of allergic reaction, or the onset of a proper illness, I shook him awake, tried to make him drink a glass of water, mopped at the vomit with one of our towels. Was it stress? Was it booze? I'll never know. Because as I came back in from the bathroom, after rinsing the vomit out into the drain, I found Nick lying on his back, happily snoring away. Well then. I suppose I got my reaction.

Telling your partner that you want to start trying for a baby isn't, of course, one single conversation. For most couples I know, the decision, or desire, seems to roll along, gathering weight and momentum, like an avalanche, for years. In the early days, you scope each other out to see if having children might ever be on the horizon. You might talk about it, as an abstract, while waiting for a bus outside Target. After spending the weekend with some friends who are pregnant you might talk about logistics, about dates, even about names. You might come off the pill, switch to the legendarily unreliable pull-out method, stop buying condoms. One woman from my prenatal group says that their decision was prompted by simple logistics: "Our landlord had given us notice, so Dave said something along the lines of 'We should try to see if we can buy somewhere and then we should have a baby.'"

Just like that! No mess, no fuss! No fireworks, no begging, no inclination to dive off a roof. I can scarcely believe it. And yet, my friend Stevo describes the conversation he had with his partner about trying for a family as "the most beautiful moment of my life." He goes on: "It was New Year's Eve. A little worse for wear, Alice and I had gone back to our room. We were chatting about life and love, and so the subject of having kids naturally came up. One of the reasons I'd split from my ex was that she didn't want to have children. I remember we were both like, 'Shall we just try for a baby?' It was a euphoric eureka moment and wonderfully exciting to have made the decision together."

When I ask my friend Becs, she is possibly most sanguine of all: "I told Cormac I was thinking of taking the coil out, and he said he was ready whenever."

There are couples who start having "potluck sex," that is, only using a condom when they can be bothered and wait for nature to make the decision for them. I mean, of course, that is actually making the decision, but fair enough, if they want to dress it up as "leaving it up to the universe," then who am I to argue? There are couples who plan the date of insemination down to the minute, using diaries and spreadsheets, in order for their child to get into a certain school on a certain date five years hence. Then there are couples who three months into dating discover that, before they've even got a toothbrush in each other's flats, they've managed to create a pregnancy.

And yet, during the Panic Years, many of us find ourselves outside of the circumstances in which we might get pregnant biologically, accidentally, or as we had once hoped. You may have just come out of a long-term relationship, you may be living abroad for work, you may be single, you may be gay, you may have suspected fertility issues, you may be undergoing medical treatment, you may have just been laid off: for a whole host of reasons you may feel that it is not the right time to try to get pregnant. And yet, running alongside that knowledge is the competing realization that your fertility is finite, that you may run out of eggs before you get your shit sorted.

For years, women in this position have been told that there is a solution: egg freezing. Pop them out and put them in a freezer until you're ready. There are adverts in magazines and on buses; companies like Facebook, Apple, and Google offer it to their employees as part of their contract; your mum not-so-subtly drops it into conversation on the way to your niece's second birthday. But what does freezing your eggs actually mean? What does it entail? How does it feel? Does it work?

At twenty-seven, my friend Eleanor Morgan found out that she was infertile. I first met Eleanor at a clothes swap party about eight years ago. I remember offering her a dress that she politely declined, saying it was "A bit too 'I-sell-organic-beetroot-and-wear-a-jade-egg-at-the-weekends.'" She offered me a pair of trousers that I said gave me "a fat cunt. Literally."

And so, one of the greatest friend romances of my twenties began. I have never yet found a question, thought, challenge, or emotion that

Eleanor couldn't open up like a Russian doll just through talking. She is one of the most eloquent, insightful, hilarious, and sensitive brains I've ever had the good fortune to slap into. In her last book, *Hormonal*, she pulled the female body apart thread by thread, rewriting the way we think about biology entirely. She is also prolifically flatulent and has awful taste in puns, but that is by the by.

"I found that I was infertile by accident," Eleanor tells me one day, as we walk her Staffordshire bull terrier, Peggy, around the park. "I'd been living with chronic pelvic pain since my appendix burst at seventeen, so they investigated and did a fertility test. I'd never planned to find out about it, but they said my tubes were scarred and so conceiving naturally would be almost impossible."

By dint of her body's own agony, Eleanor had infertility thrust upon her. Luckily, perhaps, because this infertility had an organic cause, in the shape of all that spiderweb scar tissue grafted across her womb, the doctor could offer her egg freezing or embryo freezing, for free, on the NHS. For many women, these things are rarely cheap and never simple. According to the Human Fertilization and Embryology Authority (HFEA), the average cost of having your eggs collected and frozen is £3,350 ($4,355), with another £500–£1,500 ($650–$1,950) on top of that for medication. Storage costs are between £125 ($162) and £350 ($455) per year, then thawing eggs and transferring them to the womb costs an average of £2,500 ($3,250). So, as they say themselves, "the whole process for egg freezing and thawing costs an average of £7,000–£8,000 ($9,100–$10,400)."

There are a lot of women for whom seven to eight thousand pounds or nine to ten thousand dollars is a significant, if not prohibitive, amount of money. And yet, the whole fertility industry knows that, when confronted with something as deeply felt and powerfully wanted as pregnancy, we will pay whatever it takes.

"Because of the way the private sector has monetized egg freezing, we've been fed this idea that it's a way to 'take control of your future,'" says Eleanor. "But the data for it being successful is really slim. For a woman to have a successful pregnancy after just freezing her eggs, rather than making an embryo, is quite low. It does happen, but it is low."

Let me just interrupt here to say that, according to the Human Fertilization and Embryology Authority, in 2016 (the most recent data we have) 18 percent of IVF treatments using a patient's own frozen eggs were successful, which means that in around four in five cases, the treatment was unsuccessful. The frozen eggs did not, in that event, become pregnancies.

"We're sold this idea of certainty that is just, on so many levels, playing into women's fears," says Eleanor. As is so often the case, when women's lives come crashing up against the power of capitalism, we are fed the idea that you can simply purchase your way out of anxiety, that you can buy a way out of being old, single, ugly, fat, or less fertile, rather than asking the more important questions: Who says you are, why do you believe them, and does it actually matter? Egg freezing is not, in and of itself, a silver bullet to cheat the system. Your body is aging, as are the bodies of the men around you; your fertility is decreasing, as is the fertility of your male peers; your ability to reproduce will one day pass, as will that of the men you know. You may spend eight thousand pounds ($10,400) having your eggs frozen, you may go through the significant physical and emotional upheaval of IVF, you may spend years fighting for something your friends fall into by accident. But, in the end, we are all determined by our biology. As Eleanor put it, "We can push it and tweak it and challenge it with IVF, but ultimately there is a point where we all stop. It's one of the only certainties, other than dying. That's it: your ability to make life will pass."

Of course, the urge to get pregnant is one that we can all pick at like a cheap nail polish. What do we actually mean when we say it? What do we actually want?

"My urge for pregnancy is obviously about having a child," answers

Eleanor, "but it's also about this yearning for safety and a home and stability. The fact that my potential future baby is in a freezer in Homerton Hospital, I don't know . . ." She goes quiet. "It's almost too big and
too profound," she says at last. "But then it's also not: it's a bit of jelly in
a freezer. But there's potential life in there. And I've got much better
odds of them working than many people because they're already fertil-
ized; they just need to shove them up."

In fact, I remember quite how uncomfortable Eleanor found this
whole egg-harvesting process.

"You do IVF," she explains. "They just don't put it back in the end.
Everyone experiences IVF differently, and for some people it's easier
than others, but I found it physically horrific. It was like a madness. I
felt bovine, like a bloated, seeping farm animal being dragged around.
Bulging. Fecund to a disgusting level. I had massive, hard, uncomfortable tits, I was bloated, nauseous all the time. Physically it is such a
slog because it is the same hormonal fluctuations as early pregnancy."

Suddenly, talking to Eleanor, I realize for the first time quite what
it would mean to go through all that—the madness, the anxiety-
inducing expense, the hormone fluctuations—when, say, you're twenty-
nine, grieving a recently ended relationship, living in a rented flat
with someone you barely know, unsure about your job, and worried
about your future. Suddenly freezing eggs doesn't feel like a clever
solution—it feels like an ordeal. An ordeal, yet again, that happens
in women's bodies. An ordeal that, yet again, is seen as their problem
to solve.

Lying in bed, our first night back in London after my Greek rooftop
revelation, I took Nick's hand and put it on my stomach. I could feel
his warmth, his steady breathing, hear his snores. I thought of what
I'd said, what I'd risked, and how terrified I'd been. I thought of his
steadfast silence and shaking vomit. I thought of the children I'd
walked home to their tents each day, shouting the alphabet and days

of the week, their tiny rucksacks bouncing along at knee height. I thought of all the years I'd worried about telling a man I wanted his child. I told myself that it was okay, that he was still here, that our bodies were still slotted together like bowls on a shelf. And eventually, his hand heavy on my belly, I fell asleep.

12

ANCIENT MARINER

In a small, spotlit meeting room overlooking the rooftops of Moorgate, I am sitting across the table from the woman who helped get rape defined and prosecuted as a war crime.

"They say that women hold up half the sky, but I say that during conflict they hold up the whole thing," she says. "Often they're exhausted, they're in grief, but they hold communities together."

It is early 2017, and I'm interviewing Helen Durham, the director of international law and policy at the International Committee of the Red Cross, for *Vice* about one of their new reports. We're meant to be talking about the effect of conflict on civilian populations, but somehow I feel an urge to ask her about something far more private, more personal, more specific. I know that she has two children, but I also know that she spends her life coming up against the most dangerous, violent, cruel, and destructive elements of humanity. She has stared into the faces of war criminals, murderers, and tyrants. She has seen the havoc wrought by civil and international war, the desperate fight for resources, and the domestic battles hidden within a cloak of military rule.

"As humanitarians, we can't solve the problems, we can only raise the issues for discussion," Helen concludes, resting her hand on a printout of the report.

The interview is winding down, the press officer in the room is smiling encouragingly at us and gathering his papers, the clock on the wall behind me is ticking.

Before my professional brain throws a hand across my mouth, I catch a wave of adrenaline and blurt out: "Helen, before you go, can I just ask you one thing?"

She smiles.

"Do you think I should have a baby?"

The clock stops. There is silence. I look deeply into her eyes and wait.

Upon our return to London from Berlin, I spent months desperately trying to find an objective, authoritative, political, academic answer to this question that I could both present to Nick and use to soothe my own misgivings. You see, once you've gathered together the self-awareness, confidence, and insight it takes to admit what you actually want, you then have to take the time to ask yourself if you're really right—morally, financially, environmentally, emotionally—to demand it.

You might want to break up with your partner to have sex with someone you met on Twitter; you might want to leave your well-paid job and retrain as a yoga teacher; you might want to move out of your shared flat to go and be a lodger to an elderly woman who describes herself in conversation as "proudly un-PC." But just because those desires are real, lasting, and need to be addressed, you do also have to consider if they are harmful, irresponsible, selfish, or naive before acting on them. In my case, now that I had admitted, personally and publicly, that I wanted a baby, I then had to work out if having a baby was really a sensible decision, for me, for my relationship, for my career, and for this wildly uncertain future.

I listed about my life like the Ancient Mariner, stopping every guest in three, holding them with a skinny hand, fixing them with a glittering eye and spitting out the dreaded words, again and again. Turning the tables on all those people who had once asked so casually if I wanted a baby, I now went around parties, offices, the internet, and supermarkets asking parents and nonparents if *they* thought *I* should have a baby. If I would be doing the right thing, a silly thing, or the natural thing? If they regretted having kids, regretted not having kids, regretted not having a choice over having kids? If it was fair, sensible, cruel, realistic, kind, shortsighted, or selfish to bring another child into this world? God knows, I was fun to be around.

I asked my own parents if they, knowing what they now know about climate change, the possibility of human extinction, the rise of political extremism, and social injustice, would have me all over again. I asked teachers, social workers, climate activists, fruit growers, lawyers, and doctors if they thought having a baby was an act of selfishness or selflessness. This was the Flux, and I was in utter turmoil. I became fixated with the cognitive dissonance, this apparent double-think, that allowed people to believe that we may only have sixty harvests left and yet to also have kids. To understand in detail the climate crisis we are walking into—that more than one in every four deaths among children under five is directly or indirectly related to environmental risks, that 93 percent of all children live in environments with air pollution levels above the World Health Organization guidelines—and to add another child to the picture. How did they do it? Why did they do it? Did that mean I could do it?

Recently, still fascinated by the tightrope walk of hope and fear, of family and future, I met up with the *Guardian* columnist and environmental activist George Monbiot in a café in Oxford to ask him how, in his own life, he solved this apparent contradiction. In his columns, George has for years written extensively about climate change, tyrannical governments, social inequality, the unsustainable use of natural resources, and the galloping speed of human extinction. So, knowing all this, knowing how little time we have left and how bad things have got, why did he have babies?

"It wasn't as if I really worked myself through the decision," says George, smiling over a pot of Assam tea. "I guess I didn't really want to be without children. But ever since then I've been plagued by doubt over whether it was the right thing to do."

Doubt over the world they're going to grow up in—a future of soaring temperatures, soil depletion, extreme weather events, climate-related land wars, a Britain without an NHS, lethal air pollution, rising inequality, and the rest—or because of the impact his own children will have on our planet's already overstretched natural resources?

"Well, both," says George, his sharp face flickering between humor and sadness. "I'm deeply worried about what life is going to be like when my children are my age. All the indications are that it is going to be shite. We are destroying our life-support systems, and no one in power seems to want to stop that happening. There's just this incredible incapacity to act. Between the intention and the action falls the shadow."

Oh shit, I think. *He's already paraphrasing T. S. Eliot.*

"I am also aware of the environmental impacts of having children, which are very considerable in a rich, consumerist society," continues George. "My younger daughter wants what her friends have, they want what she has, everybody wants everything, and how is that going to work? The promise of capitalism is that everyone can have everything, but we just don't have the ecological space for that—it doesn't exist. In poorer nations, having children has very little environmental impact. There's a very interesting study in India showing that people with the highest fertility were also the very poorest people, a large number of whom have a *negative* environmental impact because they are rubbish collectors. They recycle materials back into the system. But in this country, every child we have is going to make a big difference."

This, argues George, is one of the problems with the way many of us in economically developed countries use overpopulation as a way of not talking about consumerism and Western excess. It is all too easy to talk about *those* people over *there* having too many children, rather than looking at the reality of how our own lifestyle tears through water, oxygen, land, minerals, and space.

"We've just had stats come out showing that a return flight from London to Edinburgh is more than the total carbon emissions of someone living in Somalia or Uganda for a year," says George.

Maybe people in wealthy nations shouldn't be asking *if* we should have children but *how* we should raise them.

Later, as I'm frantically trying to think which would be the most ethically sound hot drink to order and instead end up just choosing tap water, I ask George whether having children can ever be a rational decision.

"It is simply impossible to make a rational decision that isn't also an emotional one," says George. "Our emotions are shortcuts that enable us to cut through the blizzard of data in order to make the right decision. Just being here, right now, what word should I use next, should I glance to the left or glance to the right, what's that noise happening behind me, should I be interacting with those people over there? There are a thousand decisions confronting me right now, but I'm only doing one thing because my emotions are telling me that talking to you now is the right thing to do."

Our whole approach, George continues, that says a decision made within a hormonal and emotional environment is somehow irrational isn't just wrong, but has been weaponized in a fundamentally sexist way. It argues that women are "of the womb": changeable, bidden by forces unseen, and their decisions are, consequently, unreliable. But we know that men experience hormonal fluctuations. Men are emotional beasts, as are women. Everybody—male, female, nonbinary—goes through the world acting on a combination of logic, thought, emotion, endocrinology, biology, psychology, and all the other -ologies you care to mention. There is no such thing as the purely rational decision. All decisions are informed by the totality of human experience. In order to make the "right" decision you must navigate a path through them all: head and heart, gut and garter.

"As a young man, I always thought I never wanted children, simply because I had this image of myself as free, of everything, forever. Which I think a lot of young people do, and it's not necessarily a bad idea to have," says George, as I pay the bill and rather conspicuously collect up my bike helmet. "But it collides with the reality of having a fulfilling, intimate, worthwhile relationship, where you obviously have to sacrifice some freedom to have that. But I think it's worth it. It has been in my case."

It was worth it.

Having a partner, a family, a baby: it might be worth it. Despite the risk and the responsibility, despite humanity's legacy of destruction, danger, and despair, it might still be worth it.

It would be frankly insane for a politically engaged, well-educated, and reasonably informed person not to question the morality of having children as the world burns all around us. As I sat in front of Helen Durham, zooming toward the crescendo of my Panic Years, asking her to effectively tell my biological fortune, I was playing a sort of double-or-quits with my own doubt. If she, as someone who had seen the very worst that humanity can wreak, thought having a baby was a bad idea, then I would have to take seriously the voice in my head that said the same.

On the other hand, if she believed, like Whitney Houston, that the children are our future, perhaps I would be finally armed with an argument that could convince both my inner critic and my reluctant boyfriend that we should start trying for a baby. Because of course I had doubts. How could I not? Ever since I was seven years old and watching *Captain Planet* on our large secondhand static-screened television, I have worried about what humanity is doing to the world and to ourselves. Sadly, instead of a set of like-minded superheroes with a jazzy collection of synchronized magical rings, the job of saving the world seemed to be up to people like, well, me. You. Us. People who care, are convinced by science, and worry about how things might turn out not just for ourselves but the people who come after.

In truth, I wasn't really looking for an objective, dispassionate answer to my question back in 2017. I didn't really want these figures of authority to tell me that having a child was an act of ecological and humanitarian irresponsibility. I didn't want to hear the bad news.

Instead, with the howl of my womb becoming ever louder, and the egg timer of my body running ever faster, what I truly wanted was someone to look across the scorched and discriminatory world in front of me and to say that it would all be okay, that I could still have a baby. I was hoping that Helen Durham would have a rational but hopeful answer to my existential crisis.

The pause only lasted a second. I exhaled slowly.

Helen broke out into a big smile, pushing her hair back from her face. "If you want to invest in the future," she said, looking me dead in the eye, "then having children is the best way to do it."

I could have kissed her. Finally I had my answer. It might be irrational, it might be self-serving, it might not even be true, but in that moment, it was precisely what I wanted to hear.

13

THE COIL UNWINDS

Lying on a blue, wipe-clean pleather bed, holding the hand of a large nurse called, ironically, Comfort, I hear the tinkle of metal instrument on metal tray. A small doctor in smart navy slacks and what I will forever think of as Math Teacher Shoes has her hand on my thigh and is gently, but efficiently, inserting the medical equivalent of an umbrella into my vagina. I stare at the window, blank-headed. Comfort strokes my hair. I want to cry, but not from pain.

These two brilliant women are acting not just as medical professionals, but also therapists, aunties, priests, called to my bedside to hear my woes. You see, I've had this particular coil, also known as an IUD, ever since I moved to London six and a half years ago. And now I genuinely can't remember if it was meant to stay in for ten years or just five, so I am having it replaced. Deep down, however, I know what I really want: I want to take my coil out. I am looking for an excuse, any excuse, to remove the copper hammerhead that sits in my uterus and stops me from being fertile. I want to have a baby. I said as much three months earlier on a rooftop in Greece and yet once again, at home, the issue seems to have been thoroughly swept under the carpet to avoid confrontation. My friends know I want a baby, I know I want a baby, but we all carry on regardless. When they inquire politely about my future plans, I mutter something about having my coil taken out in a year, maybe two years, maybe sooner than that, maybe later, perhaps, maybe, I don't know. They ask, gently, why not just have it out now, if I want a baby? The answer rolls up my throat like a snooker ball, heavy and uncomfortable. Because my boyfriend isn't ready to have children, I say, feeling as stupid and pathetic as a damp sponge.

I got the coil during my last long-term relationship—you remember, the man I bought the washing machine with, broke up with, who then DJ-ed at my thirtieth birthday party—after what my ex-boyfriend and I laughingly called the Great Cry. Oh how we laughed. During the Great Cry I would sit on my bed, my back to the window, and sob. I wept like a Victorian, in small gasping bursts, I cried like a toddler with a scraped knee, in guttural, snotty chokes, I cried like a wounded animal, howling and rocking against the headboard. But here's the thing: I had absolutely no idea why I was crying. That, in itself, was quite scary. Imagine what it's like to find your body heaving and shuddering with tears and to have no idea what's caused them. It's like being possessed. Nearly every day, for nearly two months, I would be overwhelmed by a misery, a self-pity, a physical dread that turned my face liquid and my knuckles white, and I really had no idea why.

I can't remember at what point it occurred to me that this might have to do with the pill and that I should come off it, but I do remember the feeling of being poisoned, once my mind had been made up. The daily ingestion of hormones was, I knew, making me sad, fat, lonely, cloudy, unresponsive, sexless, and bovine. My body had been hanging in a state of suspended pregnancy for years—a false pregnancy created by those little white spheres of estrogen—and suddenly, with a clarity that felt itself like madness, I realized that they were making me unwell. As we know, the pill is an important part of many women's lives and has brought millions of people a degree of control over their body, hormones, sex life, career, skin, future, and periods that simply wasn't available before. But as we also know, the effects of the contraceptive pill on women's health have been scandalously under-researched for decades. Very few meaningful studies have been undertaken to investigate suspected links between the seesaw of estrogen, progesterone, and depression.

Very little has really been done to interrogate whether the pill is even fit for purpose.

For instance, it only recently came to light that the recommended seven-day break was actually devised by the gynecologist John Rock in the hope that it would make the contraceptive pill acceptable to the Pope by imitating a natural cycle, rather than for any health and safety reason. As the clinical and molecular pharmacologist Dr. Alice Howarth wrote in the *Guardian*, "two-thirds of women aged 20–24 take the combined contraceptive pill [. . .] And yet for sixty years, few in the medical establishment questioned whether the seven-day break was necessary. No one wondered whether women really had to go through the pain, discomfort or even inconvenience of a monthly bleed." It was because of shit like this that the editor, reporter, and my occasional coffee companion Vicky Spratt launched the "Mad About The Pill" campaign in Britain in 2017.

"I had a really bad reaction to a pill called Cerazette, which is progesterone only," says Vicky as we sit in her flat eating Turkish wafer biscuits. "I suffered terrifying panic attacks, felt like I was plummeting in an elevator on a loop, couldn't leave the house, started having suicidal thoughts. I'd never experienced anything like that before, and it all happened almost instantly after I started taking Cerazette. So I researched it; I interviewed people to try and find out how hormonal contraception affects us, how they work, who had looked into their side effects."

As part of the campaign, Spratt interviewed the Copenhagen-based professor Øjvind Lidegaard, who used centralized data on more than one million Danish women aged fifteen to thirty-four over a ten-year period to study for any links between hormone contraception and mental illness. Guess what: not only did he find that women taking the pill—either the combined pill (containing both estrogen and progesterone) or the progesterone-only pill—were more likely to be prescribed an antidepressant than those not on hormonal contraception. He also found that there was a link between being on the pill and attempted suicide and suicide, particularly among adolescent women. In 2017, Angelica Lindén Hirschberg, a professor in the Department of Women's and Children's Health at Karolinska Institutet, published the results of a study in which 340 healthy women aged eighteen to thirty-five were treated randomly over the course of three months with either placebos or contraceptive pills containing ethinylestradiol and levonorgestrel (the most common form of oral contraception in Europe).

According to Hirschberg, the women who were given real contraceptive pills estimated their quality of life to be significantly lower than those who were given placebos. By quality of life they meant mood, well-being, self-control, and energy levels. They did not, specifically, find an increased rate in depressive symptoms; however, a survey carried out by *The Debrief* found that of 1,022 women aged eighteen to thirty, 93 percent had taken or were taking the pill, of whom 45 percent had experienced anxiety, 45 percent had experienced depression, 46 percent said taking the pill had decreased their sex drive, and 58 percent believed that the pill had a negative impact on their mental health. But, says Vicky, what really surprised her during these repeated deep dives into data, reports, and studies wasn't the illnesses, the suicides, the reports of anxiety and depression, but what she calls the sheer level of medical negligence.

"We know there is a subgroup of women for whom the hormones in hormonal contraception are really physically and mentally detrimental," she says, her gaze steady, her face serious. "But we don't know how big that group is because no one has ever properly checked. We simply don't have the data. And a lot of those studies that do exist are sponsored by drug companies, and so of course the work that gets published tends to show what they want."

In my case, the link between oral contraception and a mental health nosedive seemed undisputable. Like the *drip, drip, drip* of a tap in the night I was slowly, daily, regularly putting something down my throat that was making me lose control of my body and my mind. I didn't want it anymore. I didn't want any of it anymore. So I got the copper coil: a tiny, hormone-free utensil that would keep me as magically, invisibly, uncomplainingly infertile as I believed all women in their twenties must be in order to live full lives and for men to love them.

Even at seventeen, I had been conditioned to believe that it was up to me, and me alone, to not get pregnant. Never mind that I was bloated and miserable from being on the pill. Never mind that the pressure to take it every day hung over me like a threat. I couldn't rely on a man to control his fertility. Pregnancy happened in my body, and so it was up to me to make sure it didn't happen. I couldn't expect a man to carry an equal share of the discomfort, the misery, the weight. I couldn't lie back and assume he had it covered: I had to be the backstop, the sensible one, the person who carried the can. Newspapers, politicians, teachers, television dramas, and Thomas Hardy novels had all taught me that getting pregnant was what stupid, careless, or conniving women did. It was what mad women did to trap men, what poor women did to get public housing, what stupid women did because they Hadn't Known Better. Getting pregnant was something selfish, disgusting, or unfair that ruined men's lives, curtailed their youth, and was the woman's fault entirely. I may have identified as a feminist ever since my father explained the term on a bike ride beside some allotments when I was twelve years old; I may have a mother as progressive and tolerant about sex as any adult could hope to be; I may have grown up in a liberal and educated home; but still, somehow, some trace of this pregnancy-is-a-women's-problem narrative had seeped into my unconscious.

It is on this bedrock of inequality that so much of the Panic Years takes root. Fertility, freedom, what control a woman can expect over her future, the balance of power within relationships, who faces the greater sacrifice in parenthood, whose career takes precedence, what level of physical discomfort you should be expected to accept, and who, ultimately, gets to make the big decisions: all are skewed by this early view of sex, contraception, pregnancy, and parenthood.

Back on the blue pleather, as I lay back, my knees apart, a large white light shining up my holes, my voice wobbled as I explained that I wanted a baby but my boyfriend wasn't sure. Comfort started to say that if I had my own money, if I was ready, if I knew that a baby was what I wanted, then I should just do it. I could decide my own future. I was in charge of my own body.

I was shocked and bewildered by what she was saying: I couldn't decide to have a baby. I could no more tell Nick that I was going to start trying for a baby than I could tell gravity that I was going to start flying. I believed in gender equality, mutual respect, personal autonomy. If that meant weeping into a sheet of blue tissue paper as a stranger pushed a piece of wire into my vagina, making me infertile and temporarily in pain, until a theoretical time in which my boyfriend felt "ready," then that was, of course, what I had to do. If I were to become a mother, then I wanted to do it within a relationship. I had seen how hard being a single parent was, and as a result, I wanted to do it with a partner on my side. If that meant I had to be uncomfortable, unhappy, and unfulfilled in order for his life to be how he wanted it, then that was what I had to be. If I had to put on hold the one thing I wanted from life, because a man wasn't absolutely sure that the circumstances were absolutely right, then that was what I had to do. It was simple: what he wanted was in conflict with what I wanted. And if he didn't feel ready, then my own readiness was immaterial.

I see now that this ludicrous dance around my cervix—the false start of a coil replacement hiding the true desire to just rip the thing straight out—was an embarrassment to everyone in the room. We all knew that what I wanted wasn't a new coil but the freedom and self-worth to ask my boyfriend for a baby. But I couldn't. However much I loved and trusted him, I couldn't keep opening up the Pandora's box of this last, greatest desire in front of him. Because to do so would open me up to that last, greatest rejection. In short, I was scared that if I kept pushing him to have a baby, he would leave me. The risk was too great, the loss too dangerous, the consequence too permanent. The first morning I'd told Nick I was in love with him, I'd had nothing to lose. Now it felt like I could lose everything: my partner, my imagined future, my chance to become a mother.

Years of bad conditioning had taught me that men have babies only under duress, women are responsible for what happens in their womb, and that asking men for something you want makes you vulnerable to rejection. The fact was that of every single man I have ever had sex with, none of them had ever taken the whole responsibility for not getting me pregnant. Some of them might have asked if I was on the pill, some of them might have asked if I was "using anything," but a huge number of them didn't even do that.

The idea that it was their sperm, and not my womb, that should be altered in some way to prevent a pregnancy clearly didn't occur to them. They ejaculated into me, knowing full well what sperm can do, while apparently feeling not a twinge of concern, care, or caution. I can only imagine that they all assumed I would stop any fertilization, either through an oral contraceptive, the morning-after pill, or, eventually, have an abortion. Either way, it wasn't their problem and they were not going to be the ones to prevent it happening.

Honestly, I could have a dozen children by now, all fathered by men who assumed I "had it covered." All of who did nothing to prevent a pregnancy happening. Some of them might not even remember my name. Meanwhile, the man I actually wanted to have a baby with was still meeting my gentle inquiries, my fretful questions, my occasional emotional outbursts, with a heavy blanket of passivity, hesitation, or outright refusal.

Not ready. Not sure. Not the right time.

And while I knew he was in many ways right—we were both supposed to be embarking on new careers, we were living in a shared flat, we had only been together just over a year—those arguments simply didn't matter very much to me anymore. My emotional brain had its own logic, and it was pushing against his reasoning like an elephant onto an orange.

As I walked home from that clinic, pushing my bike, I felt as dejected as ever in my life. I walked past some workmen—big men, in neon vests and heavy boots, drilling into concrete and ripping up pipes. Suddenly, with a force I could barely recognize, I ached to walk over to one of them, bury my face against his chest, and tell him that I was sad. I wanted to tell this man—a stranger, a male stereotype straight from our picture books—that my vagina was bleeding, that my stomach hurt, that I wanted a baby and my boyfriend said I couldn't have one. I wanted him to scoop me up in his arms, smelling of bitumen and engine oil and sweat and roll-ups and onions, and tell me that it was all going to be okay.

I stood there for maybe twenty seconds, staring into the gaping hole in the road that was pitted with bits of metal and chunks of soil, before gripping onto my handlebars, putting one foot in front of the other, and setting off for home.

It took me another month of building up my nerve before I finally told Nick that I wanted to take my coil out. Out, out. I sat on the edge of our sofa, not breathing, alight with nerves, waiting for his response. I was taking control of my body; I was asking for what I wanted; I was pushing the issue in the only way I knew how, and it was absolutely terrifying. He agreed immediately, with almost no perceptible change in his voice. I couldn't believe it—here I'd been, twisting myself into rope over a decision that he was, apparently, entirely ready and willing for.

Until the next month came. And I made an appointment to get my new coil removed. And Nick asked if we were going to start using condoms, or if I was going on the pill. I felt like my bones had turned to lead. He hadn't understood. He hadn't understood at all. When I said I was taking my coil out, what I meant was that I wanted to start trying for a baby. But all Nick had heard was that I was taking my coil out. Nothing more. After so many years of going over and over the same ground, I thought I had finally made my case, staked my claim, and got the man I loved to come along with me on a life-changing path. But it turns out, all I'd done was give the ground some new footprints. Even when confronted with the fact that someone has removed all the bolts on her own fertility, some men will still, somehow, assume that pregnancy is a theoretical abstract, not a concern for them in the here and now.

For four more maddening, sexless weeks we talked, argued, ground against each other like pebbles on a shoreline hitting the same impasse over and over and over again. He wasn't ready. I was. He wanted to wait. I didn't want to risk waiting. He didn't have a job. I didn't know how many eggs I had left. He wasn't sure what it meant to be a father. I knew he would make a wonderful father. He wasn't ready. I was running out of time. He wanted to wait. I couldn't wait any longer. I was being asked to wait for something as intangible, ephemeral, and insubstantial as a feeling; for him to *feel* ready. But in my body, I was fighting the visceral, bloody truth that every month another egg fell out of my arse, and if I didn't move soon, I may miss my chance entirely. My mum's old joke turned sour in my mouth: if we waited for men to be ready to have babies, the human race would die out in one generation.

Of course, I come to the question of contraception as a woman who had always imagined, even hoped, that she would have a baby one day. To me, men were the source of opportunity (i.e., sperm), but also a block on that desire (i.e., never willing to have kids). For my friend Terri White, the tables are flipped. Until meeting her current partner, she'd always known she didn't want children, didn't need to be pregnant, had no great urge to be a mother. And yet still, it seems, the men in her life had assumed, accused, and attacked her for being some great, pulsating womb, desperate to steal their sperm and in so doing, steal their freedom.

"We spend our lives dodging pregnancy, trying to keep someone's sperm away from our vagina, because we know that if we get pregnant before they want to, it's our fault," she says, her batwing-black eyes rolling almost out of her head with despair and disdain. "The first time I got pregnant, I had a really good job and I was determined to become an editor before I was thirty," she explains. "But the guy who got me pregnant decided, with his friends, that I'd done it on purpose. He was furious with me. He said I'd done it to trap him. I said, 'Trap you into what? This tedious argument?'"

I love Terri. Even if you consistently and specifically argue to the contrary, as Terri has all her life, there still seems to be a residual fear among many men that the women they want to stick their dicks in are desperate for a baby, in absolute control of their fertility, and are somehow colluding with their hidden and sinister wombs to get pregnant. Never mind that these men pay as little attention to controlling their own semen as a monkey throwing peanuts off a tower block. Never mind the fact that they do literally nothing to stop a pregnancy from happening.

One afternoon, I walked up to the newsagent at the top of my street to buy a stamp. Shuffling past the dusty birthday cards, ten-pence crisp packets, and faded plastic toys I found a set of alphabetized cards, printed on stiff brown paper, sitting neglected at the back of a shelf of stationery. They might have been as old as me. They were £3.99 and as obsolete as an ear trumpet. I took them home and under each letter wrote a short paragraph about why I loved Nick and wanted him to be the father of my child. On another piece of cartography paper, bought in Berlin, I wrote him a letter, detailing all the ways in which I knew he would make a brilliant dad. On a set of graph paper bought for the purpose at great expense from a stationery shop near his childhood home, I wrote a great list of all the ways I knew we were ready to have a baby.

I presented this bundle to him that night, the minute he arrived home from work. In the face of his stolid, fleshly reluctance I had gone into a sort of paper fury, flinging words, arguments, explanations, and writing material at him in the hope that he would finally see reason. My reason. He read them. He sighed. He said he wasn't ready. I felt like a wasp, surrounding myself with a cocoon of chewed-up paper, whirling in desperate circles, trying to build something out of air.

Eventually I broke. I snapped. I cracked open like an egg under a boot. I sat on our bed, lit only by the halogen streetlights outside our window, and sobbed. I asked Nick to imagine what it must feel like to have the one person you love most in the world denying you the one thing you want more than life itself; to have your entire life put on pause by someone else's uncertainty; to be asked to keep your body on hold—knowing that time will run out, because someone else doesn't want to have to think about it right now. I pleaded. I cried. I dropped my head onto his knee and begged him to let me try to get pregnant, to see what would happen, to at least give me the chance to fail. As I broke down and soaked his leg with tears, I pointed out that I had a piece of metal in my body that I no longer wanted, that was in fact stopping me from getting what I wanted, all because he wanted to spend more time not thinking about babies. He was forcing me to put my feelings on hold because of his feelings.

With a voice that was as raw as it was wild, I explained that I had imagined having a baby since I was eight years old, six years old, maybe even longer. Could he imagine if he had wanted one thing, since he'd been a tiny boy in his Arsenal pajamas, until now? Could he imagine finding the perfect person to make that one thing happen with? And could he then imagine if that person spent a year dodging the issue, ignoring the question, or telling you that they wanted to put it off, perhaps indefinitely? That they hadn't thought about it, weren't sure what it meant, didn't know if they would ever be ready?

Between gulps and sniffs, I told him that I didn't want to carry this block, this stop, this twist of wire that was making me artificially infertile anymore. I wanted a baby. I wanted *his* baby. I knew he would be a brilliant father, that together we would be good parents. I loved him and I was terrified that loving him might make me miss my chance. I didn't have as much time as other women—I might have only six, maybe seven, fertile years left. It might take years to get pregnant. If I waited for him to feel ready, it might already be too late. He was scared of trying, but I was terrified of waiting.

Needless to say, this is only my version of events—an extremely specific, personal, and subjective version, at that. I was in the Panic Years, and, my friends, I was panicking. Talking to Nick today, I'm a little more able to see those agonizing weeks from his perspective. It turns out, that while I hammered away at him, pleading, appealing, raging, he was all the time trying to calculate the practicalities of having a child: did we have any savings, how would he manage a career change and a new baby, would he be able to dedicate enough time to training as a teacher if he was only getting four hours' sleep a night, what would I live on for that year, where were we all going to sleep? Eventually, as these questions started to resolve, he wanted to find a way of approaching the subject in a way that didn't make it seem like I'd won an argument or that he'd simply given in.

"Even when I was starting to agree with you, I probably didn't tell you for at least five more conversations because I didn't want it to seem like you'd convinced me," he said recently. "I didn't want the story for our child to be that I lost an argument. You probably remember one discussion—the one that swung it—but what I'm saying is that I had probably started to agree with you two weeks before that."

So it wasn't that I eventually broke him down with tears?

"When you were crying, I was thinking, I agree with her, so all I'm doing by sitting on this decision is being unkind. You had this worry, this upset, but at that point I agreed with you; I just hadn't told you so. I remember wanting to tell you in a better way; in the end I told you then, just to stop you crying."

And so, at last, he said yes.

To see contraception as anything other than a feminist issue is to argue that the sea isn't wet. Here we are, in 2020, still without male equivalents to almost all the common forms of contraception: pill, implant, injection, IUD. Here we are with a female pill that is simply not fit for purpose, making women in their millions—both those in the Flux and out of it—depressed, anxious, suicidal, sick, panicked, overweight, in pain, and all the other myriad side effects discussed in private WhatsApp groups and late-night confessions around the world. Here we are with a modern fuck culture that keeps men in a state of sexual immaturity their entire adult lives.

"The physical process of carrying a pregnancy and giving birth is ours," says Vicky. "But the act of conception is not ours alone. It takes two. That is why we need side-effect-free contraception for men and women; it could finally put us on a level playing field."

It might just put men and women during the Panic Years on an even footing. Would she trust men to take a male version of the pill, I ask?

"One hundred percent," she answers immediately. "I really dislike the narrative of 'Oh, men are too stupid to take the pill.' We trust men to rule the world, run the economy, have nuclear weapons, but they can't take something every day that we take?"

We both sigh. For Vicky, the answer is side-effect-free, nonhormonal contraception for both men and women. "What does that look like? I don't know," she says. "But I know they need to develop it. We can go to Mars but we can't develop side-effect-free contraception? That's mad." Talking of mad, Vicky makes the point that the way we currently use contraception encourages men and women to consider their fertility in laughably different, unhealthy, and unhelpful ways.

"Whether you acknowledge it or not, every time you get your period, it could have been a baby," she says. "It comes out of you, it's bloody, it's messy, it's sometimes painful. Meanwhile, men wank onto biscuits and make people eat it for a dare, or see how far they can project their sperm in a spunking contest: it's a very different relationship. But the substance is not so different. Each of those tiny little sperm could be a baby. They're alive. But nobody instills that in them."

It's like I'm always rapping to my pals: wombs don't make babies, eggs and sperm do.

Thanks to the wonders of modern contraception (and believe me, I know they are wonderful in comparison to what came before), we can pretend that all women are magically, invisibly, and easily infertile until they, and perhaps also their partner, decide they want to have a baby. You can still hear the phrase "tricked into having a baby" with horrifying regularity, as though ejaculation and insemination were entirely a woman's fault or choice. Or "waiting until he's ready," as though a woman's own readiness, hope, and intention were immaterial. It is just one of the many crazy-making contradictions innate to the Panic Years, one of the ways that marks out the experience between sexes.

Of course, not every woman using contraception is doing so in order to make things easier for the people she is having sex with. There is a certain security in knowing that you are unlikely to get pregnant: you can have more casual sex (though STIs are no joke); you can focus on your career without having your plans suddenly thrown awry by an unplanned pregnancy; you can hopefully avoid having an abortion; you can carve out a period of time in which to build your own life away from parenthood; you can, to some extent, control some of your body's functions.

There are also, I'm sure, plenty of men who are eager, maybe even desperate, to start a family and find their partner's reluctance hard to bear. Plenty of men who will neither experience pregnancy nor undertake labor, whose careers will march on unaffected, whose bodies will not change, who rail against their partner's hesitation without quite realizing what they're asking for. They have my sympathy. They all do.

But it is nevertheless the case that contraception has allowed two separate but parallel worlds to build up within the sexes: one in which women carry the burden of fertility and pregnancy, and the other in which men are tacitly encouraged to spend decades ignoring the reproductive potential of their sperm until they eventually decide they want to become fathers. This, of course, is grossly unfair. Human life is men's responsibility, just as much as it is women's. We know that as men get older, their fertility drops and the likelihood of congenital disorders increases. We know that older men will find it harder and more risky to conceive, not to mention father, a child. And so, the entire burden of the irreversible decision whether to have children must not be dragged along by women alone.

As I lay on that blue pleather bed, deep in the grip of the Panic Years, caught between my own desire and that of the man I loved, having my uterus pricked by a piece of metal I no longer wanted, the weight of that burden felt unbearable. Just as, years earlier, swollen and weeping, I had looked across my desk at a packet of Microgynon with pure loathing, and felt the burden to be unbearable. In order to even up the playing field, we should be forced to confront the truth about sex and fertility from the moment we start wanting to put things in each other's holes. We need to understand, viscerally, that it is sperm, as well as wombs, that cause pregnancy. We should start to see men's ability to have children as finite, just as we do women's. Men must be prepared to adjust their own bodies and sexual preferences, perhaps even their own hormones, in order to shoulder some of the contraceptive burden. Perhaps then we can get some sexual equality. Perhaps then women like me will have one less thing to cry about.

14

A TRICKY PERIOD

Looking down at my knickers, at the glossy red toad squatting across the gusset, at the smears down the inside of my thighs, at the stained toilet roll in my hand, I am unsurprised. This one was a failure from the start. Before I'd begun to hope. Before I'd even seen the blood, I suspected, maybe even knew, that it hadn't happened. A few weeks earlier I had, finally, taken my coil out. Nick and I were now "trying for a baby." Although the trying wasn't particularly strenuous, I couldn't help but feel like something seismic had shifted, that we were dancing along the edge of something monumental. It took on average a year, I knew, to get pregnant, so in the meantime I carried on making plans: getting my place to retrain as a teacher at a school up the road, moving in a new flatmate, writing for newspapers and magazines, drinking booze, swimming where I could, and occasionally getting into bed in the middle of the day for a "freelancer's lie down."

Of course, taking my coil out did have a profound effect on how I felt in my body. The first time I had sex without any hormones, any barrier, or any wiry little twist in my uterus preventing pregnancy, I'd felt a thrill that was utterly intoxicating. An envelopment of trust, possibility, love, and relief. For the first and only time in my life, I was having the kind of sex that could make a baby; could bind me to this man for the rest of our lives; could take root in my body and change our futures entirely. And yet, it hadn't. The day my period arrived, I traced that egg's failure right back up into my body, into myself. Into what never was. It wasn't the end of the world, far from it. But it wasn't the beginning of something, either.

As usual, I sought respite at my mother's. On my way home from her flat, carrying a huge *Times Atlas and Gazetteer of the World*, weighed down with self-pity, Aldi store-brand biscuits, and decaf tea, crying because my period had come—as I knew it would—I noticed a man sitting on Hackney Marshes, in the sun. His head bent slightly forward.

"Excuse me, do you have the time?" he asked.

He'd seen me crying, I knew. He'd seen my eyes tight and red against the sun.

"Two o'clock," I answered, turning toward him, stepping a little off the path and into the slightly longer grass.

"Oh, you're English," he replied, snagging me like a thorn, like a branch. I was glad of the opening—the crack that lets the light in.

"Yes," I said, walking toward him, with relief and warmth spreading across my back like sunshine.

"You could be Polish, you could be anything," he said. "They've put such a mix, now, into the aquarium."

He had that combination of dirty, pointed nails, tracksuit bottoms, smart jumper, oil-thickened hair, and grubby, pale hands that immediately speak of distress, of mental illness, poverty, or, most likely, both. He was pulling at the long, yellowed grass, working a little balding path of soil between his crossed feet. The aquarium comment was almost too studied, too obvious, but I was already sliding into this. I'd known that the moment he caught my eye.

I put down my giant atlas, dropped my rucksack on the ground, and sat down, diagonal to his right foot.

"Yes, feel free to sit and join me," he'd said, like the host at a North London tea party. "If I had a sandwich I'd offer you half."

"If I had a sandwich, I'd offer *you* half," I said, pulling the tongue of my boot round to the middle. I'd known immediately, known somehow in advance, that my conversation with this man was going to be easier than with anyone else I could have met that day. Easier than it was with my mother over lunch, as I sat weeping, a plate of barely eaten fish in breadcrumbs and white cabbage on my lap, as daytime scenes of a cozy Scottish murder washed across the telly.

"Oh, actually, I've got a cucumber if you want some?" I offered, pulling half a cucumber out of my bag. Every time my mum goes away for the weekend, my sister and I get these food parcels of market-bought, not-long-for-this-world vegetables that won't manage to stay the distance until she gets back.

"Thank you," he said, taking the proffered vegetable with that easy, no-need-to-explain familiarity of someone who knows precisely just how strange the world can feel sometimes. How the everyday is only the everyday if it happens every day. And so how relatively unsurprising, unconfusing, and unremarkable it is to go outside of the mundane.

"My name's Daniel, by the way," he said, peeling back the plastic around my cucumber. "It's okay to eat the skin, isn't it?"

"Oh yes," I replied. "My name is Nell. Like the elephant," I added as he tore off a small chunk of cucumber with his sharp, dirty nails.

"So, how are you?" he asked, cucumber water rolling off his palms and into the agitated soil at his feet.

"I'm very sad, Daniel," I said, the words coming out spotless, clean—straight from my heart, apparently unchecked by my own mouth or mind. "I got my period this morning"—and then, without so much as a pause—"but I wanted to be pregnant."

Even in talking to my own mother, I hadn't managed to finish this sentence. I hadn't told her why I felt so sad, so disappointed, such a failure. Instead, I merely wiped my sadness around her flat like a wet PE kit. She didn't know that I'd taken my coil out. I hadn't wanted to carry the burden of her excitement, expectation, and impatience as well as my own. Just another weepy, self-pitying period, she'd no doubt thought. Just another one of my dark, hormonal moods. She wasn't wrong, of course. Just not entirely right either.

When I told Daniel I had a boyfriend and wanted a baby, he said, with a cheerful shrug, "Well, that's me out then."

I replied that yes, I'm afraid it was.

He told me that he didn't get to talk to many females, that it was nice.

"Yes, females are nice, on the whole," I replied, looking down at my fingers. "I should probably get going," I said.

Although, really, I knew I had nothing to get back for. Just an empty flat, a stained gusset, the low white hum of the fridge.

"Well, it was nice to talk to you," Daniel said.

"It was nice to talk to you too," I replied.

"I'm sure I'll see you here again."

"Yes, take care," he called out, as I started to walk back to the path, the gravel, the river, my house. "And good luck!"

I tried to wave in reply, but my arm was pinned down, under the giant weight of the *Times Atlas and Gazetteer.*

We talk very little about being unpregnant in this country—the miscarriages, the unwanted periods, the short ovulation window, the years and money and hormones you can lose in the attempt to have a baby. For those people who choose to try for a baby, these can become as familiar hallmarks of the Panic Years as breakups, weddings, job interviews, or hangovers. Even if you're not trying to have a baby yourself, it is highly likely that, as you course through the Flux, many of those around you will be. Your best friend, sister, colleagues, boss, bridesmaids, girlfriend, flatmate, bus driver, new pal, and MP may well all be pulling through the grief, the disappointment, the stress, and the uncertainty of being unpregnant right beside you. They will need your support. They will appreciate your understanding. Of course, they may not tell you much, but they are far more likely to open up if you can position yourself as an ally: bring them food, let them talk, be kind, don't feel compelled to cheer them up unless they say they want to be cheered. These things are, in their own ways, all slivers of grief and can be treated accordingly. I now think back with shame at the way I forgot, stayed away, or changed the subject when friends—men and women—told me they had lost a pregnancy. They deserve an apology. I was astounded anew, in researching this book, to read quite how common it is for people not to conceive or for a pregnancy to never reach full term. They deserve recognition.

Throughout my teens and twenties I was continually threatened with the prospect of accidental pregnancy: by school, by doctors, by *Home and Away*. I particularly remember one vitriolic sexual health nurse turning to me, halfway through an appointment in which I cringingly begged for the morning-after pill, and saying, "All it takes is one sperm and then, wham, bam, you're pregnant." Wham. Bam. In truth, as the NHS website tells me, "you're most fertile within a day or two either side of an egg being released from your ovaries." A little trick known to our friends as "ovulation." You can get pregnant if you have sex at any point during the week before ovulation, as some particularly indefatigable sperm can live inside a person's body for up to seven days. But that's still only, what, a week? Ten days? Less than a fortnight of fertility every month?

As I poured the unused lining of my womb into the toilet, as I had so many times before, I remember thinking that the idea that my body was this great throbbing, barely restrained, ever-ready baby-making machine was a farce. I thought of all the morning-after pills I'd washed down with cold coffee and unanswered texts, possibly for no reason. I thought of all the hormones I'd stuffed into my swollen, unhappy body when I might never be able to get pregnant anyway. I thought of the uneasiness with which I watched my early boyfriends rip open condoms, wondering if they might have punctured the rubber and therefore be about to destroy my A-Levels. I also thought of one of my best friends, driven to such bitter fury by her endless stream of negative pregnancy tests that she started to take them in places she knew she'd never return. Of her choking, hilarious, awful story of pissing on a stick in the ladies' toilet of Walthamstow Mall and waiting, surrounded by the smell of shit and Ambi Pur as the words "NOT PREGNANT" and an unhappy face emoji slowly appeared on the display in front of her.

In an article as remarkable for its personal honesty as its depiction of female political life, the MP Stella Creasy recently wrote in the *Guardian* how "During my first miscarriage, aching and bleeding, I joined a protest for the extradition of a man who had raped and murdered a constituent of mine. The day after I found out that another baby's heartbeat had stopped, I led a public meeting on gang crime. I even scheduled the procedure to remove the body on a day I didn't have a constituency town hall. Heartbroken by all the years that I have struggled with fertility, I've kept these events to myself and made sure my constituents have never been affected."

Not many of us have the kind of caseload and public duty of a local MP, but millions of women will recognize the can't-stop-got-to-get-dressed-put-on-some-stretchy-trousers-get-to-work-on-time-don't-show-anyone-how-you're-feeling-just-have-a-little-cry-in-the-bathroom-at-lunchtime-mustn't-crack-you're-a-professional-can't-face-lunch-don't-listen-to-music-in-case-you-start-crying-remember-your-lanyard-your-heart-is-aching-your-inbox-is-full conflict between work and hurt. According to the charity Tommy's, one in four known pregnancies ends in miscarriage, which makes it highly likely that we all know someone who has gone to work the day after an unexpected bleed or a traumatic twelve-week scan. We may even have been sitting next to them.

"Now I'm pregnant once more and terrified," continues Creasy, "not just that it will go wrong again, but because I know that my resolve to keep my private and professional lives separate has become impossible."

In Brazil, according to one friend, more women tend to tell people when they're pregnant, however early they find out. Then, if you have a miscarriage, people turn up at your door with food, with flowers, with a public display of sympathy. It seems incredibly civilized to treat all pregnancies—however fleeting—as significant in this way. And strangely liberating not to have to suffer through those first nauseous, exhausting, tentative months under a shadow of secrecy. Because miscarriages really are very common: new research by evolutionary geneticist William Richard Rice of the University of California has indicated that more than half of successful fertilizations will end in miscarriage, many of which simply happen so early as to go undetected. So what of those pregnancies? The ones that don't even overreach your period? The ones that never register on a pissy strip? The ones that simply look like another missed chance to get pregnant?

These are what my friend and former boss Rebecca Holman calls the embryos that "don't plug into the matrix," as we sit over a mozzarella sandwich and enormous bun one afternoon near her office. Rebecca is telling me about her Flux, about the unique but entirely familiar course her life wound during the Panic Years: being laid off two weeks after her thirtieth birthday, living with her best mate, who had just split up with her long-term boyfriend, drinking too much, going out too much, and dating erratically. Some years later, she got together with her partner and started trying for a baby. What strikes me is the specificity with which she can still recall the details of each month, each unwanted period, after she and her partner had started shagging with intent.

"A couple of times I think there was an embryo that just didn't implant," explains Rebecca, either because those periods were late, or a little heavier. "I'd say over the course of thirteen goes, so a year of trying, that probably happened five or six times."

I think of my own sad toilet scene and let out a sympathetic sigh.

"I'm really glad it happened that way because I think having a miscarriage at six or eight weeks would have been far, far harder," Rebecca continues. "I had moments when I was panicked and upset about it, but I would just think, right, try again. And if that doesn't work we'll go for these tests."

Like many professional, career-minded, city-living women, Rebecca didn't try to get pregnant until she was thirty-five, even though she always knew she wanted to have kids. Her partner is older than her but, as she says, "There was no one else I wanted to have children with. And no one else who wanted to have children with me."

Rebecca pushed to do the tests, she explains, "Not because I necessarily thought there was a problem with one of us, but because my time was running out and so we had to know now."

Ah, the running out of time. The hunger for certainty. The pain of the unknown. Those familiar bassline notes that hum along beneath the Panic Years. In fact, the tests showed that everything was fine. And yet, she still wasn't getting pregnant.

"The first time I got my period, I was quite vague on whether we'd done it at the right time," Rebecca recalls, counting each month off on her fingers. "But the second time, I thought we'd nailed it, and my period still came early, out of nowhere. The following month I got this weird bloating about six days after I ovulated and a bit of bleeding and thought that just must be it; it was so textbook. But it turned out to just be indigestion, and my period came early a few weeks later. So I got really drunk and cried all over my friend, who started crying too."

After several months of this, Rebecca thought, *I just can't make this my life*. The swing from hope to disappointment was too great. No more pregnancy tests, no more deep dives on forums, no more panicking. She and her partner decided to start with IVF, had the appointment booked, and were preparing for the driest of Dry Januaries.

"So as a result," says Rebecca, "I was five weeks pregnant before I did a test. I remember walking home and needing a wee and thinking, 'Oh well, I'd better not waste it.'"

There was just a faint line on the test that night, but Rebecca was shocked enough that she immediately threw the entire cup of piss all over the bathroom floor. Cheers.

A couple of days after my cucumber-strewn grief at not getting pregnant, I went to therapy, told my therapist that I wasn't pregnant, cried with frustration, chewed at the corners of my fingers, and waited to see if, just once, he might offer me some words of comfort rather than simply reframe my thinking with surgical precision.

"You already know, I presume, that it might be too early to show up?" he said.

I was dumbstruck. Literally struck by how dumb I had been. Somewhere in the furthest reaches of my brain, I remembered something about pregnancy tests, false negatives, hormone changes, and waiting. But I hadn't done a test like this for years, make it a point to never read any instruction leaflets, and so had completely forgotten, genuinely hadn't realized, that the test may yet be inaccurate.

Later that week, I went into my bathroom in the middle of a pale gray afternoon and did another test. As I waited for the display to emerge, I got a feeling not unlike picking up my GCSE results: nervous excitement, trepidation, hope, yet with that ever-present second voice asking me what I was feeling, what I looked like, how I might react. Was this the way a person might feel if she was pregnant? Did I seem confident?

Oddly, as the two parallel blue lines hardened out of the pale paper background, I remember thinking that I wasn't surprised this time either. I felt lucky. This was what I'd hoped for. Unlike so many of my friends and colleagues, who I knew had been trying for years, I was pregnant after just two months. I went into our bedroom, unfolded a paper crane Nick had made me on one of our first dates, wrote "I'm pregnant" on the inside, and left it on his pillow.

Yet somehow, I couldn't quite hold on to the fact that I was pregnant. Not in my mind, nor in my body. I couldn't quite trust the fact that something so seismic had really taken hold in my womb. And so, weeks later, hovering above the toilet in a South London warehouse, surrounded by empty cans and dirty footprints, I took another test (much to the annoyance of the other people in the queue, I imagine). I watched with my breath held and knickers at half-mast as, once again, the twin lines appeared, showing that I was still, for now, pregnant. I did another at a friend's house without telling her and one more the morning I was due to my first appointment with the midwife, assuming she'd ask to see some evidence that I really was as pregnant as I claimed. For weeks I carried these four different positive pregnancy tests around in my handbag like urine-soaked amulets, trying to ward off the creeping fear that it all might disappear. I would get them out on the bus or at my kitchen table and just stare at the Tesco stripes of my fertility, trying somehow to imprint this information onto my mind.

In those early weeks, my pregnancy seemed so fragile that I couldn't tell anyone. By the time I built up the courage to tell the head of English at the school where I'd been accepted to retrain as a teacher, I was already having to hold the top of my trousers together over my swelling belly with a safety pin. Absolutely racked with nervous guilt, I went into her office with an ashen face, ready to face a wave of recrimination. I felt like I was letting somebody down; this organization had given me an opportunity, offered to support me through a change in career, had shown faith in my ability, and I was about to throw it all back in their face. I also felt guilty that, as a woman in her thirties, I was doing my bit to prove right the old, discriminatory assumption that women in the Flux are more interested in babies than their career. I was about to make a lot of people's lives very tricky: my colleagues, my boss, my students, any thirty-year-old woman who applied for a similar position in the future.

In fact, the head of department's face broke open in a big smile. "Congratulations!" she said. "That's lovely."

I couldn't believe my luck. No passive-aggressive comments, no sighing, no invasive questions, nothing but good grace and reassurance.

One day, about a year later, I was sitting on a wall on a quiet residential street breastfeeding my son when that same head of English walked past, pushing her own baby in a buggy. Turns out, just a matter of months after I had walked into her office, shamefaced and clammy, to tell her that I was pregnant, she was telling her boss the very same thing.

In that first trimester, I was also gripped with worry about how I was going to tell those friends and relatives of mine who I knew had been trying for far longer than me to get pregnant. I remembered the sensitivity with which one of my school friends had texted me personally to say that she was pregnant, before announcing it on Facebook, thus giving me time to adjust before the news flew onto the timelines. And so, weeks before I started to tell other people, I sat at my table and spent a long time drafting a group of messages to send to that handful of women who I knew would find my pregnancy more poignant than most: the friend who had recently had a miscarriage, the friend who I knew had been having fertility treatments for the last two years, the friend who wanted a baby far more than a career but simply couldn't meet the right person with whom to start a family. Someone had shown me this consideration once, and now it was my time to try and pass it on.

With the average age at which British women first get pregnant on the increase, we are becoming more susceptible to an industry trying to persuade us that fertility is something that can be controlled by money, rather than biology. Which is, sadly, complete bollocks. In a recent interview with the *Daily Telegraph*, the chairwoman of the Human Fertilization and Embryology Authority, Sally Cheshire, argued that older people in the UK are being exploited by IVF clinics "trading on hope"; that these private clinics are using "blatant" sales tactics to persuade "vulnerable" people to undergo treatment.

Just as fertility clinics target and exploit the anxiety and vulnerability of single people in their early thirties by encouraging them to get their eggs and embryos frozen, despite relatively low rates of success, so people in their forties are being sold the hope of pregnancy and upsold so-called "add-on" treatments like embryo glue and endometrial scratches, despite there being no clinical evidence that such additional "treatments" actually make any difference. According to the BBC, "The latest HFEA figures show that, among those using their own eggs, out of 2,265 embryo transfers in 2017, just seventy-five women aged forty-three to forty-four ended up with a baby. For those over forty-four, the success rate was even lower—amounting to 1 percent between 2004 and 2017."

Seventy-five women out of thousands. If it were a horse, you wouldn't bet on it. Never mind boost that bet with a two-thousand-pound hoof scratch and dab of equine velocity glue.

As is all too often the case, guilt, blame, or criticism is heaped upon women's bodies, rather than the structures in which we live. The sneering at a woman in her forties hoping to get pregnant, rather than asking why she felt unable to take time away from work, stop earning money, and go on maternity leave in her twenties and thirties. The shock and horror at women giving birth to twins or triplets as they enter middle age, rather than interrogating the way IVF was aggressively sold to her when she was at her most vulnerable. The dismay at a woman spending thousands on fertility treatments, alternative medicines, and scientifically questionable procedures rather than questioning the social, economic, financial, and sexual politics that made her and her partner put off having children until it was perhaps too late. Of course, I feel deep and genuine sympathy for anyone who cannot get pregnant whenever and however they want to. I may have had just the tiniest glimpse at that world, as I sat on my toilet and stared at the lining of my womb dripping out of me, but it was enough to give me a sense of how desperate, infuriating, and exhausting it can be.

We all can delight in those stories of people who, after years of trying, failed IVF cycles, and grim conversations in consultants' offices, simply gave up, stopped shagging-by-calendar, drank a bottle of wine one night, and two weeks later realized they were pregnant. And these stories do happen, of course. But we should not allow that version of events to overshadow the real and unavoidable alternative faced by thousands of people every year: that sometimes you simply do not, cannot, and will not get pregnant.

We need a different narrative: that sometimes people who want babies don't end up having them. Whether that's because of time, hormones, physiology, illness, or the myriad other factors that can influence fertility is often unknowable. But we can, as a culture, recognize that the child-free life, whether chosen or not, is as valid, as nuanced, and as worthy of our attention as the parenting one. That people without children often contribute a lot more—and in terms of the earth's natural resources, cost a lot less—than their parenting counterparts. We need, as my friend Ellie in Berlin puts it, better child-free role models.

It is also worth pointing out that for some people, their period is little more than a pain in the arse: messy, uncomfortable, distracting, and—factoring in the apparatus needed not to simply bleed out all over everyone's furniture—expensive. It doesn't feel like a missed opportunity, like another grain of sand passing through the egg timer of your womb, like a potential baby lost. It just feels like blood. I have friends who have never wanted children, have no desire to be pregnant, and consider their fertility the way I consider football: important to some people but of absolutely no relevance to them. To those people, my reaction to finding out I wasn't pregnant will seem somewhat alien. Which is not to say that they don't care, don't feel sympathy, don't want to help. The myth that women always exist in competition and antipathy to one another is bullshit. Sure, there are women who hate one another, disagree with one another's lifestyle, criticize one another's decisions, and take no interest in one another's lives. There are women who think my hunger to be pregnant was ridiculous; others who feel furious envy that I got pregnant so quickly. There are people who greet their period with relief because they hate the idea of pregnancy, there are women who will consider their miscarriage an escape from a future they had not planned, there are women counting down the days to menopause in order that the decision of whether to keep trying is taken away, there are women so traumatized by losing a baby that they never pursue it again.

It is possible for people with all shades of feeling toward parenthood, periods, and the pressure of fertility to coexist, offer one another support, and understand one another's position. There is room in here for all of us. Unless you're in line for a single toilet in a dank South London warehouse, in which case it's everyone for themselves. No piss-takers.

15

MOORHENS

There's a load of sticks, balanced on the seat of a rowing boat. Among the twigs and branches are strips of grass, a lily pad, someone's discarded sweet wrapper, a plastic fork handle, and what is either a piece of string or the tail end of a tampon. It looks like a badly frayed shopping basket, dropped in a canal and left to gather weeds.

This is the nest, built almost overnight by a pair of moorhens, beside the deck of the Kenwood Ladies' Pond. Just meters from the emergency hoist (on which, as part-time lifeguard, I daily lower a white-haired Austrian woman into the water) sits a nesting coot mother, apparently unfazed by the topless sunbathing, geriatric breaststroke, and occasional heron attack going on around her. Under Section 1 of the Wildlife and Countryside Act 1981, it is an offense to intentionally take, damage, or destroy the nest of any wild bird while the nest is being used or built, which means that until autumn breaks she's here sitting pretty in her wood-paneled home, while my colleagues and I are forced to undertake all heavy manual labor while wobbling on a paddleboard or thigh-deep in silt. We could probably invest in a second rowing boat.

It is April 2017 and I am working as a lifeguard at the Kenwood Ladies' Pond on Hampstead Heath, that infamous home of urban tranquility, sapphic posing, winter fortitude, literary inspiration, sweaty lounging, and indulged wildfowl so beloved by everyone from Emma Watson to Margaret Drabble. It is a pond, ostensibly. An outdoor, freshwater, brown-bottom pond full of fish and plants and ducks and women. It is open every day of the year, freezes in winter, and has a

sign on the entrance gate that reads: NO MEN, NO DOGS, NO CHIL-
DREN. To the women who swim there it is also paradise: a haven, a
lifeline, a community, a third lung.

I am dressed like the bastard love child of Ronald McDonald and
a set of traffic lights: hot-red shorts, violently yellow sweatshirt, and a
moist, pale green face. I am also two months pregnant, tired, emotional, and often to be found slipping to the back of the deck to quietly
throw up in a large red plastic bin. I'd been asked if I would ever be
interested in lifeguarding the previous winter, as I swam through rain,
ice, and snow for perhaps the sixth year in a row. I had proved myself.
I was thrilled. Working at the Pond had always been my dream job—
outdoors, a casual contract, a physical antidote to a desk-shaped life
of writing—and so I quickly signed up to a week's training course. I
paid my fees, read my training manual, and, within a matter of days,
discovered I was pregnant.

Brilliantly, when I rang Ray, the course leader, to ask him if I could
still do my lifeguard training and take the exam even though I was
eight weeks pregnant, he immediately replied, "Of course. Why not?"

When I asked the other lifeguards at the Pond if they minded
having a pregnant lifeguard on deck, they reminded me that only a
few years earlier the head lifeguard had worked right through her
pregnancy until the final trimester. You can still keep watch with a
baby beneath your ribs; you can still paddle through a crowd, clean
toilets, perform CPR, and shout at teenagers with a new person kick-
ing against your bladder.

One tea break (as likely nettle as PG Tips), I stand on the gray concrete slab of the emergency deck and stare down at this moorhen nest.
I watch as the female moorhen plumps her white breast, shakes out
her tail feathers, quickly flutters her wings, and then sits, unmoving. I
watch as she scans the edges of the pond—a lake to her—still sitting,
alone, silently, diligently waiting. I watch her quick breath pushing
small chest feathers into the sticks beneath her. I watch her sit and
wait. Then, from the far end of the pond I see her mate—a brave and
vivacious moorhen we've nicknamed Martin after he became rather

famous for his particularly dramatic showdown with a seagull—swimming doggedly along the hundred meters of bank, past lily pads, past life rings, past overhanging branches and flag irises, with a large, wet leaf in his beak. After hours away, unseen, he has finally returned. With a nimble scuttle up the oar, he jumps into the boat and clambers along the bench. A microsecond of eye contact passes between the two birds before he quickly and carefully tucks the moist, cushioning leaf beneath his partner's stomach.

All that—the swimming, the waiting, the ducking and diving—all just so she could be a little comfier, her nest a little more padded, her job a little easier. Their whole existence this spring is an act of faith: in each other, in their eggs, in that nest, in nature, and in the future. For the moment, their life has no greater purpose than to keep a collection of speckled eggs the size of walnuts warm. Until their chicks have fledged, they are woven together by duty and interdependence. Her trust, that he will return, look after her, and keep her alive, and his devotion to a family invisible, nearly winds me. I stare down into the boat with tears in my eyes.

Hours later, in the halogen dusk of East London, I will try to tell Nick about this moment, about the birds and their purpose and her reliance and his loyalty and I will be unable to get the words out. I am undone.

The truth is, I feel a little validated by those birds. For weeks, I have watched Nick go off to work, crossing London by bike, train, and tube, an hour and a half each way, and wondered, truly, if he will ever come back. In those long, empty afternoons I longed for him to come home with something—a letter, flowers, a piece of cloth—that shows he has been thinking of me despite the distance, that he would be there for us when I needed him most. I needed reassurance that I could trust him, that I existed in his interior life and that he wouldn't pull away at the first opportunity.

As someone who had spent her entire adolescent and adult life studiously building up a flinty little shell of independence and self-protection, this new feeling was terrifying. As someone who'd always believed that the only way to make a man stay was to ask for nothing, expect nothing, and plan nothing, it felt dangerous. I felt peeled open and exposed to the whipping wind of frailty, need, and hope. If Nick left me now, I wouldn't just be pregnant and heartbroken; I'd be facing six months, maybe a year, where I couldn't work. I'd have nobody to pass the baby to in moments of physical fragility or emotional distress. I'd have almost no time to see my friends, let alone meet other parents. So much of what I considered my identity as an independent woman would be compromised or lost. And yet I was scared to show him quite how much I was going to depend on him, in case it scared him off, pushed him away.

Of course, this fear is as harmful to the men kept at arm's length as it is to the women who find themselves unhappily alone. I had somehow to show Nick that I was relying on him, and trust that my relying on him wouldn't drive him away. Here I was, a human nest in Day-Glo red shorts, hoping to be tended by a mate who spent 90 percent of his day elsewhere. I had been warned about the vomit, the tiredness, and the piss of pregnancy, but nobody had warned me about this. Nobody said that I would feel so vulnerable.

Overlooking the pond, dabbing at my face with the sleeve of my XXL yellow City of London–issued Hampstead Heath Lifeguard sweatshirt, I turn to see Jane, my friend and colleague, lying prostrate across the decking, her arm stretched out like a construction digger, trying to pluck a small curled feather from the surface of the pond. She suddenly leaps up and holds it in the air like the Wimbledon trophy, beaming.

"A mandarin duck tail feather!" she hollers, her face a palette of sun lotion, eyebrows, wind burn, and pure joy. "How amazing is that!"

I first met Jane as a fellow swimmer; she was lying across the brown silk surface of the pond, staring up into the sky. Later that day I saw her, in her technicolor lifeguard garb, standing on deck, her leg hair shining in the sun, leading a rousing chorus of "Happy Birthday" to one of the women in the pond. Barefoot and topless, standing on a folded towel as I got dressed, I joined in the singing. This is the thing about Jane—she makes you join in. Whether it's dressing up as a witch to jump into the pond on a foggy Halloween morning, climbing a tree overhanging the crystal waters of Schlachtensee in Berlin, slipping into the Thames at Richmond, or thumping around London in her big white camper van: if Jane's doing it, I'll follow.

On the surface, we are quite different women. She is sixty-two, single, went to agricultural college, lives alone, nursed her partner through an aggressive and ultimately fatal form of breast cancer, is a carpenter, eats fruit sandwiches for breakfast, wanted to be a contemporary dancer, and has a body that appears to have been carved out of hardwood. She also never had children.

That summer, as I stood guard through a record-breaking heat wave, pregnant, scrubbing shit off the toilets, pulling in teenagers having asthma attacks, clearing out the drains, and picking litter off the lawn, all with my unborn son heaving and pushing against my ribs like Moby Dickhead, I wondered what Jane thought of me. What did she think of all the other pregnant women who turned up each day to bathe their swollen bellies in London's finest fresh water? Did she pity us, despair of us, envy us, or find our inflated state a mere irrelevance?

"I'm fantastically admiring of all the pregnant women who turn up here," Jane tells me one May afternoon as I sit on the meadow overlooking the pond. "I love the way they come angry, wanting to get the baby out because it's overdue. And I love the goddess stage, where they have this otherworldly glow and are double what they were. And the terrified ones, all the first pregnancies who tentatively ask if it's safe to swim here. Next time, of course, they're all trampolining with a bottle of red wine."

We laugh. I've snatched a couple of hours to come to the Pond and grill this icon of future female independence about her decision not to have children.

"It wasn't a decision in that final way," she corrects me, eating muesli soaked in orange juice out of an old Tupperware. "I've very much wanted children with the people I've fallen in love with, at the point when the relationship is all-encompassing, very close, as one."

Did she ever think she would have children with another woman? I ask. Did she imagine being a gay parent?

"No. I don't use the word gay," she explains. "I'm just me, and I fall in love with lots of different people. I've had three long-term relationships—one particularly long one. When I was with her, we'd always joke that we'd been trying for children for fifteen years but it just hadn't happened yet. It was a way of buffing off that question. I'd say, 'And it's good fun trying,' playing the fool, really."

This, I calculate, would have been in the nineties and early noughties; a time of Section 28, when same-sex parenting was rare and still fairly controversial. Did the political climate make the question of whether to have a baby more complicated?

"I don't know, really," says Jane, in a way that makes me feel like I've been unwittingly obtuse. "I had my one surge of wanting a child when I was about twenty-three and my older sister's first baby arrived," she explains, tearing a piece of grass at her feet. "I went to hospital and saw this thing and thought, *Ooh! I'd like one of those.* Much more than I thought I'd ever want one of those. But I've always loved babies and children; that's not a problem."

There is a significant pause. A cat creeps through the bushes in front of me, a woman dives into the cold, green water.

"My mum told me in graphic physical detail what it was like to have a baby from about the age of ten. Not that it would have stopped me, but I knew what it entailed. I knew how dangerous pregnancy was for the mother and the child. In my family, a lot of babies never made it to birth; of those that did, a lot died in early childhood. That was the world I grew up in. I saw the horror of it, I think, as well as the bliss."

The horror as well as the bliss. This is a phrase that will stay with me. It reminds me of my friend Jon saying, over a cup of coffee when my son was barely a year old, "Of course, having a baby is totally irrational. If it was a rational decision, nobody would do it."

Except, of course, we are not entirely rational beings. We are also emotional beasts, pack animals, storytelling monkeys. We build our lives around people, stories, and feelings. How, I wonder, did Jane feel about her own independence, her own child-free life? At what point did sex, choice, love, gender, resolve themselves into her current situation?

"I think my dad's comment to me, as I was about to leave the house to go to university was, 'If you ever get pregnant, don't darken this doorstep again,'" says Jane, her eyebrows resting somewhere above the treeline. "I also grew up with the story of my mum wanting to throw her first child off Barnes Bridge. She had a very bad reaction to her first pregnancy, what we would now call postnatal depression. They didn't have enough money for food and were all living in one room; it was very hard. I always thought, genetically I'm very like my mum and I knew she wanted to do that, so do I really want to do that? To a child, to myself? Do I want to be the one in the newspaper? I think it's also wrong to have to paint any woman as maternal or caring. Just because I'm a woman, do I have to be a mother?"

Well, quite.

Jane spends her working life looking after people, caring about their safety, feeding ducklings, entertaining, bringing together a community, making, and creating. She has also nursed someone she loves, every day, through unbearable pain and vulnerability. She has done the physical and emotional work of caring. And yet, when I ask about why she never had children, never adopted or fostered, she ends up describing the decision as selfish. This surprises me. I still consider my decision to *have* children as ultimately a selfish one. It strikes me that, whichever way you slice the decision about having a baby, a woman will ultimately end up feeling that her decision was selfish and self-centered and is therefore open to criticism. I wonder if the same is true for men.

There is, however, one corner of something like regret, something like grief that Jane still carries.

"The only thing that is a slight . . . pain," says Jane, pointing at her chest as though identifying a physical ache, "is that I was very briefly a granny to my partner's grandchild. Her daughter managed to give birth five days before Alison died. We saw him hours after he'd been born. I jokingly said, 'I'm your Granny Smith.' It was a stupid little pun, but I really liked that. Sadly we're not much in touch now, but that's life as well."

I had not even considered that, when you are not a mother, it also means you are unlikely to become a grandmother. That as your peers move through parenthood and into grandparenthood, your position will once again mark you out.

Jane swallows. "Alison's last words were, 'Isn't he beautiful? Go tell the pond,' and then she never spoke again."

If the Panic Years are characterized by a thrumming undercurrent of fertility and uncertainty, then the nature of pregnancy and early motherhood is as intrinsic to the Flux as everything that comes before it. Never in the world would I argue that a woman must have a baby in order to be fulfilled, and nothing in my life has ever made me more stridently pro-choice and pro-abortion than being pregnant and becoming a mother. But I will argue that motherhood is a Rubicon that, once passed, can never be undone.

In talking about the decision to have children, we must also talk about the decision not to have children, and in many cases that will mean an abortion.

In talking about the decision to have a baby, we must talk about the reality of pregnancy and why some people may choose to end theirs.

In order to understand the arguments in favor of reproductive choice, it might help to talk unsentimentally about what being pregnant actually involves. In the first trimester, a pregnant woman will create half of her entire volume of blood again. Just think about that: 50 percent more blood. Think about what that does to your body, your energy, your vitality. Ironically, for most women in Britain, this period of fatigue often happens just at the point when they're still keeping that pregnancy private: before you start to show, before you traditionally tell your friends, before you maybe pin on your "Baby on Board" badge. I remember standing on the light-rail, feeling more tired, more sick, more existentially exhausted than I ever have in my life and realizing that, in order to ask for a seat, I would have to explain to a group of strangers in navy blue suits that I was pregnant, before I'd told any of my various commissioning editors, before I'd even told my own mother. You see, I was very cautious about who I told during my early pregnancy—suddenly gripped by a wolfish, unfamiliar desire for privacy, to not be asked questions, to not have to carry the weight of other people's hope or expectation or opinion. I tried to control that information—as well as my own excitement—until I'd had my first scan. I asked Nick not to tell anyone either, until I was ready.

The first trimester was also, in my case, a time of near-constant nausea. Imagine the worst hangover you've ever had, on three hours' sleep, while on your period, feeling carsick, in a pair of too-tight trousers and with the taste and smell of burned onions in your mouth. For nearly sixteen weeks this was my ever-present reality. Eating didn't help, drinking didn't help, napping wasn't always an option (I may be freelance, but even I have to live my life occasionally vertically).

I threw up every single time I got the number 253 bus. One morning, while on the way to the 253 bus, I threw up in anticipation, all over the wheel and bonnet of a maroon Ford Focus, only to look up and see the driver, staring horrified right at me and the pool of vomit collecting at my feet (I had been aiming for the gutter). Meekly, I fumbled into my bag and pulled out the "Baby on Board" badge Nick had sent away for the week after I told him I was pregnant. I held it up to the driver's window and mouthed "I'm so sorry" as he waved me away, disgusted. Shamefaced, I tucked the badge back in my pocket—terrified that I might bump into someone I knew on the bus and have my new private, personal, and internal existence made public.

Of course, nobody knows exactly what causes "morning sickness" (don't be fooled—it can last all day) or how to cure it because, as always, the female body and female pain are woefully under-researched. Scientists are more likely to get funding to research male pattern baldness than first trimester pregnancy.

But, worse than all this—the vomit, the revulsion at all fresh and green foods, the tiredness, the thick snotty doubling of your discharge, the sore tits—was the constant, hovering fear that all this may slip away as quickly as it had come. Before you've had your twelve-week scan, seen that the pregnancy is viable and that this tiny collection of cells upheaving your whole body is beating as you'd hoped, you are existing in a state of tension and uncertainty. You can be pregnant without necessarily producing a living fetus; you can be reproducing cells in your womb, but they may not form a heartbeat. Similarly, that heartbeat may, at any time, for no reason, simply stop. Having something you can neither see, nor feel, nor hear, nor control, growing inside your body, but at the mercy of forces beyond your power, is an act of faith, imagination, and risk as well as biology. Suddenly, and through no fault of your own, no accident, no abuse, no choice, this pregnancy could end as uncontrollably as it began. The thought of that haunted me for months.

In the middle of the night, looking down at my flat and silent belly, I would creep over to a box file on the shelf and pull out my old, piss-soaked, positive pregnancy tests just to stare at them. Later, once the pregnancy was established, I would have moments of total fear, total panic, convinced that the baby hadn't moved for hours. With thoughts of oxygen deprivation and prenatal death screaming through my head, I would drink pints of ice water, lie down on my left-hand side, and weep, desperate to feel some kick, some twitch within my belly. When this happened in the day, when Nick was fifteen miles away, preparing a group of eleven-year-olds for their standardized tests, I would feel as lonely and frightened as a child, lost on the side of a motorway.

Back in that April of 2017, I was finding pregnancy hard. Because pregnancy *is* hard. In some ways, it is precisely as hard as what comes after. I've said it before and I'll say it again: no man who has ever voted against abortion could handle being pregnant. Not one of those ham-faced assemblages of fear, misogyny, and idiocy could handle having their skin, muscle, and bones torn apart by an unborn child. Not one of them would undergo three months of daily vomiting, existential terror, occasional bleeding, constant nausea, and unshakable fatigue, followed by another six months of aching joints, short breath, decreased mobility, near-incontinence, fear, and exhaustion for the sake of something that may not even survive. Not one of them could give up their status, their ability to work, their financial security, their freedom of thought and movement, their whole previous way of life, in order to grow something in their bodies that they never even wanted—it is hard enough when you do want it.

Never have I been more certain that such a dangerous, life-altering, difficult, and irreversible process should only ever be undertaken if the pregnant person absolutely wants to do it. No child should be born unless they are entirely wanted, and the only person who can and should judge that decision is the pregnant person themself. She who carries the baby makes the choice. Perhaps you are wondering why being pregnant, giving birth, and raising a baby made me so adamantly pro-choice. Perhaps you think such a statement makes me sound like a "bad" or uncaring mother. Maybe you're worried about how my son will feel when he reads me writing that I should have had total authority to abort him if I had wanted to. It's fine, don't worry. I know what I'm doing. I know how it feels to be the child of a pro-choice woman. And it feels pretty great.

Whether you want children or not, whether you are able to conceive or not, whether you have sex with men or women, are nonbinary or noncommittal, whether you fear it, long for it, or are revolted by the very thought of it, the possibility of creating another life beneath your bones is important. To argue otherwise—to dismiss motherhood as boring, marginal, domestic, or irrelevant—is an act of cultural violence. It allows exploitation, abuse, injustice, and dislocation to grow like mold under the systems of power. The majority of women will have at least one child by the time they are forty-one; everybody is the product of some woman's pregnancy and birth; the possibility and reality of having a baby is as important, as interesting, and as worthy of our attention as anything created, experienced, or believed by humanity.

Over the whole nine months I was pregnant, I had, probably, a total of two hours during which I could either see or hear my baby. When I say pregnancy is an act of faith and an exercise in living in uncertainty, this is what I mean. For months on end, I was entirely responsible for keeping a baby alive and yet I had no idea what was going on beneath my skin. At that first twelve-week scan, I was expecting something like a cross between the moon landings and a wedding day; Nick and I would gasp, turn to each other with tears in our eyes, and smile.

In fact, I lay across a strip of gray paper on another blue pleather bed, my heart shrieking, my hands shaking like two sweaty leaves, waiting for the bad news. Somewhere deep within me was an unquenchable feeling that something was wrong. Was its heart leaking? Did it have a skull? Would there be no brain? Was this an ectopic pregnancy about to fatally explode outside my uterus? Was it really alive? Had I imagined the whole thing?

Faith in my own body was, as I should have expected, as miserable as the wisps of hair across an adolescent boy's chin. I so wanted it to be okay, but was so sure that it wasn't. When that tiny gray skeleton man appeared on the screen, soaring down the side of my womb like a log flume and trying to turn somersaults in his liquid home, I felt some joy, but also an overwhelming terror. There it was: this tiny, ludicrous beginning of a human life that had grown, unseen, within me. My body had made it, and so, of course, my body could fail it.

So when the sonographer asked me to stay on and talk to a senior midwife after my appointment, I felt as though I were about to leave my body. Pure terror flooded through me. This was it, I thought. This was the moment when they gave me the terrible news. I was so frightened that I could barely make out what this kind, patient, cottage loaf of a woman was telling me as I shook with tears. Luckily Nick was there to explain that, because of my low levels of pregnancy-associated plasma protein-A (PAPP-A to its friends) and a problem with the blood flow to my placenta on one side, I was deemed at risk of preeclampsia and would have to take an aspirin every day of my pregnancy. I would also have to do more blood pressure and urine tests than other women.

Like a fool, I went home and googled low PAPP-A. I discovered that "low maternal serum pregnancy-associated plasma protein-A (PAPP-A), at eleven to thirteen weeks of gestation, is associated with stillbirth, infant death, intrauterine growth restriction, preterm birth, and preeclampsia in chromosomally normal fetuses, while a raised nuchal translucency is associated with specific structural abnormalities and genetic syndromes."

In a state of pure panic, I rang my cousin Eliza, a midwife, and told her what they'd said and what, stupidly, I'd read. She did everything she could to reassure me, bring me back into perspective, drag me back up to the surface. And yet, from the very moment I lay on that bed and heard the sonographers measuring and conferring about my unborn baby, perhaps even before that, I became consumed with a sort of low-level anxiety that would stay with me until the day I gave birth.

During my pregnancy I would also discover that I had group B streptococcus, a bacteria that could, if passed on to the baby during birth, result in serious complications if not death; I was told that the problems with my placenta meant I probably shouldn't have a home birth; and I was advised to speak to a consultant. Luckily for me, that consultant turned out to be a heavenly woman called Ms. Erskine, whom I will love and admire until my dying day. With a powerful mix of intelligence, competence, and humor, the selfless dedication to her job that kept her in that office for eleven hours at a time, hair like Caroline Lucas, a voice that soothed and entertained, and the sensitivity to address each of my concerns seriously but with no room for anything other than total, brutal honesty, she is everything I long for in a prime minister. Were it possible, I would put her in charge of everything, immediately.

At our first appointment, I sat trembling beside my friend Eleanor, who had come along to write notes because I'd apparently lost the ability to make and retain any new memories since getting pregnant. People call this "baby brain." I call it "gestational dementia": less cutesy, less likely to be used to patronize you. As I stared at a table of dim blood pressure results and asked about the possibility of congenital disorders, Ms. Erskine smiled, stared me dead in the eye, and said, "As women, we have control over everything: work, money, friendships, our bodies. But we have no control over our children."

There it was: I was out of control. I had stepped into a life uncertain. This hospital, my wonderful midwives, my cousin, my friends, my mother, and my partner would all do what they could to help but, ultimately, there was nothing anybody could do to change what might happen. The future of this baby and my body around it were unknowable and uncertain. That was the truth and it was inescapable. This was what I'd signed up for, apparently. Total vulnerability, interdependence, and the unknown—not a single guarantee. For the rest of my life. By existing in such a state, by bearing the risk of pregnancy and accepting that loss of control, I was preparing myself for life as a parent. The Panic Years do not end with a positive pregnancy test and a swollen belly. The Panic Years are not dissolved by a daily aspirin and the occasional *clop clop clop* of a fetal heartbeat. But perhaps the fear, the restriction, and the tiredness you feel during those nine disorienting months might just prepare you for the life that is to come.

16

LABOR OF LOVE

Walking along the River Lea, rubbing my nipples like scratch tickets and muttering, heavy-lidded, into the drizzle, I stop halfway up a footbridge, grab the rain-slick handrail, and feel my body grow tighter, thicker, and heavier than lead.

I'm wearing a pair of fluorescent yellow waterproof XXL men's trousers, given to me as a present by a man who drove a digger on building sites. From the waist down, I look like an overweight construction engineer about to drill up a mile of motorway tarmac, rather than a woman on the edge of a biological miracle. On top, I'm wearing a huge navy fisherman's jumper and padded coat that can no longer do up over my washing machine of a belly. My hair is scraped back, I'm in walking boots with the laces flapping, and the sky is like a shared towel in a student bathroom: gray, mottled, and damp. I am in labor. Finally.

Because my placenta had started to wheeze out of action on the left-hand side a few weeks earlier, like a hoover bag full of screws, my brilliant consultant was keen for me not to be pregnant for longer than forty weeks. As a result, I'd been booked in for a sweep in two days' time—a sweep, for those of you not yet in the know, is basically a medical fingering, administered with all the delicacy of a fifteen-year-old virgin, on speed, listening to Korn. According to the charity Tommy's, there is a between 25 and 50 percent chance that a sweep will start your labor within the following twenty-four hours. Which is great news if you don't want to be induced. And I didn't want to be induced. Just like you don't really want to have a rectal exam in the middle of a shopping center: if it's necessary and the only option, then of course you'll go for it, but you'd be keen to check out the other possibilities first, just in case.

I knew that being induced was likely to make your labor more painful, the contractions stronger and brought on faster; it increased your likelihood of needing an epidural and makes you more likely to need assistance during delivery—yes, I'm talking forceps and vacuum (the medical equivalent of a plunger, attached to the baby's head to help pull it out in the final stages). Which is why I spent the two weeks before my sweep date duly eating pineapple like a drunk aunt at a 1970s cocktail party, going for long waddling walks every afternoon, doing squats on Hackney Marshes at dawn most mornings, and spending my evenings having the sort of mutually unfulfilling sex that's more like trying to move furniture around a tight corner than an act of physical passion. If I could bring on this labor naturally, then by the power of agitated cervixes, I was going to try. I'd even had my back and ankles lightly impaled by a beautiful, calm, and terrifyingly strong acupuncturist called Maria.

We'll never know which out of this cocktail of delights was the one that worked. But after going to bed on Friday night with a sensation in my womb like the lapping of water at the edge of a paddling pool—I woke up and felt, well, different. I texted my cousin Eliza: "Either I'm having the world's most overdue period, or something's happening." She texted back: "WAHOOO. I've got the next three days off work. Let's get this baby out!!" By the time she arrived, I had balanced three pieces of toilet roll on the edge of the bathtub, smeared pink with mucus and blood for her to examine. I know, it's amazing I couldn't wait till Christmas.

Like snowflakes, the Jacksons, cheese sandwiches, clouds, train journeys, and cups of tea, no two labors are ever the same. The same mother, with the same father, delivering in the same room, may have entirely different experiences from birth to birth. They may have an epidural, they may deliver vaginally, they may need a caesarean, get induced, deliver without pain relief, do it on all fours, need forceps, use gas and air, scream, use ventouse, deliver on the toilet, need a pessary, get an episiotomy, have it all over within an hour, or spend three days heaving through contraction after contraction after contraction. When one of my friends had her first baby, his eyes were already peering out from between her legs by the time the midwife arrived; with her second, she had to go into hospital and have her son pulled out with forceps. You cannot prepare for labor and you cannot be judged for what happens. Any labor that results in a healthy mother and healthy baby is a successful labor. And yes, by healthy I mean physically and mentally healthy—each is as important as the other.

Birth can be joyful and it can be traumatic, it can happen in hospitals and up mountains, it can be just as you'd hoped and worse than you'd imagined. But one thing is for sure: it will change you, physically and mentally, for the rest of your life. Giving birth was, without a whisper of doubt, the single most significant and transformational thing that has ever happened to me. I will never be the person I was before; my body will never be the same again. It lasted two days and took me to the very edge of myself. And, honestly, if you told me I was to do it all again tomorrow I would do so readily.

For reasons I've never truly understood, people seem inordinately keen to tell pregnant people horror stories about labor. When I was pregnant, I had people come up to me in cafés, offices, on park benches, even on one particularly memorable occasion at a funeral, and start telling me in lurid detail about What Could Go Wrong. Of course, those experiences are real, important, and profound and should be learned from (particularly within the medical community). But they also belong to the people who experienced them; they are not my story to tell. I am simply here to point out that, whether you experience it or not, birth is intrinsic to the Flux. It is the thing we're all wondering about, talking around, preparing for, or avoiding. It is the engine that gives the whole train momentum.

You should have an idea of what it might be, before you take the decision whether you want to do it. Because it may be quite different to how you imagine.

As is fairly common during vaginal labors, my contractions would come and go; sometimes it would feel like things were getting heavier and steadier, at other times the whole thing would ease off almost completely. If I were a different, more patient person, I would have taken these lulls as a chance to sleep, lie down, have a rest. That's certainly what Nick was doing. Instead, I'd heave myself onto a birth ball or storm out into the fresh air, determined to keep things going.

Once Eliza had arrived, inspected my little mantelpiece of bodily fluids, confirmed that this probably was the passing of the mucus plug, and suggested that I could actually flush these away now if I liked, we all rather wondered what to do with ourselves. Because I had no idea how contractions would feel, I wasn't entirely convinced that this squeezing, fuzzy pressure through my back really was anything to do with labor after all. They had been going on all morning, but were nothing like the cramping stomach pain I'd always imagined contractions to be. Which reminds me: the first time my friend Josie opened her laptop after giving birth to her beautiful, tiny mouse of a baby, she found that she had fifteen tabs open, fourteen of which were various Google variations on "What are the early signs of labor" and one of which was "how long to roast a chicken." As she plowed through the first stage of labor, on one of the hottest days of the year, she'd been so unconvinced that it was happening at all that she and her partner had decided to make a full roast chicken dinner to kill some time. The image of her, swollen and throbbing, walking in and out of the toilet to check yet another website about labor signs as their basement flat transformed into a poultry inferno makes me laugh every time I think of it.

Instead of cooking, I sat on our purple plastic exercise ball, bought from Sports Direct two weeks beforehand for £7.99, and watched *Dr. No* on the television. Eliza and I had grown up watching Bond films together, sitting on her parents' huge squashy sofa, in our matching pajamas, chewing through the "Saturday sweets" I only ever got when we came to London. So it felt rather apposite to be there, in my little flat, on a drizzly Saturday afternoon, eating chicken bagels and watching Sean Connery stride up the beach in his little pale blue two-piece as my body seemed to wax and wane, unseen. As it went dark I realized that, like trying to hold on to the smell of someone's perfume after they've left the room, my labor had almost gone. Twelve hours in and the squeezing, pulsing feeling in my back was still there, but not so often.

Eliza made up a bed in our front room and I went into the bedroom, keen to keep laboring, away from the eyes and expectations of other people. Before going to bed, I remembered something about using a breast pump, rather than rubbing your nipples, to help establish labor, as it released the same hormones but caused less friction. This, honestly, is one of my best and only tips for childbirth: if you're keen to get things going, or keep that show on the road, use a breast pump. After a false start (I'd managed to put it together minus a pivotal valve, which meant I was basically holding a plastic dessert bowl over my boob with one hand and squeezing an unconnected handle with the other), the pumping started. It was amazing. With each pull of my hand, I felt a corresponding tug in my womb and a hardening in my back. It felt like I was doing something, finally.

As the night wore on, and Nick got tired, I decided to have a lie down. A few hours later, as I woke up, my body seemed to have gone quiet. The pulsing in my body had got fainter. I felt awful. Because of my stupid, lazy nap I'd managed to almost stop the whole labor in its tracks. Eliza had to go to work the day after tomorrow, and I had dropped the ball. Immediately, I pulled on my neon trousers and headed out the door. Nick was understandably a little concerned: for all he knew, his laboring partner was heading out into suburban London, alone, at five A.M. in the dark to try to give birth under a holly bush, and so he came after me. He didn't have a coat, had sleep in his eyes, but walked alongside me, squeezing my shoulder and saying nothing. An hour later, as I reached the footbridge, that familiar, low sensation kicked in across my back and I squatted, staring into the brown water below me, relieved to be here again, waiting for it to pass.

I'd read enough about hypnobirthing (by which I mean, I skim-read one book loaned to me by a friend) to know that what you need during labor is a dark, quiet space in which you feel utterly relaxed. In our bedroom, I lit three of the candles my mother seems to buy from Aldi as regularly as bread and knelt down on the bed. To this day, the smell of No. 1 Lime, Mandarin and Basil can take me straight back to that room, that day, as I tried to will my son out of my body. I'd always known I didn't want to listen to music during my labor; frankly, I can think of nothing worse than a syncopated drum fill or heartfelt vocal line as you perform the most physically demanding task of your life. But I did want to listen to something. I needed to be distracted, just enough, to stop me folding in on myself like an overloaded cardboard box.

For some inexplicable reason—some half memory of a Christmas Radio 4 takeover combined with a need for infantile comfort—I asked Nick to put on the audiobook of Harry Potter. Fuck knows where this came from. I'd never read, nor barely seen, any of Harry Potter, and yet there I was, kneeling on my bed, rotating my hips, listening to Stephen Fry intone the story of Sirius Black. About eight hours in, the official audiobook stream broke and so, understanding that this was somehow important to me, Nick found an alternative on YouTube. Which is how I spent the next four hours of my labor listening to a recording of a fifteen-year-old Asian American girl reading the second half of the second Harry Potter novel into a webcam in her bedroom.

I had been laboring for about twenty hours when things got serious. Each time another thick blur of weight, pressure, and force spread through my body, I would call out for Nick with an urgency and vulnerability that went beyond sound. I hung on to the wall, legs spread, neck arched, like someone about to get frisked by the police, as Nick rubbed the bottom of my back. I felt like I was being pushed into something unknown—something dark and heavy and utterly immense. My conscious self felt like a tiny, fluttering film, balanced on the top of something opaque and unrelenting and beyond my control. Every time a new contraction came I would open my mouth, imagine my cervix opening beneath me, and exhale all the pressure and the might like a golden, spiraling breath. Just once, a contraction came that was of such intensity that I pulled my face into a twist of pain and thought, *No. No, no, no, please no.* And then caught myself. If I started to resist this now, if I started to dread or hate or fear these convulsions going through my body every few minutes, then I would be done for. I could not fight them. I had to let them come and go. I had to go through it. And so I kept breathing, kept moving, kept imagining that light coming out of my body. As I gripped my cupboard doors and shuddered through another contraction, imagining my breath as light, I felt like a black hole, watching a tiny galaxy float off out of my great heaving body.

I threw up. Chunks of pineapple and chicken bagel hit the bottom of the bucket like so much loose change.

"Give that here. Sick is what I do," said Eliza, as Nick carried on pressing on my back, as though somehow, with enough force behind him, he could even up the great bone-shifting pressure within my body as my pelvis pulled open to allow the baby through. I crawled across the bed and clung on to the window ledge, my face pressed against the cold black glass and thought, *I will never, ever do this again.*

The candles danced against the wall, I rocked to and fro, I buried my head into my chest and held on to Nick like a woman in a sea storm. At seven P.M., Eliza said we probably could go in to the hospital if I wanted to. There was no way of knowing how close I was, and, being a little wary about the journey, I was keen to get into the hospital room and get going.

Here's a tip: if you're in labor and planning to give birth in a hospital, don't turn up during a shift change. Nick's mum had driven us, as slowly and gently as possible, the few minutes to the hospital.

I'd knelt on the car seat, facing backward, and pushed my head into the headrest, feeling the fabric dig into my eyes. After a quick walk through a side door, we got up to the reception for the maternity unit to find it glaring bright, full of other people, and with a television that took up one entire wall blaring out *X Factor*. In what world does a laboring woman want to sit on a hard plastic chair, under a fluorescent bulb, and watch a massive, flashing screen? I pulled a towel out from the bag and wrapped it around my head, trying to find some of that dark, animal quiet I'd had at home. After about twenty minutes, I was asked to give a urine sample (after nine months of pissing into plastic tubes, this seemed utterly unremarkable) and I remember glancing quickly at the small clots of blood floating through it as I passed it over to the woman behind the counter.

I was taken into the triage room and asked to lie down, under a bare white bulb, to be examined. Now, I have absolutely no issue with people looking up my hole, and I have nothing but respect and admiration for NHS staff. But it strikes me as just possible that there are better ways to do this examination than have a woman, in quite serious discomfort, lie flat, under a screaming bright bulb, while it takes place.

"I'm afraid you're only three centimeters dilated," the midwife said. "We cannot admit you until you're four centimeters along."

It was like her words were coming to me from through a wall. One centimeter. I was one centimeter off. I couldn't come in. On my notes, I'd asked for all inquiries and decisions to be directed toward Nick during labor, so I could concentrate on the matter at hand. Because of the low PAPP-A, the group B streptococcus, and my not-too-hot placenta, they had to do a series of observations before they could send me home. As all this was happening right in the middle of the staff shift change, the whole thing took at least an hour. The new midwife suggested I go home, take a Tylenol, and have a hot bath and that within a few hours I'd almost certainly be ready to be admitted. And so back we went. Back through those same dark streets, in the back of that car, feeling embarrassed, like a failure, like the sort of drama queen who demands full surgery for a splinter.

Back at home, Eliza sat in the living room, curled up on our armchair, as I dragged myself around the bedroom again, holding on to Nick, pushing against the walls, feeling this ocean inside me try to escape through my spine. The author Amy Liptrot described contractions as "an earthquake going through your body." Even before we'd got to the hospital I'd been having them regularly and for minutes at a time. By midnight, they were coming every seven minutes and lasting a minute. They were unrelenting—a near-total block on thought, a thick black noise filling every inch of my body, an unshareable weight, a central focus for all the gravity in the universe. I felt like a rigid tube, stuck in an endless, circling pattern as my limbs hung limp at my side, like strips of ribbon. I was pumping at my breasts, great golden cascades of colostrum running down my taut, solid belly, desperate to keep the labor progressing. The candles were burning low. The walls around me seemed to be getting warmer and less solid.

At one thirty A.M., we decided to go in again. This time I moaned through the car journey, on my knees, pushing my shoulders into the seat like someone trying to rugby-tackle a horse. I remembered my auntie telling me to low like a cow, rather than gritting my teeth, as it would help loosen my vagina. I moaned into the car, feeling the adrenaline scatter across my scalp like sand. This was it, I thought, I'm going to have a baby.

This time I couldn't face the stairs to the maternity ward and so stood in the lift, under an oily yellow glow from the overhead bulb. As we walked into reception, our enormous bag banging into Eliza's knees and Nick stroking my sweaty back, I realized that one of the laboring women who had been in reception last time was still here. The poor bitch had sat through six more hours of full-volume Sunday-night television. Some casino show called *Jackpot Joy* was now blaring out of that massive screen. We sat in the same seats and waited to be brought in.

After about half an hour, a midwife called me into the triage room. I lay down, the towel still over my head, and let my legs fall open. She examined me, stood up, and said, "I'm afraid you're still only three centimeters dilated."

I could have wept. All that time, the rocking, the aching, the hanging off the walls and nothing, nothing to show for it. I couldn't believe it. Under that bare white light, they made me lie, utterly still, with a pair of monitor belts tied around my belly, so they could observe two of my contractions. I can say now, any woman who is made to give birth lying down flat, on a hospital bed, on a shared ward, under a light bulb, has my enduring respect and sympathy. It was awful. I was desperate to sit up, move around. I felt like a huge, pulsating maggot, pinned to the bed.

"I'll let you think about it," the midwife said, and rushed off to answer another call. The whole unit was clearly understaffed. Thanks to years of vicious funding cuts in all health and public services, this unit, like all units throughout the country, was being held together, just, by a skeleton staff of dedicated, hardworking, but utterly harassed people who wanted nothing else but to keep the nation healthy. Our midwife was obviously dealing with too many patients, many of who were probably in more serious situations than I was. But I was still utterly dejected and pissed off, as we sat behind that thin blue curtain for more than twenty minutes, wondering what the hell was happening. Were we really being sent home? Again? Would I ever not be in labor?

With tears rolling down my face, I heard the woman in blue scrubs say that we could either go home or walk around the hospital.

"The café and everything is closed, but you can walk around the corridors," she said, looking genuinely sorry. I was done. Defeated. I couldn't do this anymore. I had been laboring for more than forty hours, had barely slept, hardly eaten, and was utterly dejected. I turned to the midwife.

"Will it harm the baby if I just give up?" I asked, feeling as hopeless and exhausted as I've ever felt in my life.

"No, darling," she said. "Your baby is fine. You can just relax."

I frowned. "He won't be stuck, or in distress, if I just stop trying to be in labor?" I asked, trying to get her to understand that I wasn't just talking about relaxing; I was giving up altogether.

"Honestly?" she said. "I think that's the best thing you can do."

And so I did. Nick's mum came back, again, to collect us, and drove slowly home. As soon as we got in through the door I walked into the bedroom and lay down quietly on the bed. Out of habit and just a smear of residual fear, I lay down on my left-hand side, shut my eyes, and tried not to cry. It was Monday. Eliza was going to work tomorrow. I'd dragged everyone to the hospital twice and wasn't even having my baby. I had failed at labor. I was giving up.

Somehow, despite the continuous waves of contractions, I must have fallen asleep. I know I was asleep because I had a dream that I was standing in front of a little rat-faced man who was wearing a white polyester shirt and lanyard, holding a clipboard. I remember saying to him, quietly, "Please, just tell me I'm not in labor."

He looked down his clipboard, back at me over his little wire-framed glasses, and said, "You're not in labor."

When I woke up, my pajamas were wet. I couldn't deal with this, not now, so I threw them in the corner of the room, pulled on another pair—this time a pale blue XL pair of men's pajamas I'd bought years earlier in a charity shop—and went back to bed. The next time I woke up, at six A.M., I felt strangely light, sharp, and completely conscious once more. These pajamas, too, were wet—much wetter than before. I crept to the toilet. Had I just pissed myself? Was this a bad sign? Was the baby okay? Bare-arsed, I padded into the front room, where Eliza was curled up asleep on our foldout bed.

"'Liza," I whispered. "I'm not sure. I think I might have wet myself. But my waters might have broken too."

Because she's family, a midwife, and one of the greatest women in my life, Eliza calmly took the pajama bottoms from my hand, peered at them under the kitchen light, gave them a sniff, and said, "Well, it doesn't smell like piss to me."

Once your waters have broken, particularly if you've been diagnosed with group B streptococcus, you are advised to either call the midwife or, if you're having a hospital birth, head in to the hospital. In that cold, bright morning I felt transformed. I was light, quiet, calm: all the heavy, sweaty, pulsing animal thickness of the night before seemed to have dissipated. I got into the car and sat, almost motionless, with my head against the window, letting the sun shine on my face. I touched Nick's arm.

"Text my mum," I said. "Tell her I love her."

In the place of that dark and churning fuzz, I felt full of something like love, like light. My poor mum had done this for me once. She'd been here, pushed through all this, just in order that I could live. In retrospect, upon reading that text, my mum probably thought I was dying. But that never occurred to me. As we walked through the hospital, on our way to the labor ward, I wondered why Nick and Eliza were trying to pull me along so fast. What was the rush? Why were we in such a hurry? I was tired, paper thin, I couldn't go any faster. Looking back over his notes (and yes, whoever you are, if you witness a labor, please write down as much of it as you can remember, as soon as you can), I realize that at that point I was walking so slowly that Nick was genuinely worried I might not make it to the end of the hallway, let alone have the energy to give birth.

When we got to the reception room, I headed straight for the nearest available chair. I could barely sit down—it felt like my body had opened up beneath me. As Nick went off to explain, for the third time, where we were due to deliver, who our consultant had been, how often the contractions were coming, and how long for, I leaned my head into the soft, familiar, family-smell of Eliza's neck. She rubbed my back—her hand was smaller than Nick's but harder, more definite. Thank god they were here, I thought.

Once again we were ushered into that dreadful triage room, with the cold hard bed and blinding, unnatural light. Once again, the midwife put a monitor to my stomach, to listen to the baby's heartbeat. It was silent. Nothing. I closed my eyes and reached out for

Nick's hand. The digital display beside my head was showing something, numbers were ticking by, but I couldn't hear anything of the horse-hoof heartbeat that told us that our baby was still alive. The midwife went out for a different device and this time we could hear it—the *thunk-a-thunk* of his tiny heartbeat, rising and falling with the coming of each contraction. I let out a long breath. The midwife started to say something about how if I was still only three centimeters dilated, I wouldn't be admitted. Which was worrying as now that my waters had broken, I knew I would have to stay in the hospital, and the last midwife had said that by the third visit I would be admitted as a matter of course.

I remember sinking back into the bed and simply giving myself up to fate. I was too tired to fight anymore. I had been laboring for forty-five hours; my body still felt like it was being pressed, gripped, wrung dry by some force bigger than me; I had gone through agitation, excitement, failure, fear, shame, and despair; I had felt my very bones and muscles be torn apart by the sheer force of what was pushing down through my womb; I had turned into a creature of sweat and night and breath and blood; I hadn't eaten or drunk anything for nearly twenty-four hours, had slept less than four hours in two days, had been forced to lie in rigid pain for nearly an hour and still had nothing to show for it but three spoiled pajama bottoms and a bucket full of sick.

As the midwife pushed her hand inside me for the examination I heard her voice crack. "Oh god," she said.

I waited, too tired to panic.

"She's fully dilated," she added. Then, shouting over her shoulder, called out, "We need to get her in a room right now."

My heart soared. I had done it. I'd fucking done it. I'd shown this cynical, three-centimeter-chatting, room-dithering world. It had taken two days and the weight of the world, but I had finally, finally stretched myself open like the mouth of a river and I was ready for my room.

Feeling almost outside of my own body, I walked through a set of double doors into a beautiful, clean, white suite. Birth Center Room C. The windows were a wash of morning sunlight, the pool was waiting to be filled. A midwife with the face and voice of an angel was holding my hands and introducing herself to me as Roisin.

"Make yourself comfortable," she trilled, in a soft Irish accent.

I immediately tore off my top, threw off my knickers, walked straight over to the window, and lay down, legs sprawled, on the cushioned seat.

Another midwife, Dorothy, started to explain that they needed to give me some intravenous antibiotics through my hand, because of the group B streptococcus. I smiled dreamily and gave her my outstretched hand. We both knew it might be too late for these to have any effect, but we also both knew that it was worth a shot. As they filled the pool, they calmly explained that, for some women, the contractions may ease off once you get into the water, so they wanted to make sure things were really established first. That meant keeping my labor at full force. I started bouncing on the ball, squeezing away at the breast pump, entirely naked, with colostrum cascading down onto the floor.

"Nell, can you feel anything in your bum?" Roisin asked, looking into my eyes with twinkling, good-humored concern.

What did she mean? I wondered. Did she mean my lower back? The part of my body that had felt like it was being reversed over by an eighteen-wheeler every five minutes for the last eight hours?

"My pooing bum?" I asked, hoping to get some clarification.

"Yes, your pooing bum," she said, utterly straight-faced and totally unfussed.

I thought about it. No. Not really. My anus, like almost all the rest of my body, felt like some sort of abstract joke; my head, my legs, my shoulders, and my feet were but a flutter of lace around this great, pulsating tube. I went into the toilet for a wee. As I stood up, I realized something tangible had shifted. Once again, my body felt transformed. Something in my bum was telling me I was ready to push. Still somehow floating on a gentle current of exhaustion and relief, I walked back into the room and, for the first time in fifty hours, made a joke.

"My bum," I said, looking around the room, "is now involved."

The two midwives, Nick, and Eliza all ushered me toward the birth pool. At that moment, I was so involved with what was happening beneath my skin that my surroundings felt almost immaterial. I genuinely could have pushed that baby out in a supermarket parking lot. And yet, as I sunk into the warm, clean water, something fundamental flooded through me. This was it, I thought. I was held, I was ready, it was happening. A huge contraction rumbled through my body like a volcano. I juddered, I quaked. I pushed my head down Nick's chest and, without even realizing what I was doing, bit down hard on the flesh of his belly like an animal. This was something. Finally, after all those hours of fruitless, meaningless pressure, something was happening.

Dorothy, my other midwife, came down to the edge of the pool and looked me in the eye. "Listen, Nell—when the next contraction comes I want you to take little, shallow brea—"

Before she'd even finished, the earth within me reared up again, pushing along my spine, against my skin, and through my entire body. With a wireless monitor in her hand, Roisin gently came alongside me and placed its cool, smooth surface against the side of my belly. Again, it was quiet. But this time I wasn't worried. I knew everything was coming, that it was going to be fine. She slipped quickly behind me and, with the monitor pressed against the very bottom of my stomach, the baby's heartbeat filled the room. Almost as soon as it came, another contraction pulled down through me like a whirlpool. I dipped my face in the water, felt it lap against my hot and purple cheeks as something deep and elemental moved within me.

I felt a ripple and then a pop around my vagina. *Right*, I thought. *There it goes. I've ripped myself into shreds.* Too late.

"That's just the seal around the baby's head coming away," said Roisin from behind me. His head? His head.

As the next contraction came, I felt myself opening out, being pulled apart. Something slipped between my legs.

"Is he out?" I asked Nick, genuinely curious.

Amazingly, Nick managed not to laugh.

He was not—he was crowning.

"Can I push?" I asked, waiting to hear that my muscle, skin, and bones were ready for what was about to happen, that I wouldn't simply shred my vagina into tatters.

I held Nick's hands in my fists and, in the next contraction, with a rush of power, of joy, of relief and strength, I tensed my entire body. This was familiar, I thought. This was right. Not unlike a shit, of course, but somehow on a scale incomparable. With the next push came, amazingly, the baby's head.

"I can see his eyes," said Roisin, somewhere behind my arse.

Suddenly, with the next contraction, I felt limbs, corners, shoulders moving down through my body. I could actually feel my baby's body sliding through my bones and down, into the world. I heaved. The water slapped. There was a wave behind me.

"You can pick up your baby," Roisin said.

And there, between my legs, rising up to the surface of the water entirely alone, was a tiny, purple person. A baby. My baby. Still kneeling, I picked him up in the wet cross of my forearms and stared down in absolute wonder. I had done it. At last, I had done it.

A few seconds later, as I climbed out of the pool, still holding this baby, my son, against my chest, I heard the scissor clamp bang against the side of the pool. Nick politely declined to cut the cord, worrying that in the tiny, wriggling detail he might accidentally snip off his son's penis instead of severing the umbilical. And so Eliza did the honors. I shuffled over to the bed and lay back, my son's tiny, purple-gray, howling body resting against my pale, mountainous front. I knew that, when it came to breastfeeding and the placenta, speed was of the essence. And so I lined his nose up with my nipple, gently tilted back his head and, with his face stretched open in a roar of anguish, he miraculously latched on. A few minutes later, Roisin came around to my side and suggested we should try to pass the placenta. Still looking down into my baby's face, at his miraculous, full-cheeked sucking and tiny, bird-like shoulders, I felt Roisin press my stomach, tensed what was left of my core, and felt something like a great, smooth bean flop out from between my legs. That was it.

"Can you get Eliza to check it's all out?" I asked Nick.

"It's fine," he replied. "That's what they're doing now."

I was emptied. It was over.

By a miraculous stroke of luck, the recovery ward was full that day, while the birth center was relatively quiet, which meant that, for the twelve hours that I needed to be observed (because of the group B streptococcus), I was able to stay in the same, cozy, quiet room in which I had given birth. Those twelve hours went by in a strange, timeless stream, punctuated by visits from other medical staff, coming to check my blood pressure, temperature, the baby's heartbeat, joints, and hearing.

At one point Eliza quietly left, going home to have a glass of red wine and cheese toastie for breakfast in bed. I washed the blood off my legs and saw, amazed, as the last evidence of what I'd just done trickled down into the drain like a delta of little red rivers. I put on a huge pair of knickers and a sanitary towel like a single mattress. Nick, topless, held the baby while I ate a piece of warm buttered toast and drank a mug of sweet tea. The sun moved across the room and I sat, quietly, trying to understand what had happened.

The weirdest interlude was when my mother, unexpected and unannounced, somehow broke all birth center protocol and came into the room, dressed in a short velvet jacket and carrying a huge bag of food. Nick must have told her it was over, I thought blearily.

"I've made you a salmon and potato salad, darling," she said.

I stared at her, wondering if this was a hallucination. She might as well have been saying, "I've brought you a little 1983 Nissan fuel injection carburetor to assemble, darling." I had just spent two days in labor; I'd just pushed a living child out of my body; I was holding my new son against my heartbeat—how and why the fuck would I want to eat a salad? Now?

As the sun set, only Nick and I were left in the room, exhausted, amazed, hardly speaking. He dozed, the baby dozed. I sat there, amazed and bewildered by what had happened. We would be going home soon, I thought. They were going to let me and this tiny, helpless creature go out into the cold, autumn tang of real-world air. Nick and I had walked in there as two people, bound together by love and fear and need and thought. We were leaving as a family.

Twelve hours after finally giving birth, sixty-two hours after my first contraction, nine months after getting pregnant, I walked down the corridor, under the banana milkshake hospital lighting, holding my little baby son in a pink car seat, utterly transformed. Everything had changed. I had changed. Nothing would ever be the same.

17

MIDNIGHT FURY

It is 2:17 A.M. and I am imagining throwing my baby at the wall.

Now, I didn't say I was *planning* to. I didn't even say I wanted to. I merely said that—after two hours of walking up and down the length of my flat, in the dark, with a tiny, screaming, inconsolable body on my shoulders—I was thinking about throwing that body, forcefully, against the wall. My arms were locked, my swaying was gentle, but my mind was racing with violence and hot fury. I could imagine the feeling of weightlessness if I were to drop him, the release of energy as I threw him into the door frame, the rush of relief as I just let go.

For many, the decision to have a baby is one preoccupied by thoughts of pregnancy and labor. But if there is ever a moment from the Panic Years more likely to break your mind and body into useless shards of despair, it is the first few months of parenthood (if you are one of those people who chooses to have a child). The disorientation, pain, anger, sadness, jealousy, regret, and fear I had felt during heartbreak, while calculating my own vanishing fertility or when considering the terrain of my career, was a mere dress rehearsal for what was to hit me in those first few weeks after my son was born. There was inexpressible love and joy to come, thank god, but those happy, milky feelings were by no means the whole of it.

At three weeks old, a baby is often little more than a helpless, anguished spasm, a vacuum of such total dependence that it sucks in all the care and energy within its orbit. No matter how much love and attention you pour into them, they will remain confused, clingy, and concerned. It is evolutionary design, of course. Without the constant, aching, fearful attention of a mother, that baby would die. So babies must evoke their own pain, fear, and disorientation within their mother, in order that she may administer to their needs. They wake you up, they make your body ache with rocking, they scream murderously in your ear, and they breathe so quietly you become convinced they are dead. This is how they communicate to you their own aches, their sensitivity to noise, and their proximity to death.

As I padded up and down my flat, the baby wrapped in the very same white shawl in which my mother had once wrapped me, he howled like his entire body was being pulled inside out. And, whatever you may think as you try to hold a conversation over the screeching of a nearby infant in a pub, grit your teeth during a cacophonous train journey, or are woken in the night by a noisy newborn neighbor, it is as nothing compared to the howling of your own baby. That noise alone can tear you limb from limb. When their cries rip through the thick, coal-colored night air, unprovoked, unpredictable, it will feel like you've woken up inside an iron lung; you will shrill with fear and pain and fury as the pressure of that helpless wail pushes down on you, agitating your every muscle, your every nerve. And let me be quite plain here: newborn babies cry a lot.

According to the pediatrician Caroline Fertleman, "A perfectly healthy baby can cry up to twelve hours, pretty much nonstop." These little people are not fucking around. You may have friends, in-laws, even parents who will smile coyly and say things like, "Oh, my son didn't cry at all for the first two months," but, my friends, they are wrong. I'm not calling them liars, I'm not calling them idiots, I'm not calling them sadistic pricks slavering at the sick thrill of seeing an already broken mother lose her last drops of faith and resistance; I'm simply telling you they are wrong. They may have forgotten. They may be thinking of their baby at six months, when they could smile and sit up and gurgle unaided. Or they are under the blanket of parental amnesia that makes people willing to have more children. They may have had a nanny or grandparents or even a night nurse on hand, so they missed some of those unrelenting hours of grisly, whinging fraction that my heavenly midwife Dawn called "the witching hours." They may simply be lying to try to make parenthood seem more attractive. But, take it from me, newborn babies cry, and sometimes, often, that crying will tear through you like a fire and make you more furious than you have ever known.

On those nights I would sway, barefoot, past the armchair that proved too narrow to breastfeed in, the sheepskin dusted with baking soda to soak up that day's vomit, the changing table whose drawers hung with muslins and flannels like scraps of meat from an enormous mouth, the fruit bowl full of biscuit wrappers. I would reach our tiny kitchen, the smell of shit and disinfectant, the cold tiles, the flicker of bushes in the streetlights, and the washing-up bowl stacked high with drying porridge. Then I would turn blindly and, in the dark, walk back past dusty bookshelves, discarded socks, the pink and stained terry diapers, the onesies the play mat and the empty cups, until I reached our back door. And then I would turn, again, and head back to the kitchen, past armchair, sheepskin, changing table, and diaper bucket. Turn. Porridge, bushes, streetlights, cups. Turn. Bookshelves, diapers, armchair, socks. Turn. Biscuits, tiles, table, shit. It was endless. It was relentless. It was all-consuming. This is the part of parenthood we never see in films, rarely read about in books, hardly ever see on television and so are blindsided by when it hits. This is the part that my child-free friends—however heartfelt their intentions, however genuine their care—could not understand.

I would rock from side to side, doing full squats, wearing a pair of pajamas that made me look like a divan. I would *shhhhhh* like blood through a placenta. I winded, I whispered, I offered milk, I rubbed, I walked, and I rocked. I was still bleeding—the unused drops of postpregnancy uterus finally leaving my body—but my legs, arms, and back were becoming stronger than they'd ever been. As the fuzzy halogen glow of the streetlights bobbed under my wavering vision and tears poured down my face, I thought, and not for the first time, that this may all have been a terrible mistake. I wasn't sure I could do this. I was being pushed to the very edge of myself and I wasn't sure how long I could cling on.

Here is the crux at the very center of the Flux: whether you have a baby or whether you don't, there will be moments when you may regret what you've done. It is very likely that, at times, you'll worry that you made the wrong call. There will be a point at which you'll mourn the fact that you cannot go back and do things differently. If, for whatever reason, you walked a child-free path, there may well come a time, a relationship, a summer holiday, a Christmas, when you regret—even just temporarily—that you didn't have a kid. And yet to admit, as a parent, that you have regrets, have doubts, have times when you waver, is still somehow the greatest taboo of all.

Parents, particularly women, are supposed to express nothing but love, contentment, happiness, and pleasure in their new identity. The very act of producing a child is meant to scrub us clean of all those other, nastier, trickier emotions like anger and resentment. We are supposed to deny them, suppress them, ignore them, or reject them, putting in their place a plump and placid face of maternal certainty. This, I know, makes many people feel unable to ever embark on parenthood; they feel cowed by the pressure to become a secure, stable, authoritative figure. They see no place for themselves in this beige seascape of calm, nonconfrontational, easygoing, all-natural, baby-oriented bliss. But, my friends, I am here to tell you that to err is human, but to doubt, hate, regret, and despair is human too.

People, particularly men, get very uncomfortable when you talk about this sort of thing. A sort of choked, squirmy silence usually follows a woman's confession of anger, irritation, an urge to hurt or to abandon. It is ten times worse when that woman is also a mother.

Tell a stranger that last night you had to call out into the torn night air, "Take this baby off me before I punch him in the face," and they will laugh nervously, look away, and try to change the subject.

Reply to someone's casual "How's it all going?" with a "This morning I wanted to leave my child in a forest and walk away," and their face may fall.

Tweet something about how, during a difficult feed or bedtime, you occasionally imagine ripping planks of wood apart with your bare hands and bloody teeth, and unknown people across the world will start to pile in telling you that you sound dangerous and insane.

As my friend the journalist and mother Saima Mir put it to me, "People don't like to talk about the seething violence women feel. It's as if talking about it will make it appear in physical form." But, as we know, the very opposite is true. Talking about your violent feelings is the very best guard against becoming physically violent. And, believe me, women are angry. We feel rage and hatred and violence and ire coarse through our bodies probably as often as men; we long to fight and destroy and burn and ransack; we imagine destruction and suffering and death. The difference is that centuries of social conditioning encouraged men to vent their anger through codified and then industrialized violence through aggressive sports, through warfare, through beer-soaked punch-ups and petty abuses, while women were shamed and distrusted for expressing the same hunger. We have been taught that female anger is somehow unnatural, even "unwomanly." Which means that our rage becomes internalized, turns putrid, or warps into some other destructive, unhealthy emotion. Had I felt ashamed of my fury that night, as my child cried, then I would have hidden it. I would have kept it a dirty secret. I would have interpreted it as a sign that, perhaps, I was not fit to be a mother at all. I would have stuffed my rage down until, eventually, it would have exploded like a volcano under the sheer pressure of denial. Because it would have. Anger will always out, in the end.

Thank god, I didn't keep quiet. I have had enough of what psychiatrists call "intrusive thoughts" to understand the mechanics of imagining throwing your baby against a wall. I have had them as long as I can remember; at school I would imagine paper worksheets slicing across my eyeball or run little imagined films of myself crushing my fingers in the hall doors. The psychoanalytic explanation is that by imagining violence, releasing that fury in fantasy, giving your mind a dress rehearsal for what that act would look like, you are building a muscle of resistance. The more you allow yourself to feel those unconscious desires—to push a nail through your tongue, to plunge a knife into your best friend's neck, to push a stranger in front of a bus—the more chance you are giving your conscious mind to guard against the impulse. Your body gets a taste of the experience, while your mind guards against it. In basic terms, you need the practice. These visions may be, in part at least, simply the by-product of your brain's particular chemical balance. Others have blamed misfiring in the amygdala—the part of the brain we identify as controlling our "fight or flight" response.

To be honest, the causes of these thoughts are less interesting to me than the ways to cope with them. I have spent my life having moments of untold violence, cruelty, and danger flash through my mind, like slices of cinematic horror, and I have never, to this point, acted in violence toward anyone. I have also never jumped off the side of a ferry, watched my son be hit by a falling tree branch as I carry him in the sling, sat by as he climbed out of a high window, or cycled into the river with him strapped to the back of my bike. But by imagining these things, I have pricked my ears and sharpened my attention to his safety and to my fears, in order that I might keep us both safe. Admitting to and talking about your feelings of seething violence, catastrophic terror, and murderous rage is the greatest defense you have against acting upon them. It also makes you an invaluable ally to any other woman—parent or not—feeling, and fearing, the same urges.

So, as the sandy grit of exhaustion rubbed along my bones, the baby reared away from my offered breast like someone in an electric chair, and the weight of my responsibility settled like iron chain around my heart, I did what I have done so many times before and since: I rang my mother. Holding my tiny infant in the crook of my elbow, I waited for three rings until, like melted butter, there was her voice down the line. My mother.

"Mum, I can't do this," I moaned—my voice matching perfectly the grinding howl of my son's. "I can't do it. He won't stop crying and I just want to drop him."

Without a heartbeat, she replied, "Just wait there, love. I'm coming. I'll be there. Get Nick. Hand the baby to him and just wait."

At 2:17 in the morning, my mother, thirty-three years into this motherhood fiasco, was still willing to walk through the winter rain of night and soothe me. Of course she was. She had held and rocked and calmed me, endlessly, through the dark December nights of my own first month of life. She had cared for me until pushed to the point of collapse. And so we had built up a bond that went far beyond simple affection. I knew she was there for me, however and whenever I needed her. The umbilical cord may be cut at birth, but the scratchy tugging rope of incontinence, indigestion, and incomprehension that winds around a baby's first years keeps you, as a mother, at their side until, one day, they feel strong enough to push you away. That was why, at thirty-three, as a mother myself, I knew I could still turn to my own mum for help. Unlike marriage, unlike a contract, unlike a mortgage, parenthood is a lifelong commitment that you cannot ever truly undo. You may have your baby adopted, move out of the family home, or lose that child to illness or accident; your children may emigrate, ignore you, or run off to join the circus. But you will never completely go back to the person you were before you had them. At times, this creamy act of nurture feels more powerful than your own breathing. But sometimes it will feel like a punishment more cruel than war.

In the end, I told my mum not to come over. The spell of anguished loneliness had been broken just by hearing her voice. I had been pulled back from the precipice. So I went into our bedroom, a slim hardboard wall away from the hours of howling that had just occurred, to find my partner sleeping peacefully beneath our mountainous red duvet. He hadn't heard a sound.

As the baby screamed and I wept, I collapsed onto the bed by Nick's side and said, in a voice that scared even me in its flatness, "You have to take him. I can't do it anymore."

Four minutes later, Nick had changed the baby's nappy, put him in a sling, and rocked him back to sleep. Shit. It was shit. Two hours of existential hell and I had somehow failed to check for shit.

On the NHS website, there is a lovely page called, simply, "Soothing a Crying Baby." Under the calm blue banner that runs along the top of every page of that glorious site, they list the most common reasons a baby will cry: hunger, a dirty or wet nappy, tiredness, wanting a cuddle, wind, being too hot or too cold, boredom, overstimulation. You will, no doubt, have spotted the fun contradictions innate to any advice about child-rearing. Your baby may be either too hot or too cold—good luck guessing which! Your baby could be bored or overstimulated—who the hell knows! The truth is, the reasons for the daily, nightly, hourly fits of newborn crying are almost always impossible to guess, so you simply run through the whole gamut, your mind a blank haze of exhaustion and distress, until something works.

During those inordinately lonely, panicked hours you will be forced to confront the change in your identity. Like a ballet-dancer-turned-bodybuilder suddenly staring down at a pair of hoover-sized thighs and mahogany-varnished ankles, you have changed beyond recognition; only, in your case, you've gone from mere individual to lifesaving caregiver. It will feel like a loss of self, like grief, and to an extent it is. Your life will never be the same again. But it will change, lighten, hopefully become easier, less bewildering, and more rewarding.

You will also build up, through the constant feedback loop of pain, attention, and relief, a deep and all-powerful empathy between you and the baby that will serve you both for the rest of your life. The dance of action and reaction between parent and child is precisely what makes it hard to leave them in a handbag on a stranger's doorstep, and in turn, makes them wipe your bum when you become decrepit.

Finally, by fumbling, helpless and unthinking, through all the

possible causes of your baby's distress you are, unconsciously, building on your natural parenting instinct so, perhaps not next time but
eventually, you will get better at recognizing why they're crying. It
is as far from an exact science as it is possible to be, but somehow
most of us start to learn when our baby is crying from fear, or from
hunger, or from something else. You will also build up a fantastic,
strong, but porous carapace that lets you react to your child a little
more proportionally, to dial down the emergency response, to give
them the opportunity to calm down without your ministrations,
to know when something really is wrong and to react accordingly.
This, along with her primal, unshakeable ability to make me feel
better, was what my mother offered on that long, dark, milk night
of the soul. She was able to hear my crying, hear my son's crying,
and react like a mother, like a creator, like a savior.

You may be wondering why it took me so long to wake Nick. Why
I cried to my mother rather than woke my boyfriend. Why was I so
desperate to have a father for this child if I wasn't willing to involve
him in these crisis points? Ah, it's a good question. A big question.
Why could I not open up the vastness of my vulnerability to the man
I loved? Well, in practical terms, because I knew he had to wake up
for work in two hours and I didn't want him to be tired. This is one
of the many problems with the way we construct the working environment in our society—we take one parent away from their child in
order to earn money, while the other's work goes unpaid and, often,
unnoticed. One person's career stalls, while the other's takes prece-
dent. But truthfully? Because I was scared.

I was scared that, were I to expose Nick to the true howling weight
of what having a baby entailed, he would regret what we'd done. After
all those years of wrangling, persuading, and begging, he would see
me as responsible for what we'd got ourselves into. And so, powered
by a regret that I could so intimately understand, he would leave
me. Leave me with the baby. The wailing, longed-for, life-changing,
utterly helpless baby. Even at the very knife-edge of my own abil-

ity to cope, I was more scared of being abandoned than of being a danger. Because here's another thing that women are conditioned into believing: that you must bear your own burden entirely. Your baby, your health, your work: they are yours to deal with and yours to fix, alone. Along with the poisonous lie that female anger is unnatural, we are all too often made to believe showing too much of our raw selves—biological, emotional, psychological, historical—will turn people against you. Your abusive ex-partner, the creepy boss who keeps "accidentally" brushing his hand against your bum, your traumatic memory of watching someone hit your mother when you were eight years old, your anxiety disorder, your menstrual blood, your two hours of housework every evening, your reliance on antidepressants, your chin hairs, your nightmares about rats, your hunger for sex, your terror of cars: we are, in subtle and not-so-subtle ways, brought up to consider these things our own problems, "women's problems," and either too disgusting, "too heavy," too abstract, or too personal to expose to other people. And so we push men out of the orbit in which these things could be solved.

We don't tell them that what they're doing hurts. We don't ask them to hang up the towels or buy our tampons or wash their own cups. We don't call them in when our babies are crying. As Nick says himself, I took on the role of primary caregiver, I breastfed, I didn't have a full-time paid job to return to, I took the lead, even when perhaps I didn't need to.

"You're the one who decides everything," he said recently, when I asked if he had any regrets. "If we have a policy about when our son goes to bed, how we rock him, what soothes him, if he has lunch before or after a nap, you will primarily have decided that. You take on the mental load. I'm quite realistic about what we've lost. I had two jobs since having a baby where I wasn't really able to make good friends at work. I'm always tired. But I don't blame you."

So many cultural tropes center on the absent fathers, the men who walk away, work long hours, forget their children's birthdays, but so little is said about why. Even the term "daddy issues" is dismissive, used by men to describe their "mad" girlfriends, used by sleazy comedians to joke about their younger girlfriends, used by everyone to cover real and specific problems with a dishcloth of derision. Instead of which, we could be asking, why do men leave and how can we stop it? How can some people feel so distant, so uninvested, so alienated from their own children, their own relationship, their own lives, that they can walk away? It took me years in therapy to discover that, embedded in my own heart, there existed a knotty fear that showing any man too much of myself, too honestly, would scare him away. It took yet more time and more talking to unravel it.

The truth is that by "protecting" men from the grit and gristle, the sleeplessness and the screaming, the regret and reality, the fear and the failure of parenting, we might, eventually, close them off from it entirely. Which makes it infinitely easier to leave, once things take a tricky turn. I am by no means blaming mothers here—in many cases, the people who walk away are simply shits; in many cases women take on the burden of the mental and parenting load because they have been conditioned since childhood to do so; in a lot of cases parents are doing everything they can just to survive. But by putting on a brave face I was pushing my partner out from his own fatherhood.

He needed the sleepless nights, the inconsolable crying, and the fear in order to bond with his child, just as I had done. He needed to be driven to the very limit, in order that he could understand the heart of it. The process of becoming a parent isn't merely biological—it is knitted together from experience and emotion, some of which can be pretty unpleasant. Fathers need the beast, as well as the beauty of babies, otherwise their love will be a flaky one—too easily crumbled by absence, rejection, and misunderstanding.

The nights when Nick strapped our tiny baby to his chest, pulled on a coat, and walked up and down the swollen river by our flat in the soaking rain, bobbing and swaying, creating a shield out of his own body in which the baby could at last relax, made him a father. Just as the sleepless, restless, carpet-stumbling, and tearstained mornings of utter loneliness and exhaustion made me a mother. It was hard, at times it was hellish, at times I wondered if we had been right to board this train at all, but it bound us together in a load-bearing unit that can, with some luck and much effort, be considered a family.

18

SLOW LOVE

Two weeks after I brought my son home, folded into a white snowsuit twice his size, my friend Hayley turned up on my doorstep with a packet of washable breast pads, a small knitted doll, a bar of chocolate, and a single sanitary pad tied up with a ribbon. She'd had her own baby just six months earlier.

Before we'd even walked the length of my hallway, she asked, "So, do you like him yet?"

Pure relief flooded through my body like rain on a forest fire. She understood. She knew. She was asking me a question I could actually answer.

"I think I like him," I said, "but I'm not sure that I love him yet."

My tongue held fast in my mouth, a fox waiting for the sound of hounds. Maybe I'd misunderstood. Maybe I'd just admitted something terrible. Maybe I was about to be put on some sort of list.

"Love him?" said Hayley, her face breaking open into a huge smile. "It's only been two weeks: you barely know him!"

In that moment, I would have given Hayley all my major organs and my record collection too.

In the dead of night, as I'd listened to the soft gruntings of my tiny son and felt the volcanic adjustments in my body, I would turn to Nick, tears streaming down my face, my heart racing, and whisper, "I think I might love you more than the baby."

I felt awful. I felt broken. I became terrified that I had somehow accidentally misfired that initial rush of oxytocin, love, and infatuation onto Nick, instead of my infant son, like those ducklings that imprint on a goose or a wheelbarrow instead of their own mother. In the first few days of motherhood, I would find myself crying with gratitude at the thought of Nick's hands on my back during labor, or of his making me a cup of tea unasked. I would feel winded at the thought of this huge sacrifice I had brought into his life; about how he would have had to bring up our son alone if I'd died in childbirth; about the way he held his son against his naked chest while I showered. I would find myself pouring with tears, remembering the days we'd spent walking through the Black Forest drinking beer and eating hard cheese, the way he'd made me laugh on that first day in Calais, of our first date in Bethnal Green Travelodge, of camping at the bottom of Snowdon when I was newly pregnant.

"I used to worry about the pressure you were putting on yourself," says Nick, during dinner one evening when our son is a year old. "I didn't love our baby as much as I loved you, but why would I? I wasn't feeding him, I didn't birth him. I didn't have a big epiphany when I first saw him during labor, because that's not how I've ever had any emotions. I remember wanting everybody to leave the room because he was ours. I was precious about him—he was amazing and beautiful and tiny—and just wanted to take him home. But I didn't have the innate level of physical attachment you had. You were his primary caregiver, he was physically dependent on you to survive."

Even as I breastfed my son, rocked him to sleep, kissed his forehead, or watched his strange, jerking arms as he slept, I would be thinking of Nick, of my mother, of Eliza, or of my friends. I loved them, adored them, knew their laughs and walks and ways of slicing bread. Had shared my life with them, grown up with them, had wrapped their words around my bones to make me into a different person. I loved them because they were people with whom I could talk, share stories, laugh, and be surprised. But this person? This little twist of muscle and skin I called my son? He offered none of these things.

Although he was physically present, somehow it felt like he hadn't yet arrived; his great glassy eyes were unseeing, his mind was un-knowable, his soul—if such a thing exists—hung suspended else-where. I cared for his body, attended to his every need, felt wolfishly protective, but for the first six weeks, until he started to focus, smile, respond to my voice, have periods of waking that were not filled with howling anguish, I found it hard to know him. Let alone love him.

The Flux is defined by a seismic shift in identity caused by deci-sions, actions, and experiences during your twenties, thirties, and forties that sometimes feel beyond your control. Early motherhood falls squarely in the very heart of that category. Whether you ever intend to be a parent or not, that experience is worth knowing about. These parents walk among you; they make up the majority of the female population aged between twenty-eight and thirty-eight; they inhabit every corner of your life; they deserve our attention and our understanding. And if you are wondering whether to have a baby, it is important that you do so in full knowledge of how early mother-hood may affect your mind. You can watch *One Born Every Min-ute* or, if you are particularly stout-hearted, look up episiotomies on Google Images until the cows come home, in order to learn about the possible physical effects of parenthood. But to understand the other half of the picture—the internal, psychological, emotional af-termath—we have to shout above the din of diaper ads, parenting manuals, and toy shops to tell a different story. A more honest, more subtle, perhaps even more unsettling story.

According to a survey carried out by the National Childbirth Trust in 2017, 50 percent of mothers experience mental health problems at some time during pregnancy or within the first year of their child's birth. These can include postpartum depression, anxiety, obsessive-compulsive disorder, post-traumatic stress disorder, and postpartum psychosis. Fifty percent. That, for the mathematicians in the room, is half of them. One in every pair of women you've ever seen pulling their great pregnant bellies around with them in the street, bouncing a newborn baby in a café, or pushing a buggy onto the bus has experienced some sort of mental health problem. I knew this. I had a therapist. I was comfortable, willing, and prepared to talk about my feelings. But what I was feeling didn't bear the hallmarks of postnatal depression or even just regular old depression: I'd been in that lonely hole before, and this wasn't it. Of course, the hormonal component of postnatal mental illness is as bewilderingly under-researched as the effects of the contraceptive pill, and so it remains almost impossible to extricate your psychological experience from your biology and your circumstances. But I am not making a claim to postnatal mental illness here. I have no authority to judge what is a "normal" reaction to becoming a mother. I am simply saying that, when I looked into my baby's eyes for the first time, it did not feel like falling in love.

"I looked into his eyes but they were little black discs," says the performance artist and writer Bryony Kimmings, describing her first few days of motherhood to me, from her studio in Brighton. I first met Bryony when she was performing her show *Sex Idiot* at Soho Theatre. I immediately loved her, fancied her, wanted to be her and wear her clothes. As well as an artist, Bryony is now also a mother. Her most recent show, *I'm a Phoenix, Bitch*, is a quite remarkable telling of the year she spent fighting with postnatal illness, relationship breakdown, and the heartbreaking illness of her tiny son, Frank. Bryony, I knew, had ground against the flinty edge of postnatal mental illness back in 2016. I wanted to ask her, had she felt instant love toward her baby? Did she know what I meant when I said that I became a physical mother before an emotional one? Did her attachment grow like weeds or explode like a firework?

"I remember thinking in the first instance, *I'm so fucking glad I met you and you're not dead*," says Bryony, recalling her early moments of maternal life. "But I remember also having a conscious thought about how I was feeling, wondering if I was feeling enough."

Perhaps it is this acute consciousness of how we are feeling, and how we think we are meant to be feeling that I struggled with during those first few days. Unlike the other mothers in my WhatsApp groups, I wasn't able to simply gaze into my baby's cot for hours on end, as he slept or twitched or stared with those huge glassy gray eyes into the ether. My mind was racing with the logistics, the ticker tape of contingencies, duties, predictions, and decisions I felt running under every minute of my life in order for my son and I to simply stay alive. When I was going to eat, where I would put him to sleep, how I would clean up that puddle of sick while also changing his bedding, brushing my teeth, changing his diaper, doing skin-to-skin by holding his naked body against my own, snatching my own hour of sleep, listening out for his breath, stopping his crying, drinking a liter of water, washing my body, changing my breast pads, changing my sanitary pad changing his Babygro, which was now also, I realized, covered in sick. I also couldn't ever quiet the voice inside my mind that was constantly weighing up my performance of this new role we call The Mother. Had I held him for long enough this morning? Did I feel anything yet? Would I consider myself a good mother? Was this love? Did he feel like my son or just a baby? Would I save him from a fire or save myself? Have I dreamed of him yet? How long would it take me to recover if he died right now? And now? And how about now?

Once she got home, Bryony felt a creeping rise in anxiety, scared that something was going to happen to Frank, someone would take him away, she'd fuck up, she'd accidentally roll over and kill him. Now, this I remember. Before anything like adoration had slid between my bones, I already felt terror at something happening to my son. Perhaps more extreme than others, I pictured shelves suddenly hurling themselves off the wall and crushing his body as he lay, utterly helpless, in his cot. I imagined our flat being broken into, my baby being stabbed, his head getting crushed beneath a falling brick. I got twitchy about people walking into my house with their shoes on, people not washing their hands after going to the toilet, people not handing the baby back when he started crying.

In the twelve hours I was alone each day (Nick had to go back to work after a grand total of five days off), the catastrophic visions were as common as the "reasonable" ones. In that fight-or-flight, sleep-deprived, hormone-flooded, fragile first few days of a baby's life, a mother's mind is as likely to be as concerned with death and destruction as she is with tea bags and cotton wool. It is, for so many women, their living reality. And yet, by saying these things out loud, you somehow open yourself up to the judgment of other people. I felt able to tell Hayley, Nick, and my therapist that I had visions of leaving my son in a wood somewhere or of accidentally suffocating him in my sleep. But pick the wrong audience and, somehow, you start to sound mad.

Bryony, eventually, started to suspect that she was suffering from postnatal depression, and told her mum.

"I felt really panicked all the time. I wasn't able to sleep; I'd just watch over him," Bryony recalls. "Then I started to realize I wasn't completing tasks. I'm quite an organized person, but I'd walk around the house and realize I'd left a trail of unfinished things. Some of that was tiredness, but some of that was just that my brain was firing so much information that I felt overwhelmed all the time. A lot of it was, *You're a bad mum, you don't know what you're doing, Tim* [her partner] *hates you.* Eventually I started to realize, *Oh, I'm not very well.*"

There were elements to her thoughts and feelings that were, as Bryony says, closer to fantasy and psychosis than what we think of as depression. She was changing as a person, as so many new parents do, but she was also losing a grip on what was real and what was not.

"For example, there was definitely a pedophile that lived in my cupboard," she explains, absolutely serious. "And if I turned my back on Frank, he would take him away."

As her son grew, and became ill, the pace of change simply never gave Bryony a chance to catch up, and so, into the cracks there started to pour fear, fantasy, and paranoia.

"I don't think anybody tells you that your identity is going to change, that who and what's important is going to shift like that," says Bryony. "If I were to do it again, I'd let myself feel things. And I'd surround myself with people I felt comfortable having feelings in front of."

Women without number have gotten in touch with me since I wrote about my experiences of early motherhood in my *Vogue* column, to say that the way I presented and seemed to cope with those early months has changed the way they feel about doing it themselves. Getting pregnant just at the point when I was supposed to be starting my course to retrain as a teacher meant that I'd had to once again throw myself back into the world of freelance journalism with gusto. I pitched articles on pregnancy, sex, childbirth, breastfeeding, and social isolation to every women's magazine and every newspaper with whom I'd ever worked. Well, they do say to write what you know, and what with spending every waking hour of my day looking after a newborn, it wasn't like I had much headspace to write about anything else. Eventually, I was asked to write the column by a former colleague; someone I had known since university; someone who could make me howl with laughter just by describing a pork pie; a woman who doesn't have a baby and is, consequently, very interested in reading about this alternative reality going on all around her. Sometimes, I'm sure, my anecdotes about sleepless nights and wayward urine filled her with horror, other times with utter relief. Women pushing headlong through their Panic Years need to hear these stories; need to see that motherhood isn't all pastel home furnishings and picnics in the park. It might take you quite a long time to fall in love with your baby, you might feel a bit broken, you might not look like the other parents around you, you might want to go outside and run through the snow at dawn. Alternatively, you might just want to stay in bed all day and bond with your baby. You might get really horny. You might lose your libido altogether. You might feel frightened at the idea of leaving the house. You might want to walk out the door and keep on walking. Motherhood is an individual experience as well as a social construct. As new parents, and friends of new parents, we need to give this transformation room to breathe; need to accept that there is no single or right way to become a parent; give people room to tell you how they're feeling, even if it's uncomfortable; and take those feelings seriously.

Postnatal mental illness is so common (remember, half of all mothers) that it seems almost remarkable to me that 50 percent of women *don't* report any symptoms. In the maelstrom of hormones, sleep deprivation, physical pain, financial uncertainty, change to your relationships, social isolation, loss of structure, and stress that almost inevitably follows having a baby, it would be absurd not to undergo some serious change in your mental state. Both mothers and fathers. And yet we are at risk of losing sight of the fact that we need to find a cause and solution to these conditions. All too often, we are told that openness, talking about our feelings, and "reaching out" will be enough.

This is what my friend Hannah Jane Parkinson calls "the Conversation." In her excellent essay "It's Nothing Like a Broken Leg," about the mishandling of mental illness in mainstream culture and published in the *Guardian* in 2018, Hannah wrote that "In recent years the discussion around mental health has hit the mainstream. I call it the Conversation. The Conversation is dominated by positivity and the memeification of a battle won. It isn't a bad thing that we are all talking more about mental health; it would be silly to argue otherwise. But this does not mean it is not infuriating to come home from a secure hospital, suicidal, to a bunch of celebrity awareness-raising selfies and thousands of people saying that all you need to do is ask for help—when you've been asking for help and not getting it."

It is all very well to tell your loved ones that you feel absent in your own body, that you cannot hold on to the lines that bind you to real life, that you think about your baby dying with every breath, that you hear voices, that you see danger in every wrinkle in every blanket, that you feel blank, that you cannot sleep, or don't want to wake up. But talking about this counts for nothing if we do not also have the services, specialists, and social care to attend to such feelings and experiences.

I was very lucky; because I have experienced depression in the past, have a family history of panic attacks and anxiety, and was already in therapy, I was offered an extended period of supervision by my midwives. The wonderful Dawn came to my house and saw me at their clinic for a whole month after I'd given birth; most women are discharged after just ten days. Without this sort of aftercare I genuinely don't know how far I may have slipped away from myself and how that slipping could have affected my relationship with my son.

Across Britain, as a result of government cuts, the privatization of public services, and the mismanagement of our institutions, that sort of support has been pulled away from millions of parents. The reduction in the number of health visitors, the closure of Sure Start centers, the hemorrhaging of midwives at the peak of their career, the reduction in public transport particularly outside the wealthy South East, the introduction of universal credit leaving so many new parents unable to afford simple things like a bus fare to a health clinic: in so many ways, new parents and particularly new mothers are being failed by the system that is supposed to protect them.

I also know—from talking to maternity staff throughout the NHS—that those dedicated, educated, specialist caregivers are being failed by the very institution that is supposed to employ them. Everywhere you look, maternity services, care services, mental health services, and social services are stretched to the breaking point after years, if not decades, of ideological underfunding, privatization, and neglect.

Even if every new mother, when first looking into her baby's eyes, fell instantly and effortlessly in love, it wouldn't solve the underlying economic, social, and political issues that can make successful parenting impossible. But they don't. Many people, myself included, fall in love with their babies after considerable time, effort, and support. They do it when they're not forced back to work by a zero-hours contract and a low-income job. They do it when they have stable housing in which to spend those vital hours sitting, sleeping, lying, and interacting with their babies. They do it when they have support- ive, sympathetic people to talk to about their physical, mental, and emotional discomfort. They do it when they are able to concentrate on the phenomenal and, frankly, essential job of parenting. You can hear it every day and yet it still bears repeating: without parents, hu- manity wouldn't exist. Without parents, there would be economy, no society, no population, and no state. Without parents, we all would surely perish. So, surely, the economy, our society, and this state can give the greater part of their resources back to the nation's parents in order to support them. Both in their bodies and in their minds.

My love for my son grew slowly. As I picked a path through the utter chaos of his new existence, soothed his tears, woke up every hour through the night to feed him, held his body against my own, watched his skin flake off (it's a thing), his eyes get clearer, his limbs uncurl, I eventually found a way to love him. Duty became devotion. Need led to nurture. Commitment turned me tender. His constant need for milk, comfort, burping, and wiping kept me close. Closer than I have ever been and will ever be to another living being. I was there, every minute of his life, for months. He grew on me, literally. And yet, I did not lose myself entirely. The old Nell was still there, fighting to push through.

Just three weeks after giving birth I swam through ice at Ken- wood Ladies' Pond, as my mother stood on the other side of the fence, holding my son. As they bobbed up and down the gravel path mere meters away, and the crystals of frozen water rippled in my slipstream, I wondered, briefly, if the breast milk could freeze inside your tits. I wondered if he could breathe. I wondered if my womb would slip out of my body in the cold. But I also slid, utterly unbur- dened, through the biting, silky water. My body was a time-share now, I knew. Yet in that moment, it was my own. I was still myself.

19

SPILLED MILK

It takes quite some doing to squirt breast milk onto the window of the number 242 bus. It's even more impressive if you're not even on the bus at the time.

One morning when my son was nearly three months old, as I walked up a street with a rucksack that weighed about the same as a photocopier on my back, the baby started howling uncontrollably in his sling. It was the sort of grinding, rusty cry that will not stop until the baby is fed. Luckily, I was two and a half months into this new lactic life, and my tits were getting more fresh air than Bear Grylls. Thanks to decades of slowly peeling myself naked in the howling wind beside freezing brown rivers and growing up in a house where locked doors were just a rumor, I've never been particularly self-conscious about getting undressed in public. One of my earliest and clearest memories is standing in the gutter of Market Drayton market, stripped down to just a pair of white knickers, in front of a long and winding line for the T. O. Williams bakery, as my mother got me to try on a variety of tracksuits. It was the nineties, as you've probably gathered. I may have always felt toward my body the way a city feels toward its sewer system—a practical necessity that really should get sorted one day—but I am nevertheless fairly unfazed by the prospect of getting partially, or even totally, nude in front of strangers.

Which is how I found myself, standing in the middle of the street, hauling my tits out of the various layers, harnesses, and fastenings that now made up my wardrobe, without so much as a postage stamp for "modesty." I could feel the skin around my nipples rising into porridge-like lumps as the milk ducts started to fill; I could feel the great cuboid pressure of my breasts pushing against the fold-down strip of fabric at the front of my nursing bra; I could feel myself start to leak—two damp circles spreading across my front like ink drops. This whole business can be triggered not just by a suckling baby but also the sight of your baby, the thought of your baby, the sound of their crying, or, in my case and on one particularly memorable occasion, the sound of a honking goose. The moment I released my left breast from its upholstery, with a number 242 bus rolling mere meters past my foot, entirely full of commuters heading to work, a thin stream of breast milk, like a brilliant white firework, screeched through the air and sprayed itself lightly against the smash-resistant windowpane in front of me.

But wait, I hear you ask, how does it actually feel to breastfeed? Is it like doing a piss? Do your nipples hurt? Does it feel like relief, like hard work, like crying? Can you hear them swallow? Do you know how much they're drinking? Does it make you tired? Can you smell the milk?

Well, of course, it feels entirely unique to each and every person breastfeeding and each and every person being breastfed. I've known women with four children who had different experiences with each baby. I've known babies crack it immediately and others who take time to learn the knack. I've known women who'd planned to breast-feed all their lives and others who found the idea terrifying. I've also known women with double mastectomies who were never going to breastfeed and had to suffer the unnecessary opinions of strangers about the evils of bottle-feeding. I am not here to tell anyone how to feed their baby. I neither want nor have the right to judge anyone for how they use their body or raise their children. But I do think that breastfeeding is—like birth—a quite remarkable physical process that has been forced into corners by centuries of squeamishness, misogyny, and oppression.

Let's start from the beginning. I remember looking down at the metallic, creamy shine of colostrum falling from my nipple as I lay across that wipe-clean bed in the hospital and thinking how funny it was that something so precious would also happen to be gold and shiny. Colostrum—the first form of breast milk, which is usually present just after the birth—is thicker than regular breast milk and is full of antibodies, to protect the baby against the pox and filth of earthly life while they frantically try to grow an immune system. I knew that babies were supposed to be instinctively drawn to the smell of colostrum, and so, if you can manage to breastfeed during those first few minutes, you may find it easier than if you approach it later. And so, with my NCT teacher's words chiming through my exhausted mind like a bell, moments after the umbilical cord had been cut, I drew my baby's tiny, violet-colored nose up to my nipple and waited for his bud-like mouth to roar open. (This forced him to open his mouth wide enough to really sucker on properly). I'd been warned that it can take some time and was prepared to ask the midwives to watch. But, amazingly, he threw his head back like a Pez dispenser and, within a few seconds, seemed to be doing the do.

I was so awash with adrenaline, so overjoyed that I had given birth, and so completely disoriented by the previous forty-eight hours that I could barely feel what was happening in my breasts. I *did* have the wherewithal to notice that, thanks to his furrowed brow, thin hair, and swollen nose, the strange little person lying in my arms looked alarmingly like my father. As a result, I could barely watch. And yet, the gold kept flowing, my son's cheeks kept bulging, and I could hear little grunting swallows and feel this tiny birdlike form against my breast. My body had almost total jurisdiction over me that day, and the thin white ropes of milk emerging from my chest were already tying my baby to me.

And yet, breastfeeding is not as straightforward as so many advocates wish to present. I absolutely understand why they do, of course. Breastfeeding is a free, natural, healthy, packaging- and plastic-free, mobile, profound, and intimate way to feed your child. You never have to remember to pack anything, don't need to boil a kettle, there's no sterilizing, it bonds you to your child, and it helps protect them against getting ill. But I, a woman who was herself breastfed and wanted to breastfeed, was often pushed to the very limit of sanity, anxiety, patience, faith, and resilience by doing it.

When Nick first asked me what breastfeeding felt like, my initial answer was, "sad." Not because I disliked it or because it hurt—years of jogging, cold swimming, and inexpert foreplay appear to have toughened my nipples into the mammary equivalent of punching bags—but because each time I felt my son latch on and the milk begin to flow, I felt a lonely, homesick sort of sadness wash through my body. It lasted only a couple of seconds, but it was palpable.

The cause was something known as D-MER or dysphoric milk ejection reflex, and it is thought to be linked to the dip in dopamine levels that allow the body to release prolactin and for your milk to "let down." I was extremely lucky in that breastfeeding never quite hurt me in the stubbed toe, reopened cut, raw blister, split skin way that I know it can hurt. My nipples did not crack, and later on, his many teeth did not get in the way or sink through my tender flesh. But all that can happen.

Women have variously described the feeling of breastfeeding to me since as "like scratching sunburn," "a binder clip on your breast," or "having your nipple shut in a hinge door." I bow down to these women, who valiantly pursued breastfeeding right through the pain, the infections, the cracked nipples, the mastitis, the tears, and the tearing. I also recognize that, as they say, hearing such descriptions and how much other women struggled may have made them feel less like, as one person put it to me, "the only woman in the world whose body didn't know how to be a mother."

If I were to try and explain breastfeeding to someone who has never done it, I would say that, in those early days particularly, it is a not-unfamiliar pull of pure relief. Each time my son would latch on to my swollen, lumpy, throbbing breasts and the milk would start to pour out of my body and into his, it was like the greatest coalescence of every tiny physical pleasure you've ever known: the release of a held-in wee, the pop of your ears when going through a change in air pressure, pulling out an ingrown hair, the lapse into unconsciousness after a long day. I would also, simultaneously, be gripped by a slaking, roaring, inescapable thirst like nothing I've known on earth. I would feel like a clay pot, cracked open, dusty, and burned.

My son also developed an interesting habit of pulling away, screaming, or failing to latch on if I sat still while trying to feed. Many is the time I have sat in a café, on a bus, or around a dinner table, both breasts fully on display, hanging in the air like an unanswered question, as my son moaned, wriggled, and flailed in my arms. I would sometimes apologize to my friends, especially the ones without babies, for this unsolicited titty show, aware that the act of breastfeeding, probably more than any other, now marked us out as different. I didn't worry that they would be offended by the sight of three square inches of naked skin—they're not seventeenth-century monks. But while we could usually pretend that our lives and friendship hadn't really changed, joking and talking as my son slept or burbled on my lap, the moment I pulled out one of my tits and started feeding a tiny mammal, it was hard not to accept that our lives were now quite different. That things had diverged. But, as is so often the case, I needn't have worried. Good friends will see you through.

One afternoon, I met my friend Eleanor in a café after my son had taken an uncharacteristically long nap. My one breast was so engorged (swollen with unused milk) I got her to touch it, in the middle of the queue for banana bread, and feel its texture.

"Fuck me," she shouted, her hand up my shirt. "It's like a concrete brain."

Despite trying over, and over again, my son never took a bottle. I can still taste the fury when, after spending an hour pumping away at my breasts like a pink and agitated bagpiper, my son would resolutely refuse to drink a drop. If I were to ever mother again, my god would I get that baby to drink from a bottle. Without it, I was locked in, day and night, to every single feed my son has ever had for eighteen months and counting. Until he was about nine months old and could finally eat food to keep him going, I was physically unable to be away from my baby for any longer than four hours at a time. I was utterly tethered to him and he to me. I couldn't go for a walk, let alone go to work. I was up all night, every night. At three A.M., when I'd been awake since seven A.M. the day before, when I was ill, when my child was crying, when I was crying, my partner still could not feed the baby. And so I would have to get up. I would have to feed our son, come what may. Nine months after giving birth, I still hadn't slept for more than two hours at a time. Most days I existed on five hours of broken sleep. I was exhausted, I was resentful, I was unable to remember words, speak in sentences, or form new memories. And yet, my body kept making milk. It kept going. I kept getting my tits out.

I have breastfed on packed trains, in busy pubs, sitting on a log in the middle of Epping Forest surrounded by fallen autumn leaves, in supermarkets, outside public toilets, on the 55 bus overlooked by disinterested schoolchildren, beside the Parthenon Marbles, beside the Mersey, halfway up Scafell, in BBC greenrooms, during therapy, on football pitches, and even during an early meeting with the editor of this book.

In order to feed my son, I've gotten my boobs out in front of bosses, builders, businessmen, ex-boyfriends, bus drivers, rude boys, and rabbis. I've done it across England, in France, in fancy restaurants, and standing up in museums. I've breastfed on the tube, while opening the door to the postman, sitting outside men's toilets, in libraries, while signing a tenancy agreement, at the swimming pool, in a private member's club, at a funeral, at weddings, under a decorative plate painted with a portrait of a bulldog, on friends' beds, in the snow, beside waterfalls, beside highways, while working, in the dead of night, at the cinema, on park benches, in the *Guardian* canteen, on a barge, at birthday parties, in a bikini, and in front of Diane Abbott.

One memorable occasion, I was on a train through Runcorn when about four hundred football supporters got on. My train car was suddenly full of men in red tops and scarves, drinking cans, shouting, chanting, cheering. In the heat and noise, my one-year-old son became fractious and started crying. Without thinking, I laid him across my bicep, undid my top, and got my tits out to feed. Suddenly, unexpectedly, a bubble of quiet emerged around me. Women tilted their heads and smiled, the football men looked down at me and smiled, the shouting stopped, my son's crying stopped. Somehow the bubble grew until the whole carriage was held in a strange state of milky sleepiness. I could hear the carriages on either side roar with laughter and banter and the crack of beers being opened, but around me all was calm.

As soon as we got into Liverpool Lime Street, the spell was broken and the red army poured out, slapping shoulders, shouting insults, holding up scarves. But in that moment, it was magic. Truly, in the eighteen months I've been breastfeeding my son I have never once encountered anything but kindness, help, or sheer disinterest in those around me. I've had strangers hold my baby while I do up my bra, had my son's feet tickled midfeed by old ladies in beige raincoats, been offered drinks by joggers running past me as I fed in the park. Once, on the 38 bus, an old and toothless Korean man adjusted my baby's hat as I breastfed beside him, before digging into the carrier bags at his feet and pulling out a box of red ginseng sweets.

He offered me one, ate one himself, pointed at the baby, and said, "Good milk. Good baby."

The sweet tasted of pure soil and the man's fingers were stained highlighter yellow from smoking, but I have rarely been so uplifted by an encounter with a stranger, nor so reassured by the way so many men seem utterly unfazed by this supposed "taboo."

According to UNICEF, the UK has some of the lowest breastfeeding rates in the entire world. But, as they write, "It is time to stop laying the blame for the UK's low breastfeeding rates in the laps of individual women and instead acknowledge that this is a public health imperative for which government, policy makers, communities and families all share responsibility."

In this country, eight out of ten women stop breastfeeding before they want to. In some cases, as with many of my friends, that is because they are forced to return to full-time, nonflexible work away from home the moment their maternity leave finishes. Some of them valiantly pumped away at their desk, in the disabled toilets, in prayer rooms, storing their breast milk up in the office fridge to take home, so a babysitter, partner, nanny, or nursery worker could continue to feed their child breast milk the next day. Others used formula; a few went back to work after a year, when you can start giving a baby straight cow's milk.

According to the last UK-wide Infant Feeding Survey, conducted in 2010, increasing the number of babies who are breastfed could cut the incidence of common childhood illnesses such as ear, chest, and gut infections and save the NHS up to £50 million each year. But it's not enough to just tell women how good breastfeeding is for their baby, for them, for society at large. It's no use me telling you how much I loved it and still love it. Women who struggle to breastfeed— myself included—already feel ashamed, guilty, angry, and insecure enough without the weight of public disapproval washing across their stretched and sorry bodies.

I wish just one of the MPs who vote in favor of cuts to health and social services could have come with me, one cold Wednesday day, to the Daubeney Children's Center in Hackney, as I turned up tearstained, wretched, and panicked at their weekly breastfeeding café. I wish those MPs could have seen the way the person who ran it took me in her arms, stroked my hair, and told me it was all going to be okay. I wish just one of them could take the time she took that day to watch my feeding son, squeeze his chubby little legs, pull out a well-thumbed textbook, and read out to me the facts about weight gain with exclusively breastfed babies. If they could take that time to think about the millions of women in this country living in poverty, miles from any form of social support, terrified and guilty that they are somehow failing their babies, and all so the government can ask the wealthiest and greediest members of society for just a little less tax.

It is thirty-eight years since Harriet Harman breastfed her daughter in the House of Commons—an act of courage and rebellion that was passed down to me by my own mother like antibodies against the patriarchy. And yet there still lingers a very real fear among women, even new mothers, of taking up room with their baby. Of "imposing" the breathing, drinking, moving, eating, shitting reality of human life upon innocent bystanders, on "real" people. It made my heart soar to see New Zealand prime minister Jacinda Ardern play with her baby at the UN General Assembly but also ache with sadness that such a sight—a high-powered woman adapting her environment to fit the demands of mothering—was still such a rarity.

Whether a parent is breastfeeding, bottle-feeding, or both, they must feed their baby. For nearly two years I fed my son anywhere, everywhere, and in whatever way I could. As a woman in the world, it is now my job to support other feeding parents as much as I can: to offer them a glass of water, give them my seat, hold their coat, meet their eye. These little acts of humanity make us feel better, but they will also start to bring parents back into the fabric of everyday life. They will bridge the gap between those who have and have not had babies. They will, at the very least, give those on either end of the Flux somewhere to meet in the middle.

20

MISTAKEN IDENTITY

The Panic Years are defined by decisions: questions that seem impossible to answer, choices that feel like no choice at all. There will be decisions about work, love, and friendship; about money, family, and home; about sex, power, and your body. All are wrought more urgent by the big decision, the mother of all decisions, the only decision that has a biological deadline: Should you have a baby?

But nestled in the heart of the Panic Years is a conundrum. You can never know what having a baby will be like unless you have a baby. You, specifically, and your baby. Because that experience will be tangibly and necessarily different to every other parent's experience of every other baby there has ever been. You can look to your parents, talk to your colleagues, observe your peers, but you can never climb into the skin of it, feel the weight of it, taste the flavor of it, without doing it yourself. And yet, unlike many of the other decisions innate to the Flux, if you do decide to have a baby and are lucky enough to get pregnant, you can never go back across that Rubicon. Unlike a change in job, a change in partner, or a change in marital status, it is the act that cannot be undone. Your life will be changed, permanently. And, whichever path you take—through choice or circumstance or a combination of the two—you will never be able to know what your life would have been like if you'd taken another. You will never know if it was the right choice because, and this is almost impossible to bear, there is no right choice. There is just the choice you made and, on the other side, the absolute unknown.

Having a baby, I now know, can do wild things to your sense of identity. Within days you have gone from city center work meetings to seven straight hours of feeding on a circular cushion designed to stop hemorrhoids. Where once you may have scrolled through Instagram for half an hour during the bus ride to work, you are now standing entirely naked under the verruca glare of your local rec center, wondering exactly how you're meant to dress an incontinent, nonverbal pudding for a swimming class. While most of your friends are still asleep, you are walking through the inky streets at 4:47 A.M. hoping that the cold air will finally send your child to sleep. There will be days when the only people you see during daylight are those collecting your bins. You will have to remember fourteen different appointments—midwife, health visitor, nursery open house, doctor, hearing unit, town registry, NCT group—in a single week, with no short-term memory and nobody to remind you. You will become one of the daytime people: the slow-moving crowd of the retired, unemployed, shift-working, and chronically ill who move between libraries, doctor's offices, cafés, parks, bus stops, shops, and benches. You will put a wash on every day and get on first-name terms with an eighteen-year-old man who works at your local pharmacy. You will walk up to total strangers in parks and ask them how old their child is, how their night was, if they live near here, and would they per-haps like to go for a cup of tea, maybe share a flapjack, and, what the hell, be your new friend? You will wear flat boots and jangle your keys as you approach the door saying, "Here we are!" in a singsong voice that seems to come from someone else entirely. Where once you carried a debit card and lip balm, your pockets will now be full of damp bibs, half-eaten packets of oatcakes, a Playmobil police-woman, two apple cores, a rattle, a teething ring, a tube of lanolin, a chocolate wrapper, a small fluffy hedgehog, two wooden bricks, a bottle of water, and a dirty wet wipe. At times, you will not know yourself. But you are still there. I promise.

Today, as I sit at my kitchen table, the milky dawn of five A.M. spreading through my flat like fog, a ten-pound Ikea high chair at my elbow and picture of my son on the wall in front of me, I am something that has been years in the making. I am now a mother. And yet, I am also recalling, slowly, the Nell I was at twenty-five, at fifteen, at nine. As my body returns to its former chunks and corners, as my son begins to sleep for longer at night and feed less during the day, as my ability to form memories and remember phrases returns, so I am finally remembering, like the smell of an ex's perfume, who I am. Not in a grandiose, I've-hiked-through-Death-Valley-and-have-stared-into-the-abyss-of-my-very-soul way. Simply that, as the constant deluge of logistics and contingencies for survival starts to ease, I am remembering the minutiae, the daily details, the prosaic truth of who I am, always was, and hope to be. It is, if you like, the sister feeling to rediscovering yourself after heartbreak: part memory, part effort, part hope.

When my son plays in his sandbox in the garden for half an hour, and I am able to chop vegetables for dinner while listening to the radio; when he goes to bed at six thirty P.M. and I use his Play-Doh spatulas to push some new grout around the bathroom tiles; when my boyfriend wheels him to sleep in the buggy and I run to the lido for a quick swim in the rain; when I tell an entire anecdote from beginning to end without getting one of my tits out; when I am able to eat a sandwich, sitting on the back step, alone: this is when I catch a handful of my old, my new, my true identity. Motherhood is permanent, irreversible, and life-changing. But rather than emerging from the Flux as a different, unrecognizable person, I am instead looking at a woman who has merely shifted one quarter turn to the right, slipped into an adjacent gear, moved into a different area of focus in the viewfinder.

Once the dust and drama of heartbreak, dating, work, pregnancy, friendship, and parenthood during my Flux began to settle, I could finally see far enough around me to recognize how much of my life was still familiar. The boiled eggs and hand-me-down bedding, the bad puns and high libido, the early mornings, hard thighs, love of company, hunger, impatience, saddle marks, and overthinking. It's all there. It was always there. But not as it was. Nor ever to be again.

What's more, my Panic Years are not quite done. I may be able to see the arc of my Flux with the ringing clarity of hindsight, but it is not yet over. Like Janus, I am looking back at the disorientation, distractions, and distress of heartbreak, chaos, work, singledom, and motherhood. But I'm simultaneously looking forward, asking if I could ever do this again. If I could sacrifice the slivers of freedom I have woven back together from my life. If I am ready to drag my partner once again across the mountains of doubt, fear, reluctance, and logic in order to make him agree to having another baby. If I am willing to postpone my career, my lucidity, my ability to form sentences and hold conversations for another year, maybe two, just when things seemed to be getting back on track. If I'm able to push my body through the herculean task of motherhood once more.

I'm still looking around me at the single friends, the married couples, the contemporaries with two kids, three kids, or no kids, the wealthy bosses, the hopeless romantics, the people who have left Britain, left their boyfriend, fallen in love, or changed career and I am still wondering: Where do I fit in?

Is this the time to concentrate on my career, on money, on picking up my place in the kinetic, competitive, self-interested world of work?

Or is this the time to pour every inch of my time and attention onto this small, blond, bubble-bellied person I have made?

Is this the time to uproot everything and move to a small Hebridean island where I can teach my son how to shear sheep with a pair of clippers and grow rhubarb in an old chimney pot?

Or should I throw it all against the wall and have an affair with a twenty-four-year-old social media manager who wears a thumb ring and pronounces his haitches?

Was this my one chance at motherhood or just the beginning? Was that my career or is this my big break? Have I finished or just got going?

The humming, debilitating mass of decisions may have moved on, changed shape, even loosened slightly, but I am still vulnerable to the panic. I can still be undone by somebody else's twelve-week scan, promotion, wedding ring, or stubble rash. Everything has changed and yet the same old feelings are still there.

Without the chaos and the loss, the fury and the fear, the depravity and the reckoning, the dependence and the hope, I would not be here now. I would not have what I have. I would not have once eaten the entire Bella Pasta Valentine's Day menu alone, I would not have slept under the stars on the Isle of Mull after a dinner of cold rice and oatcakes, I would not have had sex beside the outdoor pool of a man who looked like a horse, I would not have visited the only working windmill that is also a suburban traffic island, I would not have told a man I loved him while surrounded by my own menstrual blood, I would not have spent a summer living beside Görlitzer Park eating ice cream designed to look like spaghetti bolognese, I would not have accidentally grabbed a baby's elbow inside my own body and felt him punch me back, I would not have watched a pair of dirty pants slide out the bottom of my boyfriend's trouser leg during our first postnatal midwife visit, I would not have stockpiled eleven bottles of Calpol in anticipation of Brexit, I would not have written this book.

On my thirty-fourth birthday, I woke up under the milky dictatorship of a hot-cheeked, toy-chewing, damp-bib incarnation of love. In the pitch black, I scraped past bikes, discarded shoes, and a miniature plastic piano to lift my hot cotton prawn of a one-year-old from his bed and kiss his wet, roaring face. While heartbreak, career change, single life, marriage, and pregnancy can be, in themselves, transformative, the challenges, the irreversible changes, and the bitter joys that characterized my Flux continued once I'd had a baby, and once that baby had become a baby and not just a gray-eyed raisin.

The Panic Years were not ceased by the arrival of a partner, a pregnancy, or even a child. The conflict created by a finite but unknowable fertility, the social conditioning that urges women to fight for everything but to compromise anything, the sexism facilitated by modern employment, housing, and childcare, the injustice of contraception and the civil war between mind and body are not washed away in a wave of amniotic fluid.

In my case, the Panic Years were provoked, propelled, and eventually placated by three extremely unremarkable realizations. They are the kind of thing you can find printed on a tea towel at a seaside town. They are the kind of wisdom you can find for £2.99 in a gift shop, beside the mustache mugs and novelty toilet paper. They're the stuff of key rings. And yet, once worked through, once unpicked during hours of interrogation, experience, and thought, they quite literally changed my life. They might not change yours, of course, but here they are.

Firstly, that I have innate worth. I am allowed to want what I want, I deserve love, I can ask for help and expect to be treated as more than a bit part in the lives of people around me. Just by dint of being a living person, with an interior life, a past, feelings, and thoughts, I have as much worth as anyone else; and I can honor that worth by being honest about my interior life, my past, my thoughts, and my feelings.

Secondly, that wanting a baby is valid, acceptable, maybe even commonplace, but admitting how much you want a baby will make you feel extremely vulnerable. It will open you up to the reality of desire, of loss, of dependence, of hope that is sometimes hard to bear.

Finally, that all humans are interdependent; that we need interdependence in order to survive and so interdependence is not a dirty word. It is how society functions, how we exist, what keeps us going. Showing someone you love that you also depend on them will not drive, scare, or push them away; it will simply encourage them to depend on you in return. Whether that is a partner, a baby, or a friend. This is how bonds are made. This is how we live.

My entire Flux has been pushed forward by the slow, repetitive, maddening unraveling of these three knots. I cannot do it for you. I cannot pour these realizations into your body or weave them through your mind. I cannot teach you a single thing, in fact. But hopefully with this, this document of my Flux, these missives from the Panic Years, this tapestry of where I've been, I can force you to confront the questions. They will arrive in your life like a knock at the door, in the middle of the night, a force to be reckoned with: Who are you and what do you want? Asking them will tear you apart. But answering them will knit you back together. Good luck. I'm rooting for you.

ACKNOWLEDGMENTS

Firstly, I would like to fulfill a promise I made aged thirteen, to dedicate my first book to Alastair White: the best English teacher I ever had.

I would like to thank Darcy Nicholson for being midwife to this, my ninety-thousand-word son. What an editor. What a woman. Thank you to Jon Elek for helping me realize the idea in the first place. Thank you to Zoe for bearing my impatience, my nerves, and my irritating habit of sending WhatsApp messages before six A.M. Thank you, Rosa Schierenberg for being my champion.

To all the people who made this book possible by sharing their stories with me: Eleanor Morgan, Terri White, George Monbiot, Ellie Davey, Dolly Alderton, Freddy McConnell, Rebecca Holman, Vicky Spratt, Bryony Kimmings, Alice and Stevo Williams, Saima Mir, Amy Liptrot, Becky Barnicoat, Hayley Hatton, Raphi Randall, and the legendary Jane Smith. You are all so generous and so inspiring and I am very lucky to know you.

To everyone who contacted me privately, on Twitter, by email, and occasionally in the street, to share their poignant, honest, and illuminating experiences, many of which have found their way into this book. I won't name you, but know I appreciate you.

To Nick Scott: my best friend and my lieutenant, forever and always. To Eliza, for supporting me in pregnancy, birth, and a childhood of snazzy outfits. To Olivia Marks, for the wild move of making me a *Vogue* columnist. To Rob and Sarah Delaney for all their support in work and motherhood.

Thank you to my sister, Anna, for a lifetime of compassion and silliness. Thank you to the Auntie Army: Tonie, Jess, Molly, and Alice. God knows how I would have survived without you. Thank you, Caroline, for all those mornings you let me escape, and for being a nana extraordinaire. Thank you to my NCT mums for keeping me on the rails during that first whirlwind year. Thank you to Homerton Hospital, the Fountayne Road midwife team, the Hackney Children's Centers, and the Round Chapel for looking after my son: long live the NHS and long live social care.

Thank you to Transworld: to Ella Horne for her marketing help, to Becky Short for selling my ass so elegantly, and to Beci Kelly for her smasher of a cover. And thank you to Sophie Christopher; I wish you were here now, to read this final version.

Thank you to Nick Stanton. You are the rush between my heartbeats, the space between my skeleton, the love of my life.

Finally, thank you to my poor, long-suffering parents. I will never be able to thank you enough. I'll probably never apologize enough either. But, suffice to say, none of this would have happened without you. Thank god you made such a cock-up all those years ago. You are great parents. And superb grandparents.

NOTES

INTRODUCTION

8   "The decision to dynamite the foundations": Luke Turner, *Out of the Woods: A Memoir* (London: Orion Publishing Group, 2019).

1. SUDDENLY SINGLE

17   "freedom is just another word for nothing left to lose": "Me and Bobby McGee," lyrics by Fred L. Foster and Kris Kristofferson.

19   A survey carried out by Nationwide: Annie Lord, "How Long Is the Average Millennial Relationship?" *Vice*, October 6, 2017. https://www .vice.com/en_uk/article/wjxy74/how-long-is-the-average-millennial -relationship.

20   "Solving that question brings the priest": Philip Larkin, "Days" from *The Whitsun Weddings* (London: Faber & Faber, Ltd., 1964).

2. LET'S GO OUTSIDE

24   I was crying like a fire in the sun: "It's All Over Now Baby Blue," lyrics by Bob Dylan.

25   any difference between the sexes isn't so much biological as one of conditioning: Daniel Bergner, *What Do Women Want: Adventures in the Science of Female Desire* (New York: Ecco, 2013).

26   *Fifty Shades of Grey* became the single biggest-selling book: Zoe Williams, "Why Women Love *Fifty Shades of Grey*," *The Guardian*, July 6, 2012. https://www.theguardian.com/books/2012/jul/06/why-women-love -fifty-shades-grey.

29   make the best of a bad situation: "Making the Best of a Bad Situation," lyrics by Millie Jackson.

3. A FRIEND IN TROUBLE

43   According to the Office for National Statistics: Office for National Statistics, "Childbearing for Women Born in Different Years, England and Wales: 2016," November 24, 2017. https://www.ons.gov.uk/people populationandcommunity/birthsdeathsandmarriages/conceptionand fertilityrates/bulletins/childbearingforwomenbornindifferentyears englandandwales/2016.

45   found that after one of the women in each friendship: Nicoletta Balbo and Nicola Barban, "Does Fertility Behavior Spread Among Friends?," *American Sociological Review*, vol. 79(3) (2014), pp. 412–431.

46   renowned professor of philosophy and cognitive science at Yale University: L. A. Paul, "Transformative Choice: Discussion and Replies," *Res Philosophica*, vol. 92(2) (2015), pp. 473–545.

4. GLASS BABY

49   a hollow, handblown glass baby the size: *Not Alone* exhibition by Jennifer Rubell, shown at the Stephen Friedman Gallery, September 4– October 2, 2015.

53   I'd read the list of demands drawn up during that first conference: Sisterhood and After Research Team, "Women's Liberation: A National Movement," March 8, 2013. https://www.bl.uk/sisterhood/articles /womens-liberation-a-national-movement.

54   If I worked, I would almost certainly earn less: In 2015 the gender pay gap was 19.2 percent according to the government report. Parliament, House of Commons, Women and Equalities Committee (2016) *Gender Pay Gap: Second Report of Session 2015–16*. HC 584. https:// publications.parliament.uk/pa/cm201516/cmselect/cmwomeq/584/584.pdf.

55   My local authority nursery charges forty-three pounds: Hackney Learning Trust, "Hackney Children's Centre Nursery Fees from 1st September 2019." https://www.learningtrust.co.uk/sites/default/files /document/Childrens%20Centre%20Nursery%20Fees.pdf.

55 In the UK, the average cost of sending a child: The Money Advice Service, "Average Childcare Costs." https://www.moneyadviceservice.org.uk/en /articles/childcare-costs.

5. BIG THREE OH

65 According to the latest UN global estimates: WHO, UNICEF, UNFPA, World Bank Group and the United Nations Population Division, *Trends in Maternal Mortality: 1990–2015*. https://www.who.int/reproductive health/publications/monitoring/maternal-mortality-2015/en/

68 "Rarely mentioned is the source of the data": Jean M. Twenge, "How Long Can You Wait to Have a Baby?," *The Atlantic*, July–August 2013 issue. https://www.theatlantic.com/magazine/archive/2013/07/how-long -can-you-wait-to-have-a-baby/309374/

68 using data from 782 couples: D. B. Dunson, D. D. Baird, and B. Colombo, "Increased Infertility with Age in Men and Women," *Obstetrics and Gynaecology*, January 2004. https://www.ncbi.nlm.nih.gov /pubmed/14704244

69 "Beyond the fact that older men tend to have older female partners": I. D. Harris, C. Fronczak, L. Roth, and R. B. Meacham, "Fertility and the Aging Male," *Reviews in Urology*, 2011. https://www.ncbi.nlm.nih.gov /pubmed/22232567

69 about 10 percent of people will miscarry: *BMJ* 2019 364:l869, "Role of Maternal Age and Pregnancy History in Risk of Miscarriage: Prospective Register Based Study," March 20, 2019. https://www.bmj.com /content/364/bmj.l869

70 between 2014 and 2016, the percentage of IVF treatments: National Health Service, "Overview: IVF." https://www.nhs.uk/conditions/ivf/

6. PARENT TRAP

77 According to figures compiled by Medicare for Australia: Meka Beresford, "54 Transgender Men Have Given Birth in Australia This Year," *PinkNews*, July 12, 2017. https://www.pinknews.co.uk/2017/07/12/54 -transgender-men-have-given-birth-in-australia-this-year/

83 Rob Delaney once argued: Amanda Holpuch, "Rob Delaney: Men in Their 20s Are the Worst Thing Happening on Our Planet," *The Guardian*, June 12, 2013. https://www.theguardian.com/culture/2013/jun/12/rob-delaney-interview

83 "They fuck you up, your mum and dad": Philip Larkin, "This Be the Verse," *High Windows* (London: Faber & Faber, 2015).

7. DING-DONG

89 by 2016, 50.9 percent of British people: Office for National Statistics, "Population Estimates by Marital Status and Living Arrangements, England and Wales: 2002 to 2016," July 13, 2017. https://www.ons.gov.uk/peoplepopulationandcommunity/populationandmigration/populationestimates/bulletins/populationestimatesbymaritalstatusandlivingarrangements/2002to2016

92 there were 249,793 marriages in England and Wales in 2016: Office for National Statistics, "Marriages in England and Wales: 2016," March 28, 2019. https://www.ons.gov.uk/peoplepopulationandcommunity/birthsdeathsandmarriages/marriagecohabitationandcivilpartnerships/bulletins/marriagesinenglandandwalesprovisional/2016

92 half of UK marriages end in divorce: Office for National Statistics, "Marriages in England and Wales: 2016," March 28, 2019. https://www.ons.gov.uk/peoplepopulationandcommunity/birthsdeathsandmarriages/marriagecohabitationandcivilpartnerships/bulletins/marriagesinenglandandwalesprovisional/2016

8. MEETING THE MAN

103 According to a study by the Trades Union Congress: Trades Union Congress, "One in Five Met Their Husband or Wife at Work," February 12, 2016. https://www.tuc.org.uk/news/one-five-met-their-husband-or-wife-work-tuc-poll-reveals

9. BERLIN WALL

118 one in three British women will have an abortion: National Health Service, "Overview: abortion." https://www.nhs.uk/conditions/abortion/

119 197,533 women in England and Wales had abortions in 2017 alone: Office of National Statistics: Department of Health & Social Care, "Abortion Statistics, England and Wales: 2017." https://assets.publishing .service.gov.uk/government/uploads/system/uploads/attachment_data /file/763174/2017-abortion-statistics-for-england-and-wales-revised.pdf

120 more than 40 percent of mothers under thirty: The Co-op, "Shocking Extent of Loneliness Faced by Young Mothers Revealed," May 2, 2018. https://www.co-operative.coop/media/news-releases/shocking-extent-of -loneliness-faced-by-young-mothers-revealed

121 the local authority nursery costs £926 per month: Hackney Learning Trust, "Hackney Children's Centre Nursery Fees from 1st September 2019." https://www.learningtrust.co.uk/sites/default/files/document/Childrens %20Centre%20Nursery%20Fees.pdf

122 last year 602,000 workers were suffering from work-related stress: Health and Safety Executive, "Work-Related Stress, Anxiety or Depression Statistics in Great Britain, 2019." https://www.hse.gov.uk/statistics /causdis/stress.pdf

10. GIFT HORSE

126 It is an act of community-building, an emblem of belonging: Nicoletta Balbo and Nicola Barban, "Does Fertility Behavior Spread Among Friends?," *American Sociological Review*, 79(3) (2014), pp. 412–431. https://www .asanet.org/sites/default/files/savvy/journals/ASR/Jun14ASRFeature.pdf

131 18 percent of women in England and Wales in 2017: Office for National Statistics, "Childbearing for Women Born in Different Years, England and Wales: 2017," November 22, 2019. https://www.ons.gov .uk/peoplepopulationandcommunity/birthsdeathsandmarriages /conceptionandfertilityrates/bulletins/childbearingforwomenborn indifferentyearsenglandandwales/2017

131 more women were pregnant in their thirties: Office for National Statistics, "Conceptions in England and Wales: 2017," April 15, 2019. https://www .ons.gov.uk/peoplepopulationandcommunity/birthsdeathsandmarriages /conceptionandfertilityrates/bulletins/conceptionstatistics/2017

132 "women are waiting longer to have children": Patrick Greenfield, "More Women Getting Pregnant After 30 Than in 20s for First Time," *The Guardian*, April 15, 2019. https://www.theguardian.com/lifeandstyle/2019 /apr/15/more-women-getting-pregnant-after-30-than-in-20s-for-first-time

11. NEW YEAR'S IRRESOLUTION

134 After the 2016 EU-Turkey deal: BBC News, "Migrant Crisis: EU-Turkey Deal Comes into Effect," March 20, 2016. https://www.bbc.co.uk/news /world-europe-35854413

140 the average cost of having your eggs collected: Human Fertilisation & Embryology Authority, "Egg freezing." https://www.hfea.gov.uk/treatments /fertility-preservation/egg-freezing/

141 18 percent of IVF treatments using a patient's own frozen eggs: Human Fertilisation & Embryology Authority, "Press Release: Age Is the Key Factor for Egg Freezing Success Says New HFEA Report, as Overall Treatment Numbers Remain Low." https://www.hfea.gov.uk/about-us /news-and-press-releases/2018-news-and-press-releases/press-release -age-is-the-key-factor-for-egg-freezing-success-says-new-hfea-report-as -overall-treatment-numbers-remain-low/

12. ANCIENT MARINER

146 we may only have sixty harvests left: Chris Arsenault, "Only 60 Years of Farming Left If Soil Degradation Continues," *Scientific American*, December 5, 2014. https://www.scientificamerican.com/article/only-60 -years-of-farming-left-if-soil-degradation-continues/

146 one in every four deaths among children under five: World Health Organization, "The Cost of a Polluted Environment: 1.7 Million Child Deaths a Year, Says WHO," March 6, 2017. https://www.who.int/news-room /detail/06-03-2017-the-cost-of-a-polluted-environment-1-7-million -child-deaths-a-year-says-who

146 93 percent of all children live in environments with air pollution: World Health Organization, "More Than 90% of the World's Children Breathe Toxic Air Every Day," October 29, 2018. https://www.who.int/news-room /detail/29-10-2018-more-than-90-of-the-world%E2%80%99s-children -breathe-toxic-air-every-day

147 "There's a very interesting study in India": David Satterthwaite, "The Implications of Population Growth and Urbanization for Climate Change," *Environment & Urbanization*, vol. 21(2): 545–567, September 2009 DOI: 10.1177/0956247809344361. https://journals.sagepub.com/doi/abs /10.1177/0956247809344361

147 "We've just had stats come out": Niko Kommenda, "How Your Flight Emits as Much CO_2 as Many People Do in a Year," *The Guardian*, July 19, 2019. https://www.theguardian.com/environment/ng-interactive/2019/jul /19/carbon-calculator-how-taking-one-flight-emits-as-much-as-many -people-do-in-a-year

13. THE COIL UNWINDS

153 the recommended seven-day break was actually devised: Laura FitzPatrick, "Contraceptive Pill Can Be Taken Every Day of the Month, After Scientists Dismiss 'Pope Rule,'" *The Telegraph*, 20 January 2019. https:// www.telegraph.co.uk/news/2019/01/19/contraceptive-pill-can-taken -every-day-month-new-nhs-guidance/

153 yet for sixty years, few in the medical establishment: Alice Howarth, "Medical Advice on the Pill Was Wrong for 60 Years. How Convenient to Blame the Pope," *The Guardian*, January 23, 2019. https://www.the guardian.com/commentisfree/2019/jan/23/medical-advice-pill-pope -bleeds-women

153 women taking the pill: Olivia Petter, "Popping the Pill: Severe Mental Health Side Effects of Contraceptive Pill Revealed in New BBC Documentary," *Independent*, November 21, 2018. https://www.independent.co.uk /life-style/women/contraceptive-pill-bbc-documentary-horizon-mental -health-depression-anxiety-suicidal-thoughts-zoe-a8645151.html

154 a study in which 340 healthy women aged eighteen to thirty-five: *Science Daily*, "Oral Contraceptives Reduce General Well-Being in Healthy Women, Swedish Study Finds," April 18, 2017. https://www.sciencedaily .com/releases/2017/04/170418094245.htm

154 *The Debrief* found that, in a survey of 1,022 women: Vicky Spratt, "Is Your Contraceptive Pill Causing You Depression, Anxiety and Panic Attacks? Debrief Exclusive Investigation," *Grazia*, January 11, 2017. https://graziadaily .co.uk/life/real-life/side-effects-pill-2/

154 "a lot of those studies that do exist are sponsored by drug companies": Ibid.

155 getting pregnant was what stupid, careless, or conniving women did: Thomas Hardy, *Jude the Obscure* (Hertfordshire, UK: Wordsworth Editions, 1995).

14. A TRICKY PERIOD

167 the crack that lets the light in: "Anthem" lyrics by Leonard Cohen.

170 "you're most fertile within a day or two": National Health Service, "When Am I Most Fertile During My Cycle?" https://www.nhs.uk/common -health-questions/pregnancy/when-am-i-most-fertile-during-my-cycle/

171 "I even scheduled the procedure to remove the body": Stella Creasy, "I'm Pregnant and Forced to Choose Between Being an MP and a Mum," *The Guardian*, June 17, 2019. https://www.theguardian.com/commentisfree /2019/jun/17/pregnant-mp-maternity-leave-equality-stella-creasy

171 one in four known pregnancies ends in miscarriage: Tommy's, "Miscarriage Statistics." https://www.tommys.org/our-organisation/charity-research /pregnancy-statistics/miscarriage

172 more than half of successful fertilizations will end in miscarriage: Michael Le Page, "Women Have More Miscarriages Than Live Births over Their Lifetime," *New Scientist*, July 30, 2018. https://www.newscientist .com/article/2175534-women-have-more-miscarriages-than-live-births -over-their-lifetime/

176 older people in the UK are being exploited by IVF clinics: Laura Donnelly, "Older Women Being Exploited by IVF Clinics—When Just Two a Year Will Achieve Success After the Age of 44," *The Telegraph*, April 21, 2019. https://www.telegraph.co.uk/news/2019/04/21/older-women -exploited-ivf-clinics-just-two-year-will-achieve/

177 "out of 2,265 embryo transfers in 2017, just seventy-five women": BBC, "Older Women Exploited by IVF Clinics, Says Fertility Watchdog," April 22, 2019. https://www.bbc.co.uk/news/uk-48008635

15. MOORHENS

180 Under Section 1 of the Wildlife and Countryside Act 1981: Royal Society for the Protection of Birds, "The Wildlife & Countryside Act 1981." https://www.rspb.org.uk/birds-and-wildlife/advice/wildlife-and-the-law /wildlife-and-countryside-act/

192 I discovered that "low maternal serum": M. Patil, T. M. Panchanadikar, and G. Wagh, "Variation of Papp-A Level in the First Trimester of Pregnancy and Its Clinical Outcome," *The Journal of Obstetrics and Gynaecology of India*, April 2014, 64(2): 116–119. https://www.ncbi.nlm.nih .gov/pubmed/24757339

16. LABOR OF LOVE

194 According to the charity Tommy's, there is a between 25 and 50 percent chance: Tommy's, "What Is a Membrane Sweep?," https://www.tommys.org/pregnancy-information/labour-birth/what-membrane-sweep (Please note, this statistic no longer appears online so heed with caution.)

17. MIDNIGHT FURY

213 According to the pediatrician Caroline Fertleman, "A perfectly healthy baby": Dr. Caroline Fertleman and Simone Cave, *Your Baby Week by Week* (London: Ebury Press, 2012).

219 On the NHS website, there is a lovely page called, simply, "Soothing a Crying Baby": National Health Service, "Soothing a Crying Baby." https://www.nhs.uk/conditions/pregnancy-and-baby/soothing-crying-baby/

18. SLOW LOVE

226 50 percent of mothers experience mental health problems: National Childbirth Trust, "Nearly Half of New Mothers with Mental Health Problems Don't Get Diagnosed or Treated." https://www.nct.org.uk/about-us/news-and-views/news/nearly-half-new-mothers-mental-health-problems-dont-get-diagnosed-or-treated

231 "this does not mean it is not infuriating to come home from a secure hospital": Hannah Jane Parkinson, "'It's Nothing Like a Broken Leg': Why I'm Done with the Mental Health Conversation," *The Guardian*, June 30, 2018. https://www.theguardian.com/society/2018/jun/30/nothing-like-broken-leg-mental-health-conversation

232 The reduction in the number of health visitors, the closure of Sure Start Centres: Patrick Butler, "1,000 Sure Start Children's Centres May Have Shut Since 2010," *The Guardian*, April 5, 2018. https://www.theguardian.com/society/2018/apr/05/1000-sure-start-childrens-centres-may-have-shut-since-2010; Jon Bunn, "Warning over Budget Cuts as Health Visitor Numbers Plummet," *Nursing Times*, March 21, 2019. https://www.nursingtimes.net/news/public-health/warning-over-budget-cuts-as-health-visitor-numbers-plummet-21-03-2019/; Denis Campbell, "From Brexit to the Birth Rate: Why Midwives Are Leaving the NHS—and

Causing a Crisis," *The Guardian*, September 12, 2018. https://www
.theguardian.com/society/shortcuts/2018/sep/12/why-midwives-leaving-
nhs-causing-a-crisis; Unite the Union "Stop Universal Credit," August 1,
2019. https://unitetheunion.org/campaigns/stop-universal-credit/

19. SPILLED MILK

237 The cause was something known as D-MER or dysphoric milk ejection
reflex: Alia M. Heise and Diane Wiessinger, "Dysphoric Milk Ejection
Reflex: A Case Report," *International Breastfeeding Journal*. https://
www.ncbi.nlm.nih.gov/pmc/articles/PMC3126760/

240 the UK has some of the lowest breastfeeding rates in the entire world:
UNICEF, "Breastfeeding in the UK." https://www.unicef.org.uk
/babyfriendly/about/breastfeeding-in-the-uk/

241 increasing the number of babies who are breastfed could cut the
incidence: Ibid.

ABOUT THE AUTHOR

Nell Frizzell is a freelance journalist who writes a column for *Vogue* and also writes for *The Guardian, Elle, Vice, BuzzFeed, The Independent* (UK), *The Observer*, and *The Telegraph*. She is best known for features and columns on gender, pregnancy, and parenting, and she has been featured several times on various BBC programs. In addition to journalism, Nell has written and performed comedy and works as a lifeguard. She lives in London with her partner and child.